Open Source Solutions for Knowledge Management and Technological Ecosystems

Francisco J. Garcia–Peñalvo
University of Salamanca, Spain

Alicia García–Holgado
University of Salamanca, Spain

A volume in the Advances in Knowledge Acquisition, Transfer, and Management (AKATM) Book Series

www.igi-global.com

Published in the United States of America by
    IGI Global
    Business Science Reference (an imprint of IGI Global)
    701 E. Chocolate Avenue
    Hershey PA 17033
    Tel: 717-533-8845
    Fax: 717-533-8661
    E-mail: cust@igi-global.com
    Web site: http://www.igi-global.com

Library of Congress Cataloging-in-Publication Data

Names: García Peñalvo, Francisco José, 1971- editor. | Garcia-Holgado,
    Alicia, 1986- editor.
Title: Open source solutions for knowledge management and technological
    ecosystems / Francisco J. García Peñalvo and Alicia Garcia-Holgado,
    editors.
Description: Hershey, PA : Business Science Reference, [2017] | Series:
    Advances in knowledge acquisition, transfer, and management | Includes
    bibliographical references and index.
Identifiers: LCCN 2016028983| ISBN 9781522509059 (hardcover) | ISBN
    9781522509066 (ebook)
Subjects: LCSH: Open source software. | Software ecosystems. | Information
    technology--Management. | Knowledge management.
Classification: LCC QA76.76.S46 O6334 2017 | DDC 005.3--dc23
LC record available at https://lccn.loc.gov/2016028983

This book is published in the IGI Global book series Advances in Knowledge Acquisition, Transfer, and Management (AKATM) (ISSN: 2326-7607; eISSN: 2326-7615)

British Cataloguing in Publication Data
A Cataloguing in Publication record for this book is available from the British Library.

Advances in Knowledge Acquisition, Transfer, and Management (AKATM) Book Series

ISSN: 2326-7607
EISSN: 2326-7615

Mission

Organizations and businesses continue to utilize knowledge management practices in order to streamline processes and procedures. The emergence of web technologies has provided new methods of information usage and knowledge sharing.

The **Advances in Knowledge Acquisition, Transfer, and Management (AKATM) Book Series** brings together research on emerging technologies and their effect on information systems as well as the knowledge society. **AKATM** will provide researchers, students, practitioners, and industry leaders with research highlights surrounding the knowledge management discipline, including technology support issues and knowledge representation.

Coverage

- Cognitive Theories
- Cultural Impacts
- Information and Communication Systems
- Knowledge acquisition and transfer processes
- Knowledge management strategy
- Knowledge Sharing
- Organizational Learning
- Organizational Memory
- Small and Medium Enterprises
- Virtual Communities

IGI Global is currently accepting manuscripts for publication within this series. To submit a proposal for a volume in this series, please contact our Acquisition Editors at Acquisitions@igi-global.com or visit: http://www.igi-global.com/publish/.

Titles in this Series

For a list of additional titles in this series, please visit: www.igi-global.com

Handbook of Research on Theoretical Perspectives on Indigenous Knowledge Systems in Developing Countries
Patrick Ngulube (University of South Africa, South Africa)
Information Science Reference • copyright 2017 • 516pp • H/C (ISBN: 9781522508335) • US $275.00 (our price)

Harnessing Social Media as a Knowledge Management Tool
Ritesh Chugh (Central Queensland University, Australia)
Information Science Reference • copyright 2017 • 392pp • H/C (ISBN: 9781522504955) • US $185.00 (our price)

Contemporary Approaches to Dissertation Development and Research Methods
Valerie A. Storey (University of Central Florida, USA) and Kristina A. Hesbol (University of Denver, USA)
Information Science Reference • copyright 2016 • 360pp • H/C (ISBN: 9781522504450) • US $195.00 (our price)

Organizational Knowledge Facilitation through Communities of Practice in Emerging Markets
Sheryl Buckley (University of South Africa, South Africa) Grzegorz Majewski (University of the West of Scotland, UK) and Apostolos Giannakopoulos (University of South Africa, South Africa)
Business Science Reference • copyright 2016 • 326pp • H/C (ISBN: 9781522500131) • US $175.00 (our price)

Mixed Methods Research for Improved Scientific Study
Mette L. Baran (Cardinal Stritch University, USA) and Janice E. Jones (Cardinal Stritch University, USA)
Information Science Reference • copyright 2016 • 335pp • H/C (ISBN: 9781522500070) • US $195.00 (our price)

Handbook of Research on Innovations in Information Retrieval, Analysis, and Management
Jorge Tiago Martins (The University of Sheffield, UK) and Andreea Molnar (University of Portsmouth, UK)
Information Science Reference • copyright 2016 • 580pp • H/C (ISBN: 9781466688339) • US $325.00 (our price)

www.igi-global.com

701 E. Chocolate Ave., Hershey, PA 17033
Order online at www.igi-global.com or call 717-533-8845 x100
To place a standing order for titles released in this series,
contact: cust@igi-global.com
Mon-Fri 8:00 am - 5:00 pm (est) or fax 24 hours a day 717-533-8661

Table of Contents

Detailed Table of Contents

Chapter 1
Enhancing Education for the Knowledge Society Era with Learning
Ecosystems...1

Francisco J. García-Peñalvo, Universidad de Salamanca, Spain
Ángel Hernández-García, Universidad Politécnica de Madrid, Spain
Miguel Á. Conde, Universidad de León, Spain
Ángel Fidalgo-Blanco, Universidad Politécnica de Madrid, Spain
María Luisa Sein-Echaluce, University of Zaragoza, Spain
Marc Alier-Forment, Universitat Politècnica de Catalunya, Spain
Faraón Llorens-Largo, Universidad de Alicante, Spain
Santiago Iglesias-Pradas, Universidad Politécnica de Madrid, Spain

In order to achieve a true transition from the Information Society to the Knowledge Society, Information and Communication Technologies must play a capital role in educational and knowledge management processes. The gap between advances in technology and current teaching methods is slowing up the integration of new educational technologies into already existing technological and methodological frameworks. As a result, the combination of mature educational technologies and educational methods does not meet the demands of today's society. In the pursuit of ways to reconcile consolidated and emerging technologies with educational methods to improve educational processes, the authors propose a technological environment to support learning services: the learning ecosystem. This chapter presents an initial proposal of a learning technological ecosystem based on an architecture framework and interoperable components, and outlines the required elements, actions and methods for learning ecosystems to become a reality.

Chapter 2

Nikolas Galanis, Universitat Politècnica de Catalunya – BarcelonaTech,
  Spain
Enric Mayol, Universitat Politècnica de Catalunya – BarcelonaTech,
  Spain
María José Casany, Universitat Politècnica de Catalunya –
  BarcelonaTech, Spain
Marc Alier, Universitat Politècnica de Catalunya – BarcelonaTech,
  Spain

E-learning has experienced an extraordinary growth over the last years. We have reached a point in time when most learning institutions have adopted an LMS as an integral element of their teaching and learning infrastructure. In parallel, the number of educational tools available for learning is increasing and keeps evolving. This variety means that it is not always easy or possible to add these educational tools into LMSs to enhance the learning process. It would, however, be in everyone´s interest for these tools to interact with the LMSs. To solve the problem of interoperability between LMS and learning tools, several interoperability standards define ways so that LMSs can interface with external learning tools in order to make them accessible from within the learning platform in an intuitive and concise way. This chapter is focused on the service-oriented approach to interoperability and specifically on the IMS LTI standard and the TSUGI hosting environment that aims to simplify the integration of external learning tools.

Chapter 3

Rafael Molina-Carmona, Universidad de Alicante, Spain
Patricia Compañ-Rosique, Universidad de Alicante, Spain
Rosana Satorre-Cuerda, Universidad de Alicante, Spain
Carlos J. Villagrá-Arnedo, Universidad de Alicante, Spain
Francisco J. Gallego-Durán, Universidad de Alicante, Spain
Faraon Llorens-Largo, Universidad de Alicante, Spain

Technological ecosystems are a widespread solution to address the challenges of the information technologies in organizations. It is important to have tools to correctly and quickly evaluate them. The Technological Ecosystem Map (TEmap) is a tool to intuitively interpret complex information maintaining both a global and a detailed vision of the technologies. It is a polygonal and structured representation of the main elements of the ecosystem. Each element is evaluated according to its maturity level, indicating how it contributes to fulfil the organization objectives. Each maturity level is represented by a colour, so that the TEmap takes the form of a heat map. The particular case of the University of Alicante is chosen to illustrate its construction. The TEmap is a simple but powerful way to identify the strengths and weaknesses of a technological ecosystem and the possible actions to improve the solution to the strategic questions of the organization.

Chapter 4

Velimir Štavljanin, University of Belgrade, Serbia
Miroslav Minović, University of Belgrade, Serbia

Gamification is hot topic today. Many organizations consider the application of gamification in their processes. Therefore, to implement gamification, it's necessary to know all elements and their relationships that comprise gamification ecosystem. The aim of this chapter is to clarify all details related to that ecosystem. At the beginning we defined gamification and similar concepts. Next, we introduced different types of gamification. One of the key parts of the chapter describes various game elements taxonomies and most used game elements or building blocks of gamification. Player as an inseparable part of that ecosystem is described through player identification, player types and player life cycle. It's clear now that there is lot of different approaches available for application of games in non-leisure context. Rather than to talk about one kind of game or game system, we decided to use term ecosystem in order to be clearer and more consistent with our approach. That is to integrate different approaches and orchestrate different tools in order to make them work together.

Chapter 5

Michael Aram, Vienna University of Economics and Business, Italy
Stefan Koch, Bogazici University, Turkey
Gustaf Neumann, Vienna University of Economics and Business, Italy

The OpenACS community framework is a mature software toolkit for developing online community platforms. Originally invented at a university, it has prospered due to a high commercial demand and major investments, and subsequently settled as an open source project. In this chapter, the authors extend a previous analysis of the evolution of this software framework and its surrounding community. This long-term analysis of fourteen years of the project's evolution considers the commercial background of the members of the developer community (for-profit or non-profit), investigates the changing contribution and collaboration structures and the geographical distribution of the user community. The results reveal a continuous shift from new product development work by commercial developers to maintenance work by the open community and a relatively uniform and growing global distribution of users over the years.

Chapter 6

Dhananjay S. Deshpande, Symbiosis Institute of Computer Studies and
Research (SICSR), India
Pradeep R. Kulkarni, Kholeshwar Mahavidyalaya, India
Pravin S. Metkewar, Symbiosis Institute of Computer Studies and
Research (SICSR), India

Universities are playing main role in research and socio-economic development of the country. The University research generates lot of research information and it is physically added in to libraries. The Research information should be easily available to new Researchers. Every research is generating new knowledge, and it's just kept in the form of thesis, dissertations, research papers, articles, etc. The enormous amount of research data exists in different geographical locations, which could not be investigated by researchers because research data is not available in a central location. The research community is facing lot of problems in sharing, searching and collecting required information and knowledge for their research. Due to these issues, researchers may do work of 'reinventing a wheel'. This chapter puts a conceptual study for open source community to develop a Knowledge Management System for researchers. This study specifically focuses on Knowledge management approach and proposes the OS_KMS model for research community as an open source software.

Chapter 7

Rajeshwar Vayyavur, California Intercontinental University, USA

Software engineering for technological ecosystems also referred as Software Ecosystems (SECOs) focuses on the concept of software engineering field. The study of SECOs started in early 90s under business schools, mainly focused on software engineering based on the software product lines approach that aimed to allow external designers and developers to contribute to hitherto closed platforms. The chapter gives background, various dimensions, framework, architectural challenges of SECOs, and explains various limitations and different recommendations and solutions to provide a better and conclusive platform for the technology ecosystems.

Chapter 8

The search for more actionable knowledge lies at the core of Sustainability Science and its implicit desire to improve the lives of various stakeholders without disrupting the balance of Nature and efficient use of all available resources. In this chapter, the authors have examined current shortfalls in knowledge-centric research and proposed the creation of an Ontology-based open-source tool to create a more practical approach for researchers to facilitate both thought and decision-making process in order to solve pressing issues with place-based actions. The effectiveness of the Hozo Tool is then examined and validated using four case studies in an attempt to both refine the current models and propose the necessary steps to create a more holistic knowledge ecosystem – one that might ultimately facilitate broader collaboration worldwide.

Chapter 9

Theoretically, open source solutions are a good match with the resource scarce organization such as a young academic journal to make the publication process and the knowledge shared explicit to the participants in the system. This paper uses a case study approach to investigate how the decision to have such a system depends on a myriad of factors, and tracks how the editorial team decided to adopt an open source journal management system for their knowledge management issues. The study argues that these components should not be taken in isolation by showing how the previous decisions can become a hindrance as these components change over time. The results show that some factors, though initially thought to be unimportant, can become major forces as the journal matures, and a more holistic approach could help to side-step the problems faced.

Preface

The information systems have evolved in what today are called technological eco-systems for providing support to the management of information and knowledge in heterogeneous environments (García-Peñalvo et al., 2015a, 2015b). Recently, it has been detected a fundamental change in discussions about innovation in the current technological systems, both academic and political context, towards ecology and ecosystems (Adkins, Foth, Summerville, & Higgs, 2007; Adomavicius, Bockstedt, Gupta, & Kauffman, 2006; Aubusson, 2002; Birrer, 2006; Bollier, 2000; Crouzier, 2015; Smith, 2006; Tatnall & Davey, 2004; Watanabe & Fukuda, 2006; Zacharakis, Shepherd, & Coombs, 2003). The European Commission has begun to use the concepts of ecology and ecosystems as tools for regional innovation policy that are aimed at achieving the Lisbon Agreement goals (Dini et al., 2005; Nachira, 2002). The European Union considers digital ecosystems as a clear evolution of e-business tools and collaborative environments for organizational networks. Inside the project Digital Ecosystems promoted by the Directorate General Information Society and Media of the European Commission, a digital ecosystem has an architecture based on Open Source software components that work together to evolve and become gradually smarter through the ideas and components from the community (European Commission, 2006). In fact, the metaphor of the technology ecosystem comes from the biology area and it is transferred to the social area to better represent the evolving nature of relationships between people, their innovation activities and their environments (Papaioannou, Wield, & Chataway, 2009); to the services area as a more generic conceptualization of economic and social actors that create value in complex systems (Frow et al., 2014; Vargo & Lusch, 2011); and to the technological area, inspired by the business and biological ecosystem concepts of Moore (Moore, 1993) and Iansiti (Iansiti & Levien, 2004) in order to define the Software ECOsystems (SECO) (Yu & Deng, 2011). A software ecosystem refers to the set of businesses and their interrelationships in a common software product or service market (Jansen, Finkelstein, & Brinkkemper, 2009) or, from an architectural point of view, it is the structure or structures of the software ecosystem in terms of elements, the properties of these elements, and the relationships among these elements, where elements can be systems, system components, and actors (Manikas & Hansen, 2013).

Messerschmitt and Szyperski (2005) are the firsts to talk about software ecosystem to refer to a collection of software products that have some given degree of symbiotic relationships. According to Dhungana, Groher, Schludermann, and Biffl (2010) a software ecosystem can be compared with a biological ecosystem from the perspective of resource management and biodiversity and underline the importance of diversity, monitoring of health and supporting social interaction. This relationship between nature and technology appears in other authors, who use the definition of natural ecosystem to support its own definition of technological ecosystem (Chang & West, 2006; Chen & Chang, 2007; Laanpere, 2012; Pata, 2011). There are several definitions of natural or biological ecosystem but there are three elements that are present in all of them (Berthelemy, 2013): the organisms, the physical environment in which they carry out their basic functions, and the set of relationships among organisms and the environment. Thus, the technological ecosystem can be defined as a set of software components related to each other through information flows in a physical environment that provides support for such flows (García-Holgado & García-Peñalvo, 2013). Moreover, the users are part of any technological ecosystem, they are other key component such as the technological tools (Conde, García-Peñalvo, Rodríguez-Conde, Alier, & García-Holgado, 2014; García-Peñalvo & Conde, 2014).

The metaphor of ecosystem has been chosen to provide technological solutions to give suitable answers to knowledge management problems in heterogeneous contexts. There are several examples in the domain of Public Administration (García-Holgado & García-Peñalvo, 2014), in the informal learning management context (García-Peñalvo, Johnson, Alves, Minović, & Conde-González, 2014), in the domain of education (García-Holgado & García-Peñalvo, 2016; Llorens, Molina, Compañ, & Satorre, 2014), in the research context (for examples see chapter 6 by Dhananjay S. Deshpande et al. and chapter 10 by Özgün Imre in this book), in the domain of Libraries (Chad, 2013), etc.

DEVELOPMENT OF TECHNOLOGICAL ECOSYSTEMS

The definition of technological ecosystems is a complex process with a wide range of requirements. Each technological ecosystem is unique. It is very difficult to find two different institutions or companies that share the exact same problems and goals regarding their own knowledge management (García-Holgado & García-Peñalvo, 2013).

Technological ecosystems should have the ability to recognize a complex network of independent interrelationships among the components that compose its architecture, while offering an analytical framework for understanding the specific evolution patterns of its technology infrastructure, taking into account that its components must be able to adapt to changes suffered by the ecosystem and not collapse before them if they cannot accept the new conditions (Pickett & Cadenasso, 2002). Technological ecosystems should connect and relate the different tools and services that arise and serve for the knowledge management, building technological ecosystems, increasingly complex internally, from the semantic interoperability of its components to transparently provide more functionality and simplicity to its users. In particular, the use of service oriented architectures has increasing in the development of learning systems, as these are currently not a single system or monolithic platform (Pardo & Delgado Kloos, 2011), but more and more services and tools are used to create heterogeneous ecosystems (for a review of interoperability in learning ecosystems see Nikolas Galanis et al. chapter in this book).

Besides, to overcome the problems related to link different applications, from a technological point of view, a technological ecosystem should be developed using a technological framework that allow the evolution and adaptation of the different components of the ecosystem itself and also permit for the incorporation of new components that extend its functionality. In this book, there are several chapters focused on providing a framework to develop different types of technological ecosystems such as gamification ecosystems or learning ecosystems (see chapter 1, 4 and 5). When defining a framework for technology ecosystems we should take into account the integration, the interoperability and the evolution of its components, and a proper definition of the architecture that supports it (Bo, Qinghua, Jie, Haifei, & Mu, 2009; Bosch, 2010; García-Peñalvo, Conde, Alier, & Casany, 2011; Gustavsson & Fredriksson, 2003). The current status and technical and technological evolution of digital ecosystems has a very pronounced parallelism with all the technology that develops around the Internet and cloud services. More specifically, the evolution in making data collection, analysis procedures and decision-making are based on certain types of emerging technologies such as the Internet of Things (Domingo & Forner, 2010), processes that extract concepts of Business Intelligence (Ferguson, 2012; Long & Siemens, 2011), or data mining processes applied to knowledge management (Romero & Ventura, 2007, 2010; Yukselturk, Ozekes, & Türel, 2014).

THE CHALLENGES

Namely, the ecosystems make possible provide new and improved services that the single tools cannot be able to provide separately to resolve knowledge and information management problems inside any kind of institution or company, but the development of these technological solutions should face several challenges such as:

- The challenge of supporting decision-making processes to improve techno-logical ecosystems and the processes related to the knowledge management.
- The challenge of establishing interoperability protocols and standards be-tween the different components that compose the ecosystem.
- The challenge of defining a framework to develop technological ecosystems that can evolve and adapt to the changing needs not only of users, but also of the technology itself.

The main goal of this book is exploring the evolution of the knowledge manage-ment systems based on Open Source software in any kind of context, from companies to institutions, and providing different approaches to resolve the challenges related to technological ecosystems.

ORGANIZATION OF THE BOOK

The book is organized into ten chapters. A brief description of each of the chapters follows:

Chapter 1, "Enhancing Education for the Knowledge Society Era with Learn-ing Ecosystems", identifies the existing challenges in educational and knowledge management processes. In particular, the application of information technologies for the improvement of teaching and learning processes. The chapter proposes a new educational technology framework to support educational processes, the learning ecosystem.

Chapter 2, "Tools Interoperability for Learning Management Systems", addresses the issue of the interoperability in learning ecosystems where the main component is a virtual learning environment (VLE) or a learning management system (LMS) that is integrating with external learning tools. This chapter focuses on the service-oriented approach to interoperability and present two approaches, the OKI and the IMS standards and the TSUGI framework.

Chapter 3, "Technological Ecosystem Maps for IT Governance: Application to a Higher Education Institution", presents a model to evaluate the situation of the technological ecosystem of an organization in order to determine its features and the state of its technological ecosystem, and to identify possible improvement actions. The authors apply the model to a particular institution, the University of Alicante (Spain).

Chapter 4, "Gamification Ecosystems: Current State and Perspectives", analyses the current situation of gamification ecosystems. The authors give an overview of the gamification topics, as well as definitions of the most important terms of that domain. A theoretical base to develop an integrated framework for gamification is then established.

Chapter 5, "Long-Term Analysis of the OpenACS Community Framework", analyses the evolution of OpenACS, a high-level community framework designed for developing collaborative Internet sites. The authors review fourteen years of data from both the project's source code repository and content repository.

Chapter 6, "Need of the Research Community: Knowledge Management and Open Source Solution", studies the knowledge management processes in the research community and its problems, challenges and requirements. The authors propose an Open Source ecosystem to manage knowledge in academic research.

Chapter 7, "Software Engineering for Technological Ecosystems", reviews the architecture issues and challenges that are within the software ecosystems. The author presents several limitations and different recommendations and solutions based on software engineering to improve the development of technological ecosystems.

Chapter 8, "Knowledge Structuring for Sustainable Development and the Hozo Tool", establishes the need for a knowledge ecosystem to facilitate the decision-making process in Sustainability Science and Sustainable Development projects. The authors use an ontology exploration tool to create a practical approach of the ecosystem. They ground their arguments in four case studies that demonstrate how to apply ontology exploration for the collective thinking process.

Chapter 9, "Trying to Go Open: Knowledge Management in an Academic Journal", describes a case study on knowledge management in a scientific journal. The authors examine the decision-making process to use Open Source technologies to support knowledge management.

Francisco José García-Peñalvo
University of Salamanca, Spain

Alicia García-Holgado
University of Salamanca, Spain

REFERENCES

Adkins, B. A., Foth, M., Summerville, J. A., & Higgs, P. L. (2007). Ecologies of innovation: Symbolic aspects of cross-organizational linkages in the design sector in an Australian inner-city area. *The American Behavioral Scientist, 50*(7), 922–934. doi:10.1177/0002764206298317

Adomavicius, G., Bockstedt, J., Gupta, A., & Kauffman, R. J. (2006). Understanding patterns of technology evolution: An Ecosystem perspective. In *Proceedings of the 39th Annual Hawaii International Conference System Science* (Vol. 8). IEEE.

Aubusson, P. (2002). An ecology of science education. *International Journal of Science Education, 24*(1), 27–46. doi:10.1080/09500690110066511

Berthelemy, M. (2013). *Definition of a learning ecosystem.* Retrieved from http://www.learningconversations.co.uk/main/index.php/2010/01/10/the-characteristics-of-a-learning-ecosystem?blog=5

Birrer, A. J. F. (2006). Science-trained professionals for the innovation ecosystem: Looking back and looking ahead. *Industry and Higher Education, 20*(4), 273–277. doi:10.5367/000000006778175865

Bo, D., Qinghua, Z., Jie, Y., Haifei, L., & Mu, Q. (2009). *An e-learning ecosystem based on cloud computing infrastructure.* Paper presented at the Advanced Learning Technologies, 2009. ICALT 2009. Ninth IEEE International Conference on.

Bollier, D. (2000). *Ecologies of innovation: The role of information and communication technologies.* Washington, DC: The Aspen Institute.

Bosch, J. (2010). *Architecture challenges for software ecosystems.* Paper presented at the Fourth European Conference on Software Architecture.

Chad, K. (2013, September). The library management system is dead – Long live the library ecosystem. *CILIP Update Magazine,* 18-20.

Chang, E., & West, M. (2006). *Digital ecosystems a next generation of the collaborative environment.* Paper presented at the Eight International Conference on Information Integration and Web-Based Application & Services, Yogyakarta, Indonesia.

Chen, W., & Chang, E. (2007). *Exploring a digital ecosystem conceptual model and its simulation prototype.* Paper presented at the Industrial Electronics, 2007. ISIE 2007. IEEE International Symposium on.

Conde, M. Á., García-Peñalvo, F. J., Rodríguez-Conde, M. J., Alier, M., & García-Holgado, A. (2014). Perceived openness of learning management systems by students and teachers in education and technology courses. *Computers in Human Behavior, 31*, 517–526. doi:10.1016/j.chb.2013.05.023

Crouzier, T. (2015). *Science ecosystem 2.0: How will change occur?* Luxembourg: Publications Office of the European Union.

Dhungana, D., Groher, I., Schludermann, E., & Biffl, S. (2010). *Software ecosystems vs. natural ecosystems: Learning from the ingenious mind of nature.* Paper presented at the Fourth European Conference on Software Architecture.

Dini, P., Darking, M., Rathbone, N., Vidal, M., Hernández, P., Ferronato, P., … Hendryx, S. (2005). *The digital ecosystems research vision: 2010 and beyond*. Retrieved from http://www.digital-ecosystems.org/events/2005.05/de_position_paper_vf.pdf

Domingo, M. G., & Forner, J. A. M. (2010). Expanding the learning environment: Combining physicality and virtuality-the internet of things for elearning. In *Proceedings of 2010 IEEE 10th International Conference on Advanced Learning Technologies (ICALT)*, (pp. 730-731). IEEE.

European Commission. (2006). *Digital ecosystems: The new global commons for SMEs and local growth*. Academic Press.

Ferguson, R. (2012). Learning analytics: Drivers, developments and challenges. *International Journal of Technology Enhanced Learning*, *4*(5/6), 304–317. doi:10.1504/IJTEL.2012.051816

Frow, P., McColl-Kennedy, J. R., Hilton, T., Davidson, A., Payne, A., & Brozovic, D. (2014). Value propositions: A service ecosystems perspective. *Marketing Theory*, *14*(3), 327–351. doi:10.1177/1470593114534346

García-Holgado, A., & García-Peñalvo, F. J. (2013). The evolution of the technological ecosystems: an architectural proposal to enhancing learning processes. In *Proceedings of the First International Conference on Technological Ecosystem for Enhancing Multiculturality (TEEM'13)* (pp. 565-571). New York, NY: ACM.

García-Holgado, A., & García-Peñalvo, F. J. (2014). Knowledge management ecosystem based on drupal platform for promoting the collaboration between public administrations. In F. J. García-Peñalvo (Ed.), *Proceedings of the Second International Conference on Technological Ecosystems for Enhancing Multiculturality (TEEM'14)* (pp. 619-624). New York, NY: ACM.

García-Holgado, A., & García-Peñalvo, F. J. (2016). Architectural pattern to improve the definition and implementation of eLearning ecosystems. *Science of Computer Programming*. doi:10.1016/j.scico.2016.03.010

García-Peñalvo, F. J., & Conde, M. Á. (2014). Using informal learning for business decision making and knowledge management. *Journal of Business Research*, *67*(5), 686–691. doi:10.1016/j.jbusres.2013.11.028

García-Peñalvo, F. J., Conde, M. Á., Alier, M., & Casany, M. J. (2011). Opening learning management systems to personal learning environments. *Journal of Universal Computer Science*, *17*(9), 1222–1240. doi:10.3217/jucs-017-09-1222

García-Peñalvo, F. J., Hernández-García, Á., Conde, M. Á., Fidalgo-Blanco, Á., Sein-Echaluce, M. L., Alier, M., . . . Iglesias-Pradas, S. (2015a). *Learning services-based technological ecosystems*. Paper presented at the 3rd International Conference on Technological Ecosystems for Enhancing Multiculturality.

García-Peñalvo, F. J., Hernández-García, Á., Conde-González, M. Á., Fidalgo-Blanco, Á., Sein-Echaluce Lacleta, M. L., Alier-Forment, M., . . . Iglesias-Pradas, S. (2015b). Mirando hacia el futuro: Ecosistemas tecnológicos de aprendizaje basados en servicios. In Á. Fidalgo Blanco, M. L. Sein-Echaluce Lacleta, & F. J. García-Peñalvo (Eds.), *La Sociedad del Aprendizaje. Actas del III Congreso Internacional sobre Aprendizaje, Innovación y Competitividad. CINAIC 2015* (pp. 553-558). Madrid, Spain: Fundación General de la Universidad Politécnica de Madrid.

García-Peñalvo, F. J., Johnson, M., Alves, G. R., Minović, M., & Conde-González, M. Á. (2014). Informal learning recognition through a cloud ecosystem. *Future Generation Computer Systems*, *32*, 282–294. doi:10.1016/j.future.2013.08.004

Gustavsson, R., & Fredriksson, M. (2003). Sustainable Information Ecosystems. In A. Garcia, C. Lucena, F. Zambonelli, A. Omicini, & J. Castro (Eds.), Software Engineering for large-scale multi-agent systems (Vol. 2603, pp. 123-138). Springer Berlin Heidelberg.

Iansiti, M., & Levien, R. (2004). Strategy as ecology. *Harvard Business Review*, *82*(3), 68–78.

Jansen, S., Finkelstein, A., & Brinkkemper, S. (2009). A sense of community: A research agenda for software ecosystems. In *Proceedings of 31st International Conference on Software Engineering* (pp. 187-190). IEEE.

Laanpere, M. (2012). *Digital learning ecosystems: Rethinking virtual learning environments in the age of social media*. Paper presented at the IFIP-OST'12: Open and Social Technologies for Networked Learning, Taillin.

Llorens, F., Molina, R., Compañ, P., & Satorre, R. (2014). Technological ecosystem for open education. In R. Neves-Silva, G. A. Tsihrintzis, V. Uskov, R. J. Howlett, & L. C. Jain (Eds.), *Smart digital futures 2014: Frontiers in artificial intelligence and applications* (pp. 706–715). IOS Press.

Long, P. D., & Siemens, G. (2011). Penetrating the fog: Analytics in learning and education. *EDUCAUSE Review*, *46*(5), 30–32.

Manikas, K., & Hansen, K. M. (2013). Software ecosystems – A systematic literature review. *Journal of Systems and Software*, *86*(5), 1294–1306. doi:10.1016/j.jss.2012.12.026

Messerschmitt, D. G., & Szyperski, C. (2005). Software ecosystem: Understanding an indispensable technology and industry. *MIT Press Books, 1*.

Moore, J. F. (1993). Predators and prey: A new ecology of competition. *Harvard Business Review, 71*(3), 75–86.

Nachira, F. (2002). *Towards a network of digital business ecosystems fostering the local development*. Retrieved from http://www.digital-ecosystems.org/doc/discussionpaper.pdf

Papaioannou, T., Wield, D., & Chataway, J. (2009). Knowledge ecologies and ecosystems? An empirically grounded reflection on recent developments in innovation systems theory. *Environment and Planning. C, Government & Policy, 27*(2), 319–339. doi:10.1068/c0832

Pardo, A., & Delgado Kloos, C. (2011). Stepping out of the box: Towards analytics outside the learning management system. In *Proceedings of the 1st International Conference on Learning Analytics and Knowledge* (pp. 163-167). New York, NY: ACM.

Pata, K. (2011). *Meta-design framework for open learning ecosystems*. Paper presented at the Mash-UP Personal Learning Environments (MUP/PLE 2011), London, UK.

Pickett, S. T. A., & Cadenasso, M. L. (2002). The ecosystem as a multidimensional concept: Meaning, model, and metaphor. *Ecosystems (New York, N.Y.), 5*(1), 1–10. doi:10.1007/s10021-001-0051-y

Romero, C., & Ventura, S. (2007). Educational data mining: A survey from 1995 to 2005. *Expert Systems with Applications, 33*(1), 135–146. doi:10.1016/j.eswa.2006.04.005

Romero, C., & Ventura, S. (2010). Educational data mining: A review of the state of the art. *IEEE Transactions on Systems, Man and Cybernetics. Part C, Applications and Reviews, 40*(6), 601–618. doi:10.1109/TSMCC.2010.2053532

Smith, K. R. (2006). Building an innovation ecosystem: Process, culture and competencies. *Industry and Higher Education, 20*(4), 219–224. doi:10.5367/000000006778175801

Tatnall, A., & Davey, B. (2004). Improving the chances of getting your IT curriculum innovation successfully adopted by the application of an ecological approach to innovation. *Informing Science: International Journal of an Emerging Transdiscipline, 7*, 87–103.

Vargo, S. L., & Lusch, R. F. (2011). It's all B2B…and beyond: Toward a systems perspective of the market. *Industrial Marketing Management, 40*(2), 181–187. doi:10.1016/j.indmarman.2010.06.026

Watanabe, C., & Fukuda, K. (2006). National innovation ecosystems: The similarity and disparity of Japan-US technology policy systems toward a service oriented economy. *Journal of Service Research, 6*(1), 159–186.

Yu, E., & Deng, S. (2011). Understanding software ecosystems: A strategic modeling approach. In S. Jansen, J. Bosch, P. Campbell, & F. Ahmed (Eds.), *IWSECO-2011 Software Ecosystems 2011:Proceedings of the Third International Workshop on Software Ecosystems* (pp. 65-76). Aachen, Germany: CEUR.

Yukselturk, E., Ozekes, S., & Türel, Y. (2014). Predicting dropout student: An application of data mining methods in an online education program. *European Journal of Open, Distance and E-Learning, 17*(1).

Zacharakis, A. L., Shepherd, D. A., & Coombs, J. E. (2003). The development of venture-capital-backed Internet companies. An ecosystem perspective. *Journal of Business Venturing, 18*(2), 217–231. doi:10.1016/S0883-9026(02)00084-8

Chapter 1
Enhancing Education for the Knowledge Society Era with Learning Ecosystems

Francisco J. García-Peñalvo
Universidad de Salamanca, Spain

María Luisa Sein-Echaluce
University of Zaragoza, Spain

Ángel Hernández-García
Universidad Politécnica de Madrid, Spain

Marc Alier-Forment
Universitat Politècnica de Catalunya, Spain

Miguel Á. Conde
Universidad de León, Spain

Faraón Llorens-Largo
Universidad de Alicante, Spain

Ángel Fidalgo-Blanco
Universidad Politécnica de Madrid, Spain

Santiago Iglesias-Pradas
Universidad Politécnica de Madrid, Spain

ABSTRACT

In order to achieve a true transition from the Information Society to the Knowledge Society, Information and Communication Technologies must play a capital role in educational and knowledge management processes. The gap between advances in technology and current teaching methods is slowing up the integration of new educational technologies into already existing technological and methodological frameworks. As a result, the combination of mature educational technologies and

DOI: 10.4018/978-1-5225-0905-9.ch001

educational methods does not meet the demands of today's society. In the pursuit of ways to reconcile consolidated and emerging technologies with educational methods to improve educational processes, the authors propose a technological environment to support learning services: the learning ecosystem. This chapter presents an initial proposal of a learning technological ecosystem based on an architecture framework and interoperable components, and outlines the required elements, actions and methods for learning ecosystems to become a reality.

INTRODUCTION

Authors' reflections upon the current state of the art on the application of information technologies to teaching and learning processes (Conde-González, Hernández-García, García-Peñalvo & Sein-Echaluce, 2015; García-Holgado & García-Peñalvo, 2014; García-Holgado, García-Peñalvo, Hernández-García & Llorens-Largo, 2015; García-Peñalvo et al., 2015a; 2015b; Sein-Echaluce, Fidalgo-Blanco, García-Peñalvo & Conde-González, 2015) reveal that we are not making the most of the potential of educational technologies for the improvement of learning and learning processes to meet the expectations and needs of a Digital Society willing to evolve to a Knowledge Society.

In the educational landscape, few technical innovations reach an adequate level of maturity as to permeate society. As a consequence, in many occasions most of them disappear at early stages of their lifecycle. Other innovations appear surrounded by a halo of hype and fascination that induces new practices, often followed by adopters without any systematization or aspiration to last in time. This kind of innovations usually ends up not living up to the expectations, and fade away once their novelty is gone.

The moment an innovation enters the end of the hype cycle may be precisely the ideal moment to get it back in track towards its adequate maturity point, because a technology may be most effective when it is put at the disposal of process innovation after it is no longer in the spotlight.

This also holds true in the case of education and information technologies. Learning Management Systems (LMS) constitute a perfect example of this hype-cycle paradigm. LMS are widely used and completely established in education, and they have deeply transformed online and IT-supported learning. Yet, despite their relevance, most researchers seem to have lost interest in LMS, as newer technologies become the new "last thing" –e.g. MOOCs, gamified learning, learning analytics, adaptive systems, etc. However, these newer trends have not had a disrupting effect, and therefore they have not been able to transform learning processes on their own.

This discussion leads to two important conclusions. First, LMS are no longer valid as a single component of technical innovation in education. Second, new technical frameworks for education should nonetheless incorporate consolidated technologies such as LMS, and integrate them with existing technical components that have earned enough acceptance but have not yet fully realized the hopes that learning agents have put in them.

This study proposes the basic components of such a new educational technology framework to support educational processes: the learning ecosystem. The framework needs to give response to educational institutions' needs in terms of flexibility and adaptability, in order to allow deployment of new processes due to component addition or evolution. Previous experiences (Alier Forment, Casañ Guerrero, Conde González, García-Peñalvo & Severance, 2010; Alier et al., 2012) further confirm additional characteristics that the learning ecosystem must have:

1. Provision of interoperability, which must be transparent and guaranteed at all times; this way, components may evolve in a seamless way, allowing teachers and students to focus on learning processes;
2. Device-independency, which opens doors not just to mobility, but also to the incorporation of devices that can bring new ways to interact to make users part of the ecosystem;
3. Integration of both emerging and established technologies;
4. Guaranteed data flow to, from and within the framework, by using data adapters that enable data semantic integration; and
5. On-demand presentation of data to any actor within the ecosystem.

BACKGROUND

Information Technology and Education

Learning is a fundamental part of human beings. While instructors may create a favorable climate for learning, in the end it all comes to students adopting an active role. Motivation and engagement are essential in the regard: no matter the amount of effort made by teachers, if students do not work and commit, they will not learn. Admittedly, each individual has particular characteristics, and people also have different learning styles and paces, or develop some aspects of their intelligence more than others (Gardner, 1999; 2011). The transition to the Knowledge Society demands changes and transformation of educational processes and educational methods to achieve active education, a term that involves "educating in a different way, letting the young take the stage, making students responsible for making the most of their time, swaying routine away, worrying more about educating than grading." (Michavila, 2013)

The application of information technologies to educational processes induces transformations that affect both the way we learn and the digital and informational competences required for learning (García-Peñalvo & Seoane-Pardo, 2015); furthermore, technology may help customization of learning and favor active involvement of students.

Technical advances promote the irruption of the digital world and foster the use of tools that connect users in social networks and facilitate collaboration and workgroup. Information is originated nowadays from multiple sources, may come in different formats and media, and is almost immediately accessible. Learning and education, and especially Higher Education due to its bridging role between students and the labor market, cannot fall behind the constant technical evolution (García-Peñalvo, 2008). More particularly, in educational settings technological evolution needs to have a direct reflect on learning processes (Illanas & Llorens, 2011). The use of information technologies in education offers new possibilities and unexplored paths that may complement traditional education.

High-quality technology-supported education needs to address two main elements: instructional methods and the technical platform that supports learning processes. The increasing complexity of information technologies and high adoption ratios make it necessary to study both elements from an integral view, to observe and understand the problems, challenges and relevance of information technologies in the development of learning and business strategies, and their execution and management. Only then will institutions achieve the goal of improving overall performance and profitability: digitalization entails process re-engineering and reconsideration of the organization's goals.

The Innovation Diffusion Theory (Rogers, 2003) analyzes why some ideas and products are successful and become trends while others go out of style. According to Moore (2014), an innovation becomes successful when it can "cross the chasm" and reach a majority of users. Early adopters, on the other hand, abandon a new product as soon as it becomes accepted by the general population and a replaces it with a newer product. Gartner's (2015) Hype Cycle offers a graphic representation of technology adoption and maturity, and how the different technologies may be employed to solve real business opportunities and explore new opportunities. Being able to forecast technology adoption allows prediction of passing fads and social contagion that can go beyond technology itself (information cascades) (Friedkin & Johnsen, 2011). IT-based practices in a global, connected and complex world fit perfectly in the "black swan theory" (Taleb & Mosquera, 2008), but changes in the educational landscape cannot be dependent on trends as the effect of such changes are only observable in the long term. Therefore, it is necessary to advance research on educational technologies by combining research on application of information technologies to learning processes, educational research and technology innovation.

The existence of a growing number of projects on open educational resources and the "open movement" itself make it easier to create open systems that facilitate participation and collaboration (García-Peñalvo, García de Figuerola & Merlo, 2010). Virtual campuses and LMS, for instance, have gained high popularity in academic (Arroway, Davenport, Guangning & Updegrove, 2010; Browne et al, 2010; CRUE TIC, 2014) and business (Wexler et al., 2007) contexts. LMS provide users with tools that extend and support the traditional concept of "classroom", by helping instructors to manage learning more effectively (Avgeriou, Papasalouros, Retalis & Skordalakis, 2003). For students, LMS comprise the virtual space where they learn or where they find resources that may complement traditional classes.

However, and despite the usefulness of LMS as a mediator between teachers and students, LMS are too oriented toward learning management; thus, communication flows are predetermined, which highly limits interaction. Teachers and students try to circumvent this problem by using additional tools and services, offered by the institution or freely available online, blurring the boundaries between formal and informal learning (García-Peñalvo, Colomo-Palacios & Lytras, 2012).

The difficulty to integrate formal and informal learning poses a big challenge and give way to the concept of Personal Learning Environment (PLE) (Wilson et al., 2007). PLEs aim to facilitate learning by providing students with the tools they choose to use –usually, those more familiar to them– without any tie to any institution or specific time frame (Adell & Castañeda, 2010). By choosing the tools they will use, PLEs also make students responsible for their own learning. Students then pass from learning consumers to learning providers, and along the whole process they also learn to relate with other students depending on their needs (Schaffert & Hilzensauer, 2008).

When the set of available tools for learning is supported by an institution, a greater effort for integration is needed to control the evolution of the different tools –that now become system components–, leading to a new concept that aims to overcome the pure accumulation of trending technologies (Llorens, 2009; 2011): the learning technological ecosystem, or learning ecosystem (García-Holgado & García-Peñalvo, 2013).

LEARNING ECOSYSTEMS

An ecosystem is a community of living organisms whose vital processes are interrelated and whose development is contingent on the physical factors of the environment. The translation of the concept to a technological setting leads to definition of technological ecosystem. These definitions vary from one author to another, but all authors agree on one thing: there is a clear relation between the characteristics of a natural ecosystem and a technological ecosystem (Chen & Chang, 2007; Laanpere, 2012; Pata, 2011). Therefore, we propose a learning technological ecosystem where a community –with their educational methods, policies, rules and regulations, applications and work teams– may coexist in a way that the processes are inter-related, and the implementation and execution of such processes is based on physical factors of the technological environment (Llorens, Molina, Compañ & Satorre, 2014).

The European Union considers that digital ecosystems are the evolution of e-business tools and platforms for collaboration in organizations. Under the Digital Ecosystems Project promoted by the European Commission's Directorate General Information Society and Media, the architecture of a digital ecosystem is based on Open Source software components, which combine to jointly enable gradual evolution of the system by the addition of new components created by the community (European Commission, 2006).

If the past of IT-based learning was characterized by automation –which led to the development of LMS–, the present is characterized by integration. The real challenge is to connect the different tools and services that support learning, creating technological ecosystems of increasing internal complexity through semantic interoperability of its components in a seamless way, in order to offer more functionality –but also more simplicity– to users.

Framework for Learning Ecosystems

When defining a framework for learning services-based ecosystems there are some important aspects to observe: component integration, interoperability and evolution, and a correct definition of the underlying architecture (Bo, Qinghua, Jie, Haifei & Mu, 2009; Bosch, 2010; García-Peñalvo, Conde-González, Alier & Casany, 2011; Gustavsson, & Fredriksson, 2003). In that sense, it would be possible to establish a parallelism between the current state of learning ecosystems –and their technological evolution– and the development of cloud services. Furthermore, learning ecosystems should also incorporate elements like data collection, analytics procedures and decision making rules and processes from other technological innovations like the Internet of Things (Domingo & Forner, 2010), Business Intelligence (Long & Siemens, 2011; Ferguson, 2012), or educational data mining (Romero & Ventura, 2007; Romero & Ventura, 2010; Yukselturk, Ozekes, & Türel, 2014).

There are two elements in a learning [technological] ecosystem: the architecture framework and the components. Making an analogy with a human body, the architecture framework would comprise the veins and brain, and the components would be the different organs. That is, the architecture framework provides the structure that connects the different components, while each component adds a distinctive functionality to the ecosystem. A requisite of the learning ecosystem is component inter-operability to ensure flexibility in a way that addition, removal or modification of one component does not affect the ecosystem.

In order for the ecosystem to be efficient, the architecture framework must guarantee communication and data flows among the different components. Our proposal (Figure 1) is completed by a data bus managed by the architecture framework –in our analogy, it would be the equivalent of the neural system of the body– that enables data flows and communication between the different components, and an interaction layer for the different learning actors to interact with the ecosystem.

Figure 1. Structure of the learning ecosystem with some examples of interoperable components at the bottom

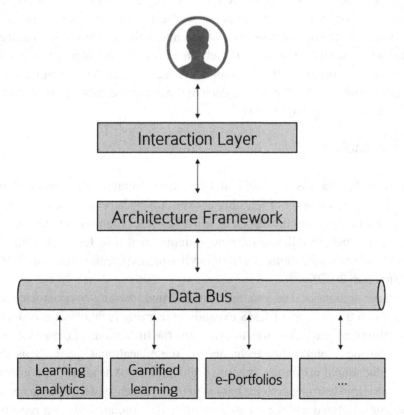

Components of the Learning Ecosystem

Most prevalent software environments, like cloud-based services, are supported by interchangeable components and architectures that connect different systems, using communication protocols and standards. IT-supported learning is also following this trend, leading to the implementation of an increasing number of service-oriented architectures in learning systems. Therefore, it is logical to propose a deployment of components as learning-based services that provide all the needed functionalities in the learning ecosystem.

Service-oriented architectures overcome the limitations of using a single system, by allowing the use of more services and tools (Pardo & Delgado Kloos, 2001). Connection of the different services requires the use of protocols, interfaces and data description standards that preserve the meaning and contexts of the data being transmitted. The specification of these protocols is based on platform interoperability and standard semantic descriptors, enabling their use by sensors and collectors of learning evidences.

As we state in the introductory section, new technical frameworks for education –i.e. learning ecosystems– should integrate well-establish technologies such as LMS with existing technical components that are interesting for learning practices but have not developed their full potential yet. Therefore, our initial proposal of a learning ecosystem incorporates three components: learning analytics, gamification –or gamified learning– and e-Portfolios. Each of the components are explained in more detail in the following subsections.

Learning Analytics

Research on the analysis of educational data is essential for the development and successful implementation of learning ecosystems because data have become the fundamental elements for the design of learning cycles (data-driven design), learning task assessment (intelligent tutoring systems), real-time feedback (data-driven feedback) and personalization of learning environments (Bienkowski, Feng & Means, 2012; Siemens, 2012).

The large amount of data generated by a virtual learning environment, and especially when the concept of LMS expands to learning technological ecosystems, forces institutions and instructors to overcome the limitations of these systems and translate business intelligence techniques to the educational sphere. This shift in the way educational institution may use high volumes of academic and interaction information from learning systems has led to the emergence of a new concept, learning analytics, defined as "the measurement, collection, analysis and reporting of data about learners and their contexts, for purposes of understanding and optimising learning and the environments in which it occurs." (Long & Siemens, 2011; p.34)

Despite some voices from experts claiming that interaction records from virtual environments have been under-utilized in e-learning research (Phillips, Maor, Preston & Cumming-Potvin, 2012), the emergence of MOOCs (Massive Online Open Courses) in 2012 brought special attention to the field of learning analytics, in an effort to manage courses with thousands of students enrolled. Recent advances in learning analytics are not exempt from perils. For example, Agudo-Peregrina, Iglesias-Pradas, Conde-González and Hernández-García (2014) warn that there is a high risk of fragmentation in learning analytics research. Agudo-Peregrina et al. (2014) note that a common theoretical framework is necessary in order to apply system-independent learning analytics techniques, and that agreement on variable selection criteria are critical for effective learning analytics –an idea they share with (Duval & Verbert, 2012).

In the past years, and owing to the drive of a growing research community, learning analytics has gained traction, with the creation of networks at national and international scale –e.g. SNOLA (2016) in Spain and SOLAR (2016) at an international level– (Conde-González & Hernández-García, 2013), and project-oriented task forces like ROLE (n.d.) and LACE (n.d.). In parallel, we have witnessed the appearance of frameworks (IMS Caliper Analytics, xAPI), technologies (Pentaho Data Integration) and data mining analytics techniques (rule-based association, matrix factoring, etc.) for the analysis of educational data from different sources.

Effective deployment of learning analytics foster learning personalization and adaptability. This personalization goes beyond approaches focused on student knowledge and incorporate other aspects, such as profiles, learning styles, behavior, competences and skills, providing real-time information about student progress and factors influencing motivation and academic performance (Lerís & Sein-Echaluce, 2011).

Gamification and Gamified Learning

Learning adaptation can be strengthened with the introduction of gamification-based rules. Video-games have changed the way younger people understand reality and relate with each other (McGonigal, 2011; Turkle, 2011). Video-games have been used in learning processes through game-based learning and learning objects like educational video-games and serious games (Prensky, 2006; 2007). However, new approaches propose the application of techniques and tools used in video-game design to other fields, a process known as gamification (Werbach, & Hunter, 2012). Application of gamification to learning processes, or gamified learning, is one of the most promising lines in gamification (Kapp, 2012).

There are many tools available to use gamification elements –e.g. Mozilla Foundation's Open Badges Project (Mozilla OpenBadges, n.d.)–, recent experiences –e.g. BBVA Game (Equipo BBVA España, 2012), a simple web page that provides an entertaining way to learn about the services offered by a bank; Karmacracy (c2013), where users receive points and badges every time they share contents in social media; Duolingo (n.d.), where students learn by playing for free in a fun way; or Stackoverflow (n.d.), a Q&A web site for programmers that incorporates authority and popularity indexes dependent on the number and quality –through a peer-voting system– of contributions from participants.

Despite the increasing interest from researchers and practitioners in gamification, the fact is that gamified learning is still on the earlier stages of development. Experiences are still unique –although there may be some overlapping between them– and thus there is still a need of a gamification core for learning processes; that is to say, to define and develop a component that implements the necessary functionalities for gamified learning in a learning ecosystem.

e-Portfolios

A good example where gamified learning may improve learning processes is the collection of evidence relative to the competences an individual develops along his or her life, both in formal and informal learning contexts. These evidences should then be registered in an institutional –if appropriate circumstances apply– or personal portfolio.

A portfolio, or e-Portfolio, is a tool for personal learning process development. e-Portfolios include different evidences –class notes, grades, tasks, essays, diagrams, feedback, progress reports, etc.–, ordered and structured according to different criteria (Barrios, 2000).

Various proposals of e-Portfolios have been made at different educational levels, including projects –e.g. TRAILER (García-Peñalvo, García de Figuerola & Merlo, 2010; García-Peñalvo et al., 2013), ePEL (Pitarch, Álvarez, & Monferrer, 2007) and TENCompetence (Berlanga, Sloep, Brouns, Bitter-Rijpkema & Koper, 2008)– and communities of interest –e.g. CAES at Universitat Autònoma de Barcelona (Blanch Gelabert et al., 2011)– oriented toward competence-based learning. These proposals include tools to create a profile of the individual's competences (Berlanga, Sloep, Brouns, Bitter-Rijpkema & Koper, 2008), or the design and development of a platform where users can save and show evidences of informal learning (García-Peñalvo, García de Figuerola & Merlo, 2010), but none of them has achieved a big success. One of the main reasons of this lack of success is the complexity involved in reaching to an agreement on the definition of the different competences.

TOWARDS THE LEARNING ECOSYSTEM

So far, our proposals of the learning ecosystem (Conde-González, Hernández-García, García-Peñalvo & Sein-Echaluce, 2015; García-Holgado, García-Peñalvo, Hernández-García & Llorens-Largo, 2015; García-Peñalvo et al., 2015a; 2015b; Sein-Echaluce et al. 2015) have been circumscribed to a theoretical proposal and a description of its main elements –namely, the architecture framework and three fundamental components: learning analytics, gamified learning and e-Portfolios. In this section we explain the different actions, objectives and methods that should be covered in order to turn the conceptual idea of learning ecosystems into a working, real system.

Architecture Framework

The architecture framework should cover the proposal of a technological environment to support learning services; and the definition of the learning ecosystem.

The definition of a learning ecosystem must be independent of specific implementations of learning and knowledge management processes. That is, they must be independent of learning modes –face-to-face, b-learning, e-learning, m-learning–, number of students or degree of formality –formal or informal learning. This independence helps overcoming the constraints associated with the use of existing LMS by providing transparent and semantic support that guarantees interoperability and evolution of the components.

The architecture framework should support, implement and deploy the learning ecosystem, including dynamic integration of different tools and services. The architecture framework provides a structure upon which the different services may be adapted to learning needs of teachers and students, in a seamless way for end-users. This structure requires the definition of functionalities, consistent mechanisms of data exchanges among components, and tools that enable user activity tracking. More specifically, building the architecture framework of the learning ecosystem entails the following actions:

1. Definition of the factory wrappers and connectors that represent the components/service of the learning ecosystem, both at a data description and functionality levels.
2. Definition of a supporting architecture template for the deployment of learning ecosystems.
3. Definition of adaptability elements and mechanisms to facilitate the evolution of the learning ecosystem. These elements should enable inclusion of

new components/services, changes in functionality or information of existing services, and elimination of outdated or no longer required services.

4. Semantic definition of data flows between components.
5. Definition of logging systems to record user interactions.
6. Definition of instructional methods that optimize the use of components.

Learning Analytics

The incorporation of learning analytics services to the learning ecosystem should aim to cover two objectives:

1. The definition of a common reference framework to support collection and analysis of educational data and learning evidences from the different components of the ecosystem through interoperable standards; the reference framework must act as a facilitator to other components, providing the necessary information to adapt learning processes to each student's individual needs;
2. The definition of methods to ensure adaptability, such as early-warning systems, custom search results or recommender systems of learning contents), and the application of learning analytics techniques to support educational decision making by all learning actors. In order to achieve these objectives, the following actions must take place:
    a. Definition of a service- and platform-independent general framework for learning analytics based on interoperable standards –e.g. Caliper Analytics, xAPI. The framework need to address behavioral –identification of teaching/learning patterns–, social –analysis of the effects of interactions between learning processes and agents– and semantic –analysis of content from information exchanges– aspects of learning.
    b. Design and implementation of technical elements to collect and integrate data from the different components of the ecosystem in a way that is consistent with the general framework using ETL (Extract, Transform and Load) processes –e.g. Pentaho Data Integration.
    c. Design of a classification system to categorize learning processes-related data, regardless of the source they originated from.
    d. Identification of patterns from information exchanges between different processes and services –i.e. components– in different learning types –online learning, blended learning, communities of practice, informal learning, MOOCs, etc.
    e. Development of tools to generate new patterns and enable adaptability and delivery of personalized educational contents and processes to the different components of the ecosystem.

f.   Design of analytics systems and the communication protocols and interfaces with other components to support educational decision making.

Gamified Learning

Implementation of gamification elements in the learning ecosystem has to be oriented toward autonomous learning, with a strong focus on automation and usability. A successful implementation of gamified learning comprises the following actions:

1.   Definition of a gamified learning model suitable for formal and informal training, both academic and professional. The gamified learning model needs to be inspired in video-gaming characteristics –interactivity, real-time feedback, engagement, progression, reward systems, levels, challenges, etc.–, be easily integrated in any platform and adapted to different user profiles.
2.   Definition of indicators for the assessment of learning results, such as level of participation in the different activities, satisfaction, user experience and generation of knowledge.
3.   Design of a set of patterns and templates for the development of gamification tools in order to make the model extensible and to facilitate collaboration with third-party providers. The templates should then be scalable, modular and configurable.
4.   Development of a set of gamified tools using the templates.

e-Portfolios

An e-Portfolio component should provide collection of online and offline learning evidences and send them to a personal or institutional portfolio. e-Portfolios need to include semantic contextual information, allow interoperability between other portfolios and the rest of the components of the ecosystem, while adhering to privacy policies. More precisely, an e-Portfolio component for a learning ecosystem involves the following actions:

1.   Creation of a service model to define a portfolio for service-oriented architectures, including: communication methods –protocols, APIs, etc.–, security and privacy elements, and interoperability mechanisms.
2.   Creation or selection of a semantic model.
3.   Design of the system for collection of online and offline evidences, semantic tagging and classification, and automatic processing and storing methods.
4.   Identification of best practices.

Methods

Given the variety of actions necessary to define the learning ecosystem and get it fully functioning, it is necessary to apply different methodologies. This subsection details the different approaches that are required for a successful implementation of the ecosystem.

First of all, we suggest that the global design and implementation of the learning ecosystem is covered by action research (Baskerville, 1999). Action research is a method that is commonly employed in information systems and education research. Action research is focused on action and change, which makes it suitable for research on learning ecosystems because of the evolutionary nature of a technological ecosystem. Moreover, action research encompasses systematic and iterative exchanges, and fosters collaboration between researchers; therefore, it is adequate for the definition and modelling of complex systems that require the effort of researchers from different disciplines, as is the case of learning ecosystems.

The first stages of characterization of the learning ecosystem –both architecture framework and components– include actions oriented toward the definition of requirements and model design. A systematic review will be appropriate to further refine those requirements and to identify existing technology and models that may be incorporated to the first prototype of the ecosystem. Particularly, Kitchenham et al.'s (Kitchenham & Charters, 2007; Kitchenham et al., 2009;) indications to perform systematic reviews in the field of software engineering will be useful to summarize the evidences related to a specific procedure or technology, to anticipate possible sources of problems, to define the different frameworks, and to confront and complement theory and empirical findings.

The intermediate and final stages of creation of the architecture framework and components involve software development. In this regard, we propose the use of agile software development techniques to provide with the necessary flexibility. More particularly, Scrum (Schwaber, 2007) offers the processes, sets of rules, practices, roles and artifacts required for the deployment of the learning ecosystem based on an incremental and iterative software development cycle.

CONCLUSION AND FUTURE RESEARCH DIRECTIONS

Information and communication technologies take a prominent role in the transition from the Information Society to the Knowledge Society, but the gap between advances in technology and current teaching methods makes it difficult to integrate new educational technologies into already existing technological and methodological frameworks and to make use of the potential of technology for the improvement of learning. As a result, there is a technological imbalance, often causing mature educational technologies and educational methods to not meet the demands of today's society. As an alternative solution to this problem, in this chapter we propose a way to reconcile consolidated and emerging technologies with educational methods: the learning ecosystem.

Learning ecosystems overcome the barriers imposed of current learning management systems and encompass different educational practices by providing transparent support for interoperability and evolution of its components.

Learning ecosystems rely on the deployment of flexible framework architectures that enable seamless incorporation and adaptation of learning services. Our theoretical proposal for a learning ecosystem in this chapter includes a common reference framework for collection and analysis of educational data originated in the different components of the ecosystem, an innovative model of adaptive gamified learning, and lifelong-learning based on semantic portfolios. Such an ecosystem would facilitate both adaptability of the information regarding learning processes and support to educational decision making.

The proposal aims to define a new technological framework that promotes the definition of new educational methods in line with the profound social changes in, and in response to the many challenges of, the Digital Society and the Knowledge Society. The learning ecosystem becomes a framework that integrates existing and emerging technologies, which interoperate and evolve in a seamless way for users.

This proposal includes an initial selection of technologies, techniques and methods that should be implemented as components of the ecosystem:

- Learning analytics to support educational decision making and facilitate adaptability of learning content and processes.
- Gamification as a means to define innovative models of flexible gamified learning.
- e-Portfolios to extract and collect learning and competence development evidences from formal and informal settings.

In the same way as cloud-based services are transforming the way businesses and organizations operate, the proposal of the learning ecosystem aims to transform the educational landscape and give response to the current challenges for learning in the Knowledge Society. The learning ecosystem does not render previous systems –e.g. LMS– obsolete and unusable, but rather evolves from them to take advantage of their benefits and overcome their limitations. The result is an open and interoperable platform where new functionalities and services may be added effortlessly, to foster the transition toward smarter systems and advanced interactions.

We are aware that our selection of three components for this initial proposal is limited and somewhat discretionary. However, this choice is not arbitrary because it addresses some of the most demanded needs of current education: the introduction of new instructional methods and approaches –gamified learning–, different learning settings and competence-based learning –e-Portfolios– and adaptable learning and educational decision making support systems –learning analytics. However, the only limit to new applications and services for the learning ecosystem is the imagination. In that sense, current and emerging trends in IT-supported education, like mobile (Fulantelli, Taibi & Arrigo, 2015) and multimodal (Garaizar & Guenaga, 2014) learning can be easily added to the ecosystem due to the evolving nature of its own definition.

REFERENCES

Adell, J., & Castañeda, L. (2010). Los Entornos Personales de Aprendizaje (PLEs): una nueva manera de entender el aprendizaje. In R. Roig Vila & M. Fiorucci (Eds.), Claves para la investigación en innovación y calidad educativas. La integración de las Tecnologías de la Información y la Comunicación y la Interculturalidad en las aulas. Stumenti di ricerca per l'innovaziones e la qualità in ámbito educativo. La Tecnologie dell'informazione e della Comunicazione e l'interculturalità nella scuola. Alcoy, Spain: Marfil – Roma TRE Universita degli studi.

Agudo-Peregrina, Á. F., Iglesias-Pradas, S., Conde-González, M. Á., & Hernández-García, Á. (2014). Can we predict success from log data in VLEs? Classification of interactions for learning analytics and their relation with performance in VLE-supported F2F and online learning. *Computers in Human Behavior, 31,* 542–550. doi:10.1016/j.chb.2013.05.031

Alier, M., Mayol, E., Casañ, M. J., Piguillem, J., Merriman, J. W., & Conde González, M. Á. et al. (2012). Clustering Projects for eLearning Interoperability. *Journal of Universal Computer Science, 18*(1), 106–122.

Alier Forment, M., Casañ Guerrero, M. J., Conde González, M. Á., García-Peñalvo, F. J., & Severance, C. (2010). Interoperability for LMS: The missing piece to become the common place for e-learning innovation.[IJKL]. *International Journal of Knowledge and Learning, 6*(2/3), 130–141. doi:10.1504/IJKL.2010.034749

Arroway, P., Davenport, E., Guangning, X., & Updegrove, D. (2010). *Educause Core Data Service Fiscal Year 2009 summary report.* EDUCAUSE White Paper. EDUCAUSE.

Avgeriou, P., Papasalouros, A., Retalis, S., & Skordalakis, M. (2003). Towards a Pattern Language for Learning Management Systems. *Journal of Educational Technology & Society, 6*(2), 11–24.

Barrios, O. (2000). *Estrategia del portafolio del alumnado. In Estrategias didácticas innovadoras* (pp. 294–301). Barcelona: Octaedro.

Baskerville, R. L. (1999). Investigating information systems with action research. *Communications of the AIS, 2*(3es), 4.

Berlanga, A. J., Sloep, P. B., Brouns, F., Bitter-Rijpkema, M. E., & Koper, R. (2008). Towards a TENCompetence ePortfolio. *International Journal of Emerging Technologies in Learning, 3*, 24–28.

Bienkowski, M., Feng, M., & Means, B. (2012). Enhancing teaching and learning through educational data mining and learning analytics: An issue brief. US Department of Education, Office of Educational Technology.

Blanch Gelabert, S., Bosco Paniagua, A., Gimeno Soria, X., González Monfort, N., Fuentes Agustí, M., Jariot Garcia, M., … Forestello, A. M. (2011). *Carpetas de aprendizaje en la educación superior: una oportunidad para repensar la docencia.* Bellaterra: Servei de Publicacions Universitat Autònoma de Barcelona.

Bo, D., Qinghua, Z., Jie, Y., Haifei, L., & Mu, Q. (2009). An E-learning Ecosystem Based on Cloud Computing Infrastructure.*Ninth IEEE International Conference on Advanced Learning Technologies, 2009. ICALT 2009.* Riga, Latvia: IEEE.

Bosch, J. (2010). Architecture challenges for software ecosystems. In *Proceedings of the Fourth European Conference on Software Architecture: Companion Volume* (pp. 93-95). New York, NY: ACM.

Browne, T., Hewitt, R., Jenkins, M., Voce, J., Walker, R., & Yip, H. (2010). *Survey of Technology Enhanced Learning for higher education in the UK.* Oxford, UK: UCISA - Universities and Colleges Information System Association.

Chen, W., & Chang, E. (2007). Exploring a Digital Ecosystem Conceptual Model and Its Simulation Prototype.*Proceedings of IEEE International Symposium on Industrial Electronics, 2007 (ISIE 2007)* (pp. 2933 - 2938). IEEE.

Conde-González, M. Á., García-Peñalvo, F. J., Casany, M. J., & Alier, M. (2009). Adapting LMS architecture to the SOA: an Architectural Approach. In H. Sasaki, G. O. Bellot, M. Ehmann, & O. Dini (Eds.), *Proceedings of the Fourth International Conference on Internet and Web Applications and Services – ICIW 2009* (pp. 322-327). Los Alamitos, CA: IEEE Computer Society. doi:10.1109/ICIW.2009.54

Conde-González, M. Á., & Hernández-García, Á. (2013). A promised land for educational decision-making? Present and future of learning analytics.*Proceedings of the First International Conference on Technological Ecosystem for Enhancing Multiculturality* (pp. 239-243). ACM. doi:10.1145/2536536.2536573

Conde-González, M. Á., Hernández-García, Á., García-Peñalvo, F. J., & Sein-Echaluce Lacleta, M. L. (2015). Exploring student interactions: Learning analytics tools for student tracking.*Proceedings of the 17th International Conference, HCI International 2015*. Los Angeles, CA: Springer International Publishing.

CRUE TIC. (2014). *UNIVERSITIC 2014: Descripción, Gestión y Gobierno de las TI en el Sistema Universitario Español*. Madrid, España: Conferencia de Rectores de las Universidades Españolas (CRUE).

Domingo, M. G., & Forner, J. A. M. (2010). Expanding the Learning Environment: Combining Physicality and Virtuality-The Internet of Things for eLearning.*Proceedings of the IEEE 10th International Conference on Advanced Learning Technologies (ICALT 2010)* (pp. 730-731). IEEE. doi:10.1109/ICALT.2010.211

Duolingo. (n.d.). *Duolingo: Learn Spanish, French and other languages for free*. Retrieved 21 April 2016 from https://www.duolingo.com

Duval, E., & Verbert, K. (2012). Learning analytics. *E-Learning and Education, 1*(8).

Equipo BBVA España. (2012). *BBVA game: juega, gana y aprende*. Retrieved 21 April 2016 from https://www.blogbbva.es/bbva-game-juega-gana-y-aprende

European Commission. (2006). *Digital Ecosystems: The New Global Commons for SMEs and local growth*. Author.

Ferguson, R. (2012). Learning analytics: Drivers, developments and challenges. *International Journal of Technology Enhanced Learning, 4*(5/6), 304–317. doi:10.1504/IJTEL.2012.051816

Friedkin, N. E., & Johnsen, E. C. (2011). *Social Influence Network Theory: A Sociological Examination of Small Group Dynamics*. Cambridge University Press. doi:10.1017/CBO9780511976735

Fulantelli, G., Taibi, D., & Arrigo, M. (2015). A framework to support educational decision making in mobile learning. *Computers in Human Behavior, 47*, 50–59. doi:10.1016/j.chb.2014.05.045

Garaizar, P., & Guenaga, M. (2014). A multimodal learning analytics view of HTML5 APIs: technical benefits and privacy risks. In F. J. García-Peñalvo (Ed.), *Proceedings of the Second International Conference on Technological Ecosystem for Enhancing Multiculturality (TEEM'14)* (pp. 275-281). New York, NY: ACM. doi:10.1145/2669711.2669911

García-Holgado, A., & García-Peñalvo, F. J. (2013). The evolution of the technological ecosystems: An architectural proposal to enhancing learning processes. In F. J. García-Peñalvo (Ed.), *Proceedings of the First International Conference on Technological Ecosystems for Enhancing Multiculturality (TEEM'13)*. New York, NY: ACM. doi:10.1145/2536536.2536623

García-Holgado, A., & García-Peñalvo, F. J. (2014). Architectural pattern for the definition of eLearning ecosystems based on Open Source developments. In J. L. Sierra-Rodríguez, J. M. Dodero-Beardo, & D. Burgos (Eds.), *Proceedings of 2014 International Symposium on Computers in Education (SIIE)* (pp. 93-98). Institute of Electrical and Electronics Engineers. doi:10.1109/SIIE.2014.7017711

García-Holgado, A., García-Peñalvo, F. J., Hernández-García, Á., & Llorens-Largo, F. (2015). Analysis and Improvement of Knowledge Management Processes in Organizations Using the Business Process Model Notation. In D. Palacios-Marqués, D. Ribeiro Soriano, & K. H. Huarng (Eds.), *New Information and Communication Technologies for Knowledge Management in Organizations* (pp. 93–101). Springer International Publishing. doi:10.1007/978-3-319-22204-2_9

García-Peñalvo, F. J. (2008). *Advances in E-Learning: Experiences and Methodologies*. Hershey, PA: Information Science Reference. doi:10.4018/978-1-59904-756-0

García-Peñalvo, F. J., Colomo-Palacios, R., & Lytras, M. D. (2012). Informal learning in work environments: Training with the Social Web in the workplace. *Behaviour & Information Technology, 31*(8), 753–755. doi:10.1080/0144929X.2012.661548

García-Peñalvo, F. J., Conde-González, M. A., Alier, M., & Casany, M. J. (2011). Opening Learning Management Systems to Personal Learning Environments. *Journal of Universal Computer Science, 17*(9), 1222–1240.

García-Peñalvo, F. J., Conde-González, M. Á., Zangrando, V., García-Holgado, A., Seoane, A. M., Forment, M. A., & Minović, M. (2013). TRAILER project (Tagging, recognition, acknowledgment of informal learning experiences). A Methodology to make visible learners' informal learning activities to the institutions. *Journal of Universal Computer Science, 19*(11), 1661.

García-Peñalvo, F. J., García de Figuerola, C., & Merlo, J. A. (2010). Open knowledge: Challenges and facts. *Online Information Review, 34*(4), 520–539. doi:10.1108/14684521011072963

García-Peñalvo, F. J., Hernández-García, Á., Conde-González, M. Á., Fidalgo-Blanco, Á., Sein-Echaluce Lacleta, M. L., & Alier-Forment, M. et al. (2015a). Learning services-based technological ecosystems.*Proceedings of the Third International Conference on Technological Ecosystems for Enhancing Multiculturality (TEEM'15)*. New York: ACM. doi:10.1145/2808580.2808650

García-Peñalvo, F. J., Hernández-García, Á., Conde-González, M. Á., Fidalgo-Blanco, Á., Sein-Echaluce Lacleta, M. L., Alier-Forment, M., et al. (2015b). Mirando hacia el futuro: Ecosistemas tecnológicos de aprendizaje basados en servicios.*Actas del III Congreso Internacional sobre Aprendizaje, Innovación y Competitividad (CINAIC 2015)*. Madrid, Spain: Fundación General de la UPM.

García-Peñalvo, F. J., & Seoane-Pardo, A. M. (2015). Una revisión actualizada del concepto de eLearning. Décimo Aniversario. *Education in the Knowledge Society, 16*(1), 119–144. doi:10.14201/eks2015161119144

Gardner, H. (1999). *Intelligence Reframed: Multiple Intelligences for the 21st Century*. Basic Books.

Gardner, H. (2011). *Multiple intelligences: Reflections after thirty years*. Washington, DC: National Association of Gifted Children Parent and Community Network Newsletter.

Gartner. (2015). *Gartner Hype Cycle*. Retrieved 11/07/2015, from http://www.gartner.com/technology/research/methodologies/hype-cycle.jsp

Gustavsson, R., & Fredriksson, M. (2003). Sustainable Information Ecosystems. In A. Garcia, C. Lucena, F. Zambonelli, A. Omicini, & J. Castro (Eds.), Software Engineering for Large-Scale Multi-Agent Systems (Vol. 2603, pp. 123-138). Springer Berlin Heidelberg.

Illanas, A., & Llorens, F. (2011). Los retos Web 2.0 de cara al EEES. In C. Suarez-Guerrero & F. J. García-Peñalvo (Eds.), *Universidad y Desarrollo Social de la Web* (pp. 13–34). Editandum.

Kapp, K. M. (2012). *The Gamification of Learning and Instruction: Game-based Methods and Strategies for Training and Education*. San Francisco, CA: Wiley.

Karmacracy. (2013). *Karmacracy*. Retrieved 21 April 2016 from https://karmacracy.com

Kitchenham, B., Brereton, O. P., Budgen, D., Turner, M., Bailey, J., & Linkman, S. (2009). Systematic literature reviews in software engineering – A systematic literature review. *Information and Software Technology*, *51*(1), 7–15. doi:10.1016/j.infsof.2008.09.009

Kitchenham, B., & Charters, S. (2007). *Guidelines for performing Systematic Literature Reviews in Software Engineering. Version 2.3*. School of Computer Science and Mathematics, Keele University.

Laanpere, M. (2012). *Digital Learning ecosystems: rethinking virtual learning environments in the age of social media*. Paper presented at the IFIP-OST'12: Open and Social Technologies for Networked Learning, Taillinn, Estonia.

LACE. (n.d.). *LACE – Learning Analytics Community Exchange*. Retrieved 21 April 2016 from http://www.laceproject.eu

Lerís, D., & Sein-Echaluce, M. L. (2011). La personalización del aprendizaje: Un objetivo del paradigma educativo centrado en el aprendizaje. *Arbor*, *187*(3), 123-134.

Llorens, F. (2009). La tecnología como motor de la innovación educativa. Estrategia y política institucional de la Universidad de Alicante. *Arbor*, *185*, 21-32.

Llorens, F. (2011). La biblioteca universitaria como difusor de la innovación educativa. Estrategia y política institucional de la Universidad de Alicante. *Arbor*, *187*(3), 89-100.

Llorens, F., Molina, R., Compañ, P., & Satorre, R. (2014). Technological Ecosystem for Open Education. In R. Neves-Silva, G. A. Tsihrintzis, V. Uskov, R. J. Howlett, & L. C. Jain (Eds.), *Smart Digital Futures 2014* (Vol. 262, pp. 706–715). IOS Press.

Long, P. D., & Siemens, G. (2011). Penetrating the Fog: Analytics in Learning and Education. *EDUCAUSE Review*, *46*(5), 30–32.

McGonigal, J. (2011). *Reality Is Broken: Why Games Make Us Better and How They Can Change the World*. Penguin Group US.

Michavila, F. (2013). Prólogo del informe Tendencias Universidad: En pos de la educación activa. In F. Llorens Largo (Ed.), *En pos de la educación activa* (pp. 5–7). Madrid: Cátedra UNESCO de Gestión y Política Universitaria de la Universidad Politécnica de Madrid.

Moore, G. A. (2014). *Crossing the Chasm* (3rd ed.). HarperCollins.

Mozilla OpenBadges. (n.d.). *Open Badges*. Retrieved 21 April 2016 from http://openbadges.org

Pardo, A., & Delgado Kloos, C. (2011). Stepping out of the box: Towards analytics outside the learning management system. In *Proceedings of the 1st International Conference on Learning Analytics and Knowledge* (pp. 163-167). ACM.

Pata, K. (2011). *Meta-design framework for open learning ecosystems*. Paper presented at the Mash-UP Personal Learning Environments (MUP/PLE 2011), London, UK.

Phillips, R., Maor, D., Preston, G., & Cumming-Potvin, W. (2012). *Exploring Learning Analytics as Indicators of Study Behaviour*. Paper presented at the World Conference on Educational Multimedia, Hypermedia and Telecommunications 2012, Denver, CO.

Pitarch, A., Álvarez, A., & Monferrer, J. (2007). *e-PEL: paradigma de gestión de portfolios educativos*. Paper presented at the Congreso Español de Informática (CEDI 2007).

Prensky, M. (2006). *"Don't bother me Mom, I'm learning!": how computer and video games are preparing your kids for twenty-first century success and how you can help!* St. Paul, MN: Paragon House.

Prensky, M. (2007). *Digital Game-Based Learning*. St. Paul, MN: Paragon House.

Rogers, E. M. (2003). *Diffusion of Innovations* (5th ed.). Free Press.

ROLE. (n.d.). *Project*. Retrieved 21 April 2016 from http://www.role-project.eu

Romero, C., & Ventura, S. (2007). Educational data mining: A survey from 1995 to 2005. *Expert Systems with Applications*, *33*(1), 135–146. doi:10.1016/j.eswa.2006.04.005

Romero, C., & Ventura, S. (2010). Educational Data Mining: A Review of the State of the Art. *Systems, Man, and Cybernetics, Part C: Applications and Reviews. IEEE Transactions on*, *40*(6), 601–618.

Schaffert, R., & Hilzensauer, W. (2008). On the way towards Personal Learning Environments: Seven crucial aspects. *eLearning Papers*, *2*(9), 1-11.

Schwaber, K. (2007). SCRUM Development Process. In J. Sutherland, C. Casanave, J. Miller, P. Patel, & G. Hollowell (Eds.), *Business Object Design and Implementation. OOPSLA '95 Workshop Proceedings* (pp. 117-134). London, UK: Springer London. doi:10.1007/978-1-4471-0947-1_11

Sein-Echaluce Lacleta, M. L., Fidalgo-Blanco, Á., García-Peñalvo, F. J., & Conde-González, M. Á. (2015). A knowledge management system to classify social educational resources within a subject using teamwork techniques.*Proceedings of the 17th International Conference, HCI International 2015*. Los Angeles, CA: Springer International Publishing. doi:10.1007/978-3-319-20609-7_48

Siemens, G. (2012). Learning analytics: envisioning a research discipline and a domain of practice. In *Proceedings of the 2nd International Conference on Learning Analytics and Knowledge* (pp. 4-8). New York, NY: ACM.

SNOLA. (2016). *SNOLA*. Retrieved 21 April 2016 from http://snola.net

SOLAR. (2016). *Society for Learning Analytics Research (SoLAR)*. Retrieved 21 April from https://solaresearch.org

Stackoverflow. (n.d.). *Stack Overflow*. Retrieved 21 April 2016 from http://stackoverflow.com

Taleb, N. N., & Mosquera, A. S. (2008). *El cisne negro: El impacto de lo altamente improbable*. Barcelona: Paidós Ibérica.

Turkle, S. (2011). *Alone Together: Why We Expect More from Technology and Less from Each Other*. Basic Books.

Wexler, S., Dublin, L., Grey, N., Jagannathan, S., Karrer, T., Martinez, M., & van Barneveld, A. (2007). *Learning management systems. The good, the bad, the ugly,... and the truth. Guild Research 360 Degree Report*. Santa Rosa, CA: The eLearning Guild.

Wilson, S., Liber, O., Johnson, M., Beauvoir, P., Sharples, P., & Milligan, C. (2007). Personal Learning Environments: Challenging the dominant design of educational systems. *Journal of e-Learning and Knowledge Society, 3*(3), 27-38.

Yukselturk, E., Ozekes, S., & Türel, Y. (2014). Predicting Dropout Student: An Application of Data Mining Methods in an Online Education Program. *European Journal of Open, Distance and E-Learning, 17*(1).

KEY TERMS AND DEFINITIONS

Architecture Framework: The structural element of the learning ecosystem that connects and guarantees communication and data flows between the different components. The architecture framework supports, implements and deploys the learning ecosystem, by ensuring interoperability and dynamic integration of different tools and services.

Components: Interoperable learning-based services based on standard semantic descriptors that add functionalities to the learning ecosystem.

e-Portfolios: Tools for personal learning process development that include different learning evidences, ordered and structured according to different criteria, to create a profile of the individual's competences and to store and display evidences of informal learning.

Gamified Learning: Application of gamification-based design rules, techniques and tools to learning processes.

Interoperability: Property of a product or system, whose interfaces are completely understood, to work with other products or systems, present or future, without any restricted access or implementation.

Learning Analytics: The measurement, collection, analysis and reporting of data about learners and their contexts, for purposes of understanding and optimising learning and the environments in which it occurs.

Learning Ecosystem: Also named learning technological ecosystem or learning service-based technological ecosystem, this term refer to a configuration of architecture framework and interoperable service components where a community –with their educational methods, policies, rules and regulations, applications and work teams– may coexist in a way that the learning processes are inter-related, and the implementation and execution of such processes is based on physical factors of the technological environment.

Chapter 2
Tools Interoperability for Learning Management Systems

Nikolas Galanis
*Universitat Politècnica de Catalunya –
BarcelonaTech, Spain*

María José Casany
*Universitat Politècnica de Catalunya –
BarcelonaTech, Spain*

Enric Mayol
*Universitat Politècnica de Catalunya –
BarcelonaTech, Spain*

Marc Alier
*Universitat Politècnica de Catalunya –
BarcelonaTech, Spain*

ABSTRACT

E-learning has experienced an extraordinary growth over the last years. We have reached a point in time when most learning institutions have adopted an LMS as an integral element of their teaching and learning infrastructure. In parallel, the number of educational tools available for learning is increasing and keeps evolving. This variety means that it is not always easy or possible to add these educational tools into LMSs to enhance the learning process. It would, however, be in everyone's interest for these tools to interact with the LMSs. To solve the problem of interoperability between LMS and learning tools, several interoperability standards define ways so that LMSs can interface with external learning tools in order to make them accessible from within the learning platform in an intuitive and concise way. This chapter is focused on the service-oriented approach to interoperability and specifically on the IMS LTI standard and the TSUGI hosting environment that aims to simplify the integration of external learning tools.

DOI: 10.4018/978-1-5225-0905-9.ch002

1. INTRODUCTION

Innovation on ICT-based learning depends on the ability of the content creators and providers to develop new tools and services and making them available to the general public. The broad adoption of ICT in the education process, means that educators are increasingly on the lookout for new content and methods to adopt into their teaching process or, in some cases, they even go as far as to adapt their entire process to these contents.

This abundance of learning content is a product of social constructivism and social constructionism (Berger and Luckman, 1991), where with the help of technology, learners have transformed from simple consumers of learning contents to producers and creators of contents that they make available to the world for consumption. Social constructionism refers to the knowledge artifacts created by learners through social interaction, while social constructivism refers to an individual´s learning that is attributed to their participation within such a social group.

Formal ICT-based learning, however, usually takes place within a virtual learning environment (VLE) or learning management system (LMS). Usually, once an LMS is installed and integrated into the workflow of an organization, it is very difficult to convince any governance team to replace it with a new one, because of costs in software integration, data migrations, user training and the inherent risks of any software migration procedure. So we can assume that the current install base of the various LMSs is going to be very stable, and changes will mostly come from new organizations or new kind of activities (like the use of new platforms as support for MOOCS). The variety of existing VLEs, means that the availability of learning contents within each platform depends on the author´s or a third party´s ability and willingness to provide a compatible implementation. This inevitably leads to fragmentation of the content availability among the available platforms since creators usually only develop on the platform they themselves use.

On top of that, contrary to the relative stability of the VLEs/LMSs, the teaching tools offered to the educators tend to suffer a lot of changes. These tools keep evolving and new ones are constantly introduced and it is only normal that teachers will want to incorporate them in their teaching. Usually VLEs offer software development kits that allow the creation of extensions - learning activities, visual styles, widgets, even complete virtual classroom frameworks. But these extensions are created, bound and tested for a version of the VLE/LMS and need to be revised and re-tested for each new version. Due to all these compatibility concerns, many big installations avoid installing unofficial extensions (even the ones developed within the organization), and teachers and students have to deal with a stock version of the VLE/LMS.

Even if we extend a VLE/LMS with extensions we are bound to miss learning tools and contents hosted in the Cloud, a fairly recent tendency that was not on the table when the most successful VLEs/LMSs where on the drawing board. In order to try to avoid this fragmentation, a number of organizations have proposed interoperability standards to be implemented and followed by LMSs and content creators alike. These standards define ways that LMSs/VLEs can interface with external tools in order to make them accessible from within the learning platform in an intuitive and concise way.

This chapter discusses the concept of interoperability. The focus is on the service-oriented approach (SOA) to interoperability and present two approaches: the Open Knowledge Initiative (OKI) and the IMS approach.

2. INTEROPERABILITY

2.1 The SOA Approach to Interoperability

The IEEE defines interoperability as "the ability of two or more systems, or components to exchange information and to use the information that has been exchanged" (Prensky, 2001). However, the IEEE definition for interoperability is 16 years old, and hardly applies to modern software systems that can do more things concurrently than just exchange information, like for example share functionality. The Open Knowledge Initiative (OKI) provides a new, more up-to-date definition for interoperability: "the measure of ease of integration between two systems or software components to achieve a functional goal. A highly interoperable integration is one that can easily achieved by the individual who requires the result". According to this definition, interoperability is about making the integration as simple and cost effective as technologically possible (Merriman, 2003).

The Service Oriented Architecture (SOA) provides an approach to achieving such interoperability. SOA is a software engineering approach that provides a separation between the interface of a service, and its underlying implementation. For the end users of these services the implementation details, how contents are stored and how they are structured are not important. In the SOA approach consumer applications can interoperate across the widest set of service providers (implementations), and providers can easily be swapped on-the-fly without modification to application code.

SOA preserves the investment in software development as the whole idea rests on that underlying technologies and mechanisms evolve and can be replaced by newer ones developed internally or externally without compromising interoperability.

For these reasons SOA architectures are a perfect fit for Learning Management Systems (LMS) by offering a solution that help reinforce their interoperability with new and future generations of learning applications. Using a SOA architecture to integrate new generations of learning applications into the Web-based LMS, provides the following benefits:

1. The students gain access to a variety of modern tools accessed directly from their institution's LMS.
2. The teachers do not need to look outside the LMS they are used to, to create new tasks for their students. These new tasks can be done using an external application from the LMS interface.
3. There is no need of any confusing interface changes. Everything stays consistent using the usual LMS's interface.

2.2 Interoperability Specifications

2.2.1 The Open Knowledge Initiative

The Open Knowledge Initiative (OKI) was born in 2003 with the purpose of creating a standard architecture of common services across software systems that need to share, such as Authentication, Authorization, Logging (Merriman, 2003). The OKI project has developed and published a suite of interfaces know as Open Service Interface Definitions (OSIDs) whose design has been informed by a broad architectural view. The OSIDs specifications provide interoperability among applications across a varied base of underlying and changing technologies. They provide general software contracts between service consumers and service providers. The OSIDs open up a wide range of choice among end-user tools. As long as the tools offer support for these interface definitions, interoperability is easily achieved. It is worth noting that OSIDs are software contracts only and are therefore compatible with most other technologies and specifications, such a SOAP, WSDL. They can be used with existing technology, open source or commercial solutions.

Each OSID describes a logical service. They separate program logic from underlying technology using software interfaces. The separation between the software consumer and provider is done at the application level so as to separate consumers from specific protocols. This enables applications to be designed and developed independently from any particular service environment.

As an example, services such as authentication that are common functions required by many systems, do not need to be built specifically for each system. A single implementation following the OKI standards will work for all systems and will further help guarantee homogeneity and parity of features. On top of that, in the case of a composite system, the OKI approach separates the authentication function from the rest of the system and provides a central authentication service for all the applications.

OKI uses OSIDs to describe the basic services already available in e-learning platforms. Some of the most common services are:

- The authentication OSID for registering new users or logging existing users in the system. This is a basic service in any software system.
- The authorization OSID is used to know if a user has rights to access a service or function. This service is necessary in any system using roles.
- The logging OSID is used to capture usage information for performance and diagnostics reasons.
- The internationalization OSID is used to change the language of the application or add new languages.
- The configuration OSID is used to change configuration parameters.

Thus using the OKI OSIDs has the following advantages:

- Ease to develop software. The developers only have to concentrate in the part of the problem where they can add value. Common functions can be shared among the systems.
- Common service factoring. OKI provides a general service factory so that services can be reused.
- Reduce integration cost. The cost of integration is usually the main factor that prevents new solutions from being easily adopted. OSIDs are a neutral open interface that provides well-understood integration points. This way integration costs are kept to a minimum, plus there is no need to build a dependency on a particular vendor.
- Software usable across a wider range of environments, because OKI is a SOA architecture.

2.2.2 The IMS Global Learning Consortium Initiatives for Interoperability in Learning Systems

The IMS Global Learning Consortium (IMS GLC) is also working since 2005 in standards towards the interoperability and integration of learning services and systems. Among these standards, IMS GLC developed the IMS Abstract Framework (IMS AF), a set of (abstract) specifications to build a generic e-learning framework, capable of interoperating with other systems following the same specifications. IMS AF describes an e-learning system as the set of services that need to be offered (IMS AF, 2003).

Another specification created by IMS that became an interoperability standard is the IMS Learning Tools for Interoperability (IMS-LTI). The specification called Tool Interoperability (TI) aims to integrate external applications into an LMS through Service-Oriented Architectures (SOA) (IMS LTI, 2013).

IMS TI created a new approach regarding interoperability between external applications and LMSs. IMS TI proposed an architecture where the LMS is a generic player of applications. The LMS is able to interact with any external application that follows the specification proposed by IMS TI. IMS TI is based on three pillars; the first one is a proxy of external applications. As its name suggests, it is a proxy or a front-end in the LMS associated with an external application. The second one is the execution of the external application. This application must accept an alternative invocation method proposed by the IMs TI standard. Finally, web services that are provided by the LMS and invoked by the external application.

IMS TI offers several advantages in the integration between applications and LMSs. On one hand it provides a generic mechanism to integrate external applications within an LMS as if they were native to the LMS. The use of this standard simplifies the integration of LMS-external application because it does not require a bilateral development. The use of IMS TI as an interoperability protocol between LMS and external applications allows external applications (that make certain adaptations in their code) to be used by all the LMSs that follow the standard. Moreover, it simplifies the administrative tasks in the LMS when deploying new modules because in IMS TI the process consists in configuring a new proxy instance.

The first version of IMS LTI was IMS Simple LTI (2010), developed under the supervision of Dr. Charles Severance. This early version focused on the process on how a remote tool is installed on a web based learning system (IMS LTI, 2013). SimpleLTI is neither a standard nor a specification. It is a minimal expression of an implementation guide of the LTI protocol. SimpleLTI was created so that LMS developers could create a quick implementation of the protocol and provide feedback to improve the LTI specification.

Afterwards, BasicLTI (or LTI v1.0) (released in May 2010) was created as an expanded version of SimpleLTI by IMS GLC. BasicLTI can be considered a standard and is a simplified version of the LTI specification. An important difference between simpleLTI and basicLTI is that basicLTI is a formal specification and not an implementation guide. Its main contribution is that it provides a simple but standard method to establish a secure link to an external tool from the LMS.

LTI v1.0 evolved to LTI 1.1 that adds the ability to pass back an outcome from the external tool to the LMS. This allows students to receive a grade or score from their interaction with the learning application.

Learning Tools Interoperability 2.0 (2012) is the name of the second version of the standard for interoperability of IMS GLC. LTI 2.0 is a major rewrite of LTI 1. It is designed to extend interoperability to the entire lifecycle of the tool not just to the launch point. Therefore, LTI 2.0 becomes a platform not just for embedding a tool but also for creating very smart and adaptive tools, or even general-purpose educational web applications. A detailed explanation of LTI 2.0 is presented in section 3.

An example of an application using IMS LTI to connect an external tool to an LMS is the Docs4Learning project. The authors implemented an LTI bridge to make the Google Docs (currently Google Drive) authoring tools available from within an LMS. Although the Docs4Learning platform was tested using Moodle, its LTI implementation means that it should be accessible from any LMS that provides support for IMS LTI.

Summering up, the main goal of this architecture is to provide a framework that allows integrating easily educational tools within LMSs transparently. The intention of IMS GLC is that developers have all the specification of the protocol and system architecture so that the difference between an LMS native-activity and an external-activity is not visible.

Now, IMs TI has become well adopted as a simple but effective mechanism for integrating third party content and applications with LMSs. For example, it is now part of the core product for all major LMSs, including Moodle, Blackboard Learn 9, Desire2Learn and Canvas from Instructure (Vickers & Booth, 2014).

2.2.3 SOA Initiatives

There have been several other initiatives to adapt SOA services for LMS and the integration of external applications into the LMS (Kurz, 2008), (Luisa, n.d), (Pätzold et al, 2008). But all these initiatives have some notable limitations:

- **A Defined Application Domain:** Not all LMS services are provided, only those, which are useful to a specific application domain.
- **Unidirectional Interoperability:** Architectures work only in one direction, which is, provide information from the LMS to other applications or integrate it with other tools. It not possible to provide information from external applications to the LMS.
- **Interoperability Specifications:** Definition of a service structure that does not use specifications for interoperability.

3. IMS-LTI 2.0

This section introduces main features of LTI 2 by examining the characteristics of its predecessors and calling out the forces that has led to its redesign. This summary is based on best practices of the celLTIc project (CeLTIc Project Wiki, 2014), (Vickers & Both, 2014), tutorials provided by the IMS consortium for developers (IMS Tutorials, 2015) and the final draft specification of LTI 2 (IMS LTI 2.0, 2015).

LTI 2 has been under development for several years, and the final specification has been released on February 2014. LTI 2 provides a more sophisticated and extensible platform to enable deeper integrations and greater support for services and events. LTI 2 builds on LTI 1 by incorporating more sophisticated outcomes reporting and a rich extensions architecture allowing additional services to be added gradually. LTI 2 uses REST and JSON-LD to deliver this new functionality (IMS LTI 2.0, 2015).

3.1 LTI Basic Concepts

This section is used to introduce some basic terminology and concepts to help follow the analysis that follows.

3.1.1 Basic LTI workflow

In the context of an LMS that want to access to an externally hosted tool, the basic workflow for using LTI starts when an LMS administrator gains access to the external tool. This access is obtained when the external tool's administrator provides the LMS administrator a URL, key, and secret for the Tool.

From the point of view of a LMS Instructor, he generally adds a LTI tool into their course structure as a resource link using the LMS control panel. The instructor enters the URL, secret, and key into as meta data for the resource link. When students select the tool, the LMS uses the URL, secret, and key information to seamlessly launch the student into the remote tool in an iframe or a new browser window.

From the Administrator point of view, he generally adds a "virtual tool" to the LMS, entering the URL, secret and key. Once this is done, Instructors simply see the newly configured LTI tool as another tool or activity to be placed as a resource link in their course structure. The Instructors and students may not even be aware that the tool they are using is running out side of the LMS. They simply select and use the tool like any other tool that is built-into the LMS.

In both cases, the external tool receives a Launch request that includes user identity, course information, role information, and the key and signature. The launch information is sent using an HTTP form generated in the user's browser with the

LTI data elements in hidden form fields and automatically submitted to the external tool using JavaScript. The data in the HTTP form is signed using the OAuth (Oauth, n.d.) security standard so the external tool can be assured that the launch data was not modified between time the LMS generated and signed the data and the time that the Tool received the data.

3.1.2 LTI Basic Concepts

- **Tool Consumer (TC):** Typically, this refers to the LMs or Virtual Learning Environment (VLE); it is the system which users (instructor, students, …) are logged into and from which they will be redirected to the external tool being integrated with it.
- **Tool Provider (TP):** The external tool, like a web-based learning application or a content delivery system, which is being integrated with the tool consumer (TC).
- **Consumer Key (CK):** A string generated by the tool provider that identifies it, to allow them to uniquely identify the source of requests being received.
- **Shared Secret (SS):** States that communications between the tool provider (TP) and the tool consumer (TC) are secured using the OAuth protocol with the shared secret (which should be known only to the tool provider and the tool consumer).
- **Context Information (CI):** The context in the tool consumer from where tool provider is launched. Tool Consumers (TC) are typically organised into courses, with users being enrolled into each course for which they are permitted to access; thus, in this case, the course is the context from which users launch into tool providers.
- **Resource Link (RL):** The actual link provided within a context which users follow to access the tool provider; there may be multiple resource links to each tool provider within the same context and across the whole tool consumer, but each resource link is uniquely identified.

3.1.3 Launch Request

The mechanism used by a tool consumer (TC) to redirect a user to a tool provider (TP) is performed by means of a launch request. The fundamentals of this process are:

- Redirection is done via the user's browser using an HTTP POST request;
- Data is passed using POST data parameters with prescribed names;

- Parameters may include data about the context and resource link from which the launch request originates, the user making the request, and the role of the user within the context;
- The connection is secured by a timestamp, a nonce value and an OAuth signature.

A tool consumer (TC) will typically implement a launch by returning an HTML page to the user's browser consisting of a form containing all the launch parameters as hidden input elements. The form would be submitted automatically by a JavaScript function run when the page is loaded or by the user clicking a submit button.

3.1.4 Launch Parameters

The names of supported parameters depend on the LTI version, and can be found in the different IMS-LTI specifications (IMS LTI, 2010). But the only required parameters are:

- **lti_message_type:** Basic-lti-launch-request | ToolProxyRegistrationRequest. This parameter indicates the type of the message. This allows a Tool Provider to accept a number of different LTI message types at the same endpoint
- **lti_version:** LTI-2p0. This parameter indicates which version of the specification is being used for this particular message.
- **Resource_link_id:** This parameter is an opaque unique identifier that the Tool Consumer guarantees will be unique within the Tool Consumer for every placement of the link. If the tool / activity is placed multiple times in the same context, each of those placements will be distinct. This value will also change if the item is exported from one system or context and imported into another system or context.

Additionally, the following OAuth parameters are required:

- **Oauth_consumer_key:** A plain text that identifies which tool consumer (TC) is sending the message allowing the tool provider (TP) to look up the appropriate secret for validation
- **Oauth_signature_method:** Indicates the signing method with OAuth fields coming from POST parameters for launch requests

- **Oauth_timestamp:** Indicates when the request was created in terms of the number of seconds since the Unix epoch at the point the request is generated. It is used to reject requests that were created too far in the past.
- **Oauth_nonce:** A unique token generated for each unique request. It is used to determine whether a request has been submitted multiple times.
- **Oauth_version:** Indicates OAuth version used to sign.
- **Oauth_signature:** Contains a value which is generated by running all of the other request parameters and secret key through a signing algorithm. The purpose of the signature is so that tool provider (TP) can verify that the request has not been modified in transit, verify the tool consumer (TC) sending the request, and verify that tool provider and consumer have authorization to interact.
- **Oauth_callback:** Corresponds to the absolute URL to which the tool provider (TP) will redirect the user back when the user identification step is completed.

As you can see, a launch request can be extremely minimal and need not to include any data about the context, user or role. When a tool consumer (TC) or tool provider (TP) has been certified by IMS, some of the parameters recommended by the specification will also be present. These additional demands for certification are designed to enhance interoperability, whilst still allowing flexibility in the specification.

3.1.5 Receiving a Launch Request

The tool consumer (TC) receiving a LTI launches will need to be a script that is capable of processing the request. A typical script would perform the following actions:

1. Ensure all the required LTI parameters are present and have appropriate values.
2. Check that the request comes from a known tool consumer looking up the consumer key.
3. Verify the authenticity of the request: checking timestamp, nonce values and OAuth signature.
4. Ensure that all additional parameters that your system depends upon are present.

If you reach this point it means that you have a valid launch request from a known customer with all the data you require. Hence it is now safe to process the request and provide access to the user.

3.2 How to Launch a Request in the Different LTI Versions

This section summarizes how a tool consumer (TC) launches a request to an external tool provider (TP) using different versions of LTI (from v.1.0 to v.2.0). This summary is based on the tutorial provided by IMS Consortium (IMS Tutorials, 2015).

3.2.1 LTI v1.0: The Beginnings

The success of LTI is due mainly to simple reasons. The most relevant is that it allows a learning system, particularly a Learning Management System (LMS), to launch an external learning tool and run it as if it were an integrated part of the learning system. This fact has opened a big opportunity to extend LMS functionality in a simple and powerful way, without introducing the necessity to redesign or re-implement the learning system. Moreover, this launch is performed with the sufficient security that it protected the learning tool from misuse, and it took the simplest approach possible to achieve these goals. It benefited from strong early advocacy, especially from the tireless promotion of Dr. Chuck Severance. The key to understanding LTI 1.0 is to realize that it focuses on one, and only one, aspect of tool interoperability, the tool's launch.

3.2.1.1 Use Case

A very common use case for LTI is the opening of an e-textbook from within the LMS. This is such a widely used case it's often been called the 'killer app' of LTI. For example, a student logs into his LMS, proceeds to one of his courses and finds that his instructor has placed a link to a text document. He clicks on the link and the document opens to the page of the next assigned reading. Then, the student reads, advances through other pages, jumps to references, leaves notes, etc. as the document was stored into the LMS course.

3.2.1.2 Architecture

Figure 1 shows the schema of the LTI 1.0 launch.

1. A user, perhaps a student, clicks on an LTI link that requests a tool launch.
2. The Tool Consumer (TC) prepares a bundle of launch parameters including standard, optional, and custom parameters that are part of the 'envelope' of the launch message.
3. OAuth digitally signs the payload to ensure its integrity.
4. The TC then sends this message back to the browser and a tiny piece of javascript auto-POSTs the message to the Tool Provider. The peculiar piece of orchestration (step 4) is essential to the LTI launch; it ensures that the source

Figure 1. Launch interaction using LTI v.1.0

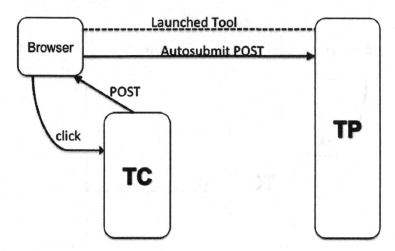

of the launch is the user (actually the browser, the user's agent) rather than the TC server.

5.   The Tool Provider (TP) responds with a presentation of the tool in the browser.

LTI 1.0 is solely about tool launch. The bundle of parameters contained in the launch determines likewise everything about the textbook appearance, its size, position, and its page.

3.2.2 LTI v1.1: Course Correction

After LTI 1.0 established itself as the premier interoperability standard, a particular need arose that caused a change to its specification. Some learning tools return a grade from the tool provider (TP) that would like to pass back into the grade book of the tool consumer. Since LTI 1.0 lost contact between TC and TP after launch another communication channel was required to get a tool outcome back from the launch and redirected to the grade book.

3.2.2.1 Use Case

At week's end, the student is ready to take a weekly assessment. She presses the link and it now directs his to an exercise within the document (or possibly in a separate standalone assessment tool). He takes the exercise, feels good about the results, and submits the result. When he goes over to his LMS grade book he sees the grade he's accrued.

3.2.2.2 Architecture

The LTI 1.1 launch diagram is shown in Figure 2.

Figure 2. Launch interaction using LTI v.1.1

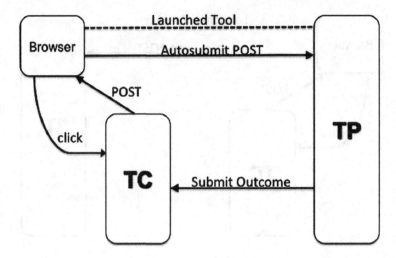

The launch phase is structurally identical to a LTI 1.0 launch. (The dotted line is a shorthand for the multiple arrows in the 1.0 launch). However at least two extra parameters are passed in the launch:

- **lis_outcome_service_url:** The return point to which an outcome may be placed into the grade book.
- **lis_result_sourced_id:** An encrypted ticket provided by the LMS to ensure that the outcome is properly labelled for the particular user, course, and link that are involved in this interaction

It's not obvious from the diagram, but the message with the returned outcome is completely asynchronous from the launch. That is, any time after the launch, whether seconds or weeks, it can return the outcome to the grade book.

3.2.3 LTI v2.0: Learning Tools (with Full) Interoperability

LTI 2.0 is a major rewrite of LTI 1. It is designed to extend interoperability to the entire lifecycle of the tool not just to the launch point. Therefore, LTI 2.0 becomes a platform not just for embedding a tool but also for creating very smart and adaptive tools, or even general-purpose educational web applications.

3.2.3.1 User Story

One of the most desired issues by course instructors is to easily open books within an LMS. Using LTI, this may be performed in minutes rather than weeks. But, the challenge lies in provisioning the books in the LMS so that the right books would be available to the right courses. A school might have hundreds of courses each of which might adopt several books. Some of them are adopted course-books by the school, meanwhile others are recommended by individual professors.

Provisioning thousands of links using custom LTI parameters was not a good design. A best practice of creating book adoption applications evolved but required lots of proprietary web services. LTI 2 and LTI 1.2 can fix this situation by supporting an LTI-launched application that is a book adoption application. This external application allows instructors browsing the book catalog, selecting books, storing with the LMS course using a ToolSettings service, and probably, billing model might require invoking a Roster service in the institution to get a census of students to determine billing.

Observe that this use case is more complex than a launch request since it requires some additional negotiation.

3.2.3.2 Architecture

The LTI 2.0 launch diagram is shown in Figure 3.

The major deliverable in LTI 2 is standardized, architected, REST services that are implemented using industry best-practices. These services and on the Registration phase in the launch are presented below.

- **REST-Level 3 Web Service Model:** REST web services are the preferred technique for implementing distributed services within web applications.

Figure 3. Launch interaction using LTI v.2.0

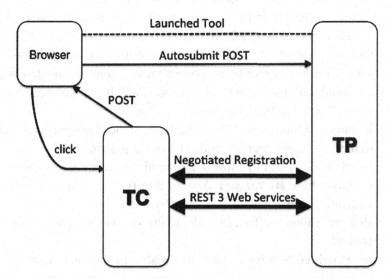

LTI has used a precise recipe for REST services based on the Richardson Maturity Model, where Level 3 REST requires: Resources as basis for HTTP addressing, Proper use of HTTP intrinsic methods and Media type definitions supporting Linked Data.

- **JSON-LD for Payload Definition:** JSON is widely used because it is light-weight and simple to use. The Linked Data (LD) extensions provide hyper-media linking between media types.

- **Discoverable Services:** In any particular pairing of tool consumer and tool provider, a specific interface contract needs to be struck and recorded. This contract is called a Tool Proxy. The Tool Proxy is negotiated by the two parties (TC and TP) automatically but allows human workflows on either side to intervene if necessary. This negotiation is performed during the Registration phase in the LTI 2 Architecture diagram above.

- **Automatic Credential Exchange and Management:** The Registration phase also bakes the LTI key and secret into the Tool Proxy itself. The Tool Consumer defines the key and Tool Provider the corresponding secret. This Registration process and credential exchange can be very fast, usually only requiring the enrolling institution to provide the provider's public registration endpoint. This replaces the cumbersome, out-of-band credential exchange of LTI 1.

- **Architected Services:** LTI 2 not only defines some common services, such as Tool Settings, but also provides the architecture for bi-directional web services. This means that new services can be defined quickly without affecting the core standard. All that's needed to incorporate a new service is to modify the metadata in the TC or TP and re-register. The available services are:
  - **Tool Settings:** Allows a Tool Provider to store data in the Tool Consumer and associate that data with either the Tool Proxy itself, a Course, or a Link. This has extraordinary power; for example, an adopted book can be stored with the course object in an LMS. If that course is copied or deleted, so is the book adoption.
  - **Enhanced Outcomes:** Allows the Tool Provider to send outcomes back to the Tool Consumer but with a) a richer palette of value types than a simple number and b) allow other learning metrics to be provided.
  - **Organization Hierarchy:** Allows the Tool Provider to inspect the structure of departments, courses, course sections etc.
  - **Roster:** Allows the Tool Provider to inspect who's enrolled in a specific course.

- **Partner-Provided Services:** One of the really revolutionary features of LTI 2 is that it allows custom services to be created by partners and used either among themselves, or among any distinct sub-community. These services snap right into LTI 2. Another benefit of partner-provided services it that it allows new services to evolve organically before being submitted for full inclusion as an architected service.

3.2.4 LTI v1.2

LTI 1.2 was co-developed with LTI 2.0. It is a subset of LTI 2.0 that some LTI 1.0 vendors may use it as a steppingstone to LTI 2.0. In fact, LTI 1.2 is a hybrid of LTI 1 and LTI 2.

Here are the characteristics of LTI 1.2.

- The LTI 1.0 launch is virtually identical. No change needs to be made to support the LTI 1.2 launch.
- It defines the ToolConsumerProfile (the TC metadata) and makes it available to the ToolProvider.
- There's no definition of a Tool Profile, nor creation of a Tool Proxy.
- Only TC-based services (e.g., Roster and ToolSettings) are supported.
- It is a declarative rather than negotiated interface. That only means that services are presented by the TC and are not modified by any Tool Provider concern.

LTI 1.2 can provide a transitional step to LTI 1 based TCs by just adding a ToolConsumerProfile with no Registration phase required.

3.2.5 Comparison Chart of LTI Versions

As a summary, Table 1 provides a comparison table of the main features of each LTI version. This table is a reproduction of the table shown in (IMS Tutorials, 2015).

4. TSUGI

4.1 Overview

The ongoing evolution of LTI framework means that either tool consumers need to provide support for all past, present and future versions, or that tool providers need to keep updating their tools to comply to the latest specifications in order to be accessible. Either case requires a lot of dedication and resources that are not always available.

Table 1. Comparison of LTI features

Feature	LTI 1.0	LTI 1.1	LTI 1.2	LTI 2.0	Comment
Basic Launch	X	X	X	X	LTI 2+ greatly reduces requirements for optional data to be carried in every launch.
Simple Outcomes		X	X	X	Return single numeric value that scores the value of launch activity.
Tool Consumer Profile			X	X	TCP is metadata that describes attributes and available services of the Tool Consumer (TC). It's made available by a REST service.
Tool Proxy				X	Tool Proxy is metadata that describes the negotiated interface contract between a particular Tool Consumer (TC) and Tool Provider (TP).
Credential Management				X	Automatic secure exchange of key/secret
Registration Flow				X	LMS Admin initiates new tool provisioning including tool proxy creation and credential management.
Reregistration Flow					LMS Admin initiates an existing tool re-provisioning.
Model-driven documentation			X	X	Tool-generated, exhaustive, reference documentation generated from UML
REST services			X	X	REST level 3 services for a variety of server-to-server tasks. Note that LTI 1.2 limits REST service implementation to be on Tool Consumer (TC) only.

IMS Tutorials, 2015.

Identifying this problem, Dr. Charles Severance proposed the TSUGI framework (http://www.tsugi.org) (Galanis et al., 2014). Essentially, TSUGI is a learning tool hosting environment developed in PHP, with a Java version in the works. TSUGI provides support for all IMS-LTI versions but hides all implementation details behind an API so that tools running on it may be LTI version agnostic. In short, the goal of the TSUGI framework is to make it as simple as possible to write IMS Learning Tools Interoperability™ (LTI)™ tools supporting LTI 1.x and soon 2.x and put them into production. The use of this framework does not automatically imply any type of IMS certification. Tools and products that use this framework must still go through the formal certification process through IMS.

The overall goal behind this framework is to create a learning ecosystem that spans all the LMS systems including Sakai, Moodle, Blackboard, Desire2Learn, Canvas, Coursera, EdX, NovoEd, and perhaps even Google Classroom. Content creators and consumers need to move away from the one-off LTI implementations and move towards a shared hosting container for learning tools. With the emergence of IMS standards for Analytics, Gradebook, Roster, App Store, and a myriad of other services, we cannot afford to do independent implementations for each of these standards. TSUGI hopes to provide one sharable implementation of all of these standards as they are developed, completed, and approved.

4.2 Design

As mentioned above, TSUGI is essentially a hosting container that allows users to get a third-party tool and install it locally on their campus computer or server (Figure 4).

This way, an educational institution can have its own, privately managed TSUGI installation, thus guaranteeing privacy for their users and total control over all the data within. Figure 5 shows a typical TSUGI installation, where a number of external tools have been acquired from their sources (a repository, a web page, an app store, etc.) and installed locally within the institution´s TSUGI container. TSUGI in turn, provides all the necessary LTI APIs for these tools to communicate with any number of VLEs/LMSs the institution requires.

Figure 4. TSUGI container

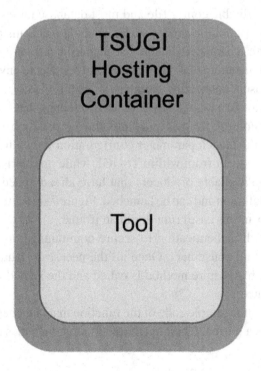

Figure 5. A typical TSUGI installation

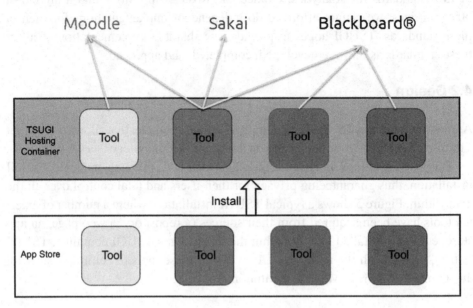

TSUGI has a simple and greatly automated install process. All configuration data are kept in an editable config file and most database tables are automatically created during the installation process. The same database installation procedure can be used to repair a damaged database structure in case of an accident. TSUGI is also multi-tenant, meaning that one instance can connect to any number of VLEs/LMSs and accept users connecting from any of them. Finally, it does not use any cookies in order to avoid a lot of small problems and bugs that tend to appear when combining session control, iframes and simultaneous access from various clients.

Figure 6 shows the launch parameter configuration screen for connecting to an external LTI tool producer from within TSUGI, while on the right hand, the drop-down list shows the available producers that have already been configured in the current TSUGI installation and can be launched. Figure 7 shows the selected external tool (a video player in this case) running in an iframe.

Tsugi uses OAuth authentication to secure communications between the tool producers and the tool consumers. Once all the necessary launch parameters are collected, the OAuth signature method is called and the signed request is ready to be sent to the producer.

Figure 8 shows some sample code of the function that launches the LTI tool from within TSUGI. It is a normal LTI launch function that launches the tool within the

Figure 6. LTI launch parameters in TSUGI

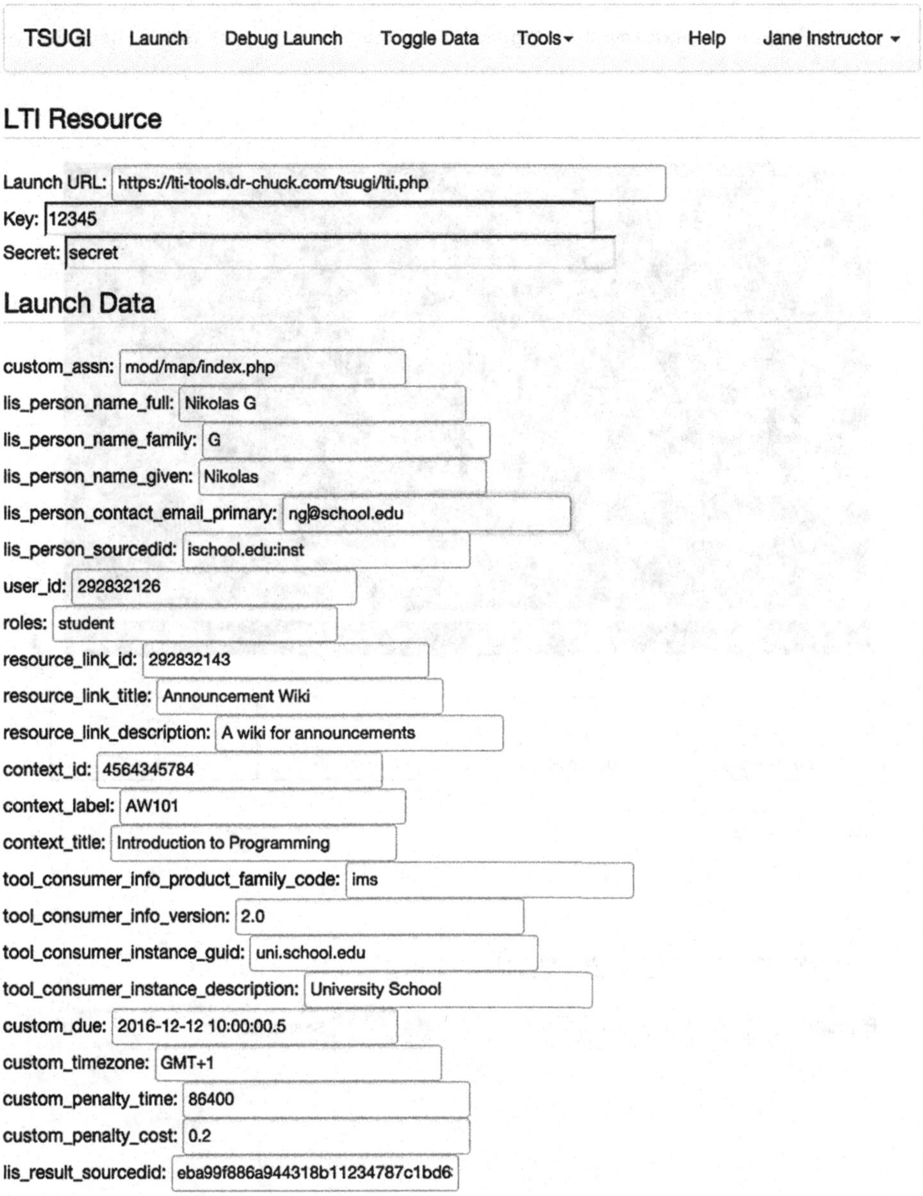

| TSUGI | Launch | Debug Launch | Toggle Data | Tools ▾ | | Help | Jane Instructor ▾ |

LTI Resource

Launch URL: `https://lti-tools.dr-chuck.com/tsugi/lti.php`
Key: `12345`
Secret: `secret`

Launch Data

custom_assn: `mod/map/index.php`

lis_person_name_full: `Nikolas G`

lis_person_name_family: `G`

lis_person_name_given: `Nikolas`

lis_person_contact_email_primary: `ng@school.edu`

lis_person_sourcedid: `ischool.edu:inst`

user_id: `292832126`

roles: `student`

resource_link_id: `292832143`

resource_link_title: `Announcement Wiki`

resource_link_description: `A wiki for announcements`

context_id: `4564345784`

context_label: `AW101`

context_title: `Introduction to Programming`

tool_consumer_info_product_family_code: `ims`

tool_consumer_info_version: `2.0`

tool_consumer_instance_guid: `uni.school.edu`

tool_consumer_instance_description: `University School`

custom_due: `2016-12-12 10:00:00.5`

custom_timezone: `GMT+1`

custom_penalty_time: `86400`

custom_penalty_cost: `0.2`

lis_result_sourcedid: `eba99f886a944318b11234787c1bd6`

Figure 7. Video player launched from TSUGI

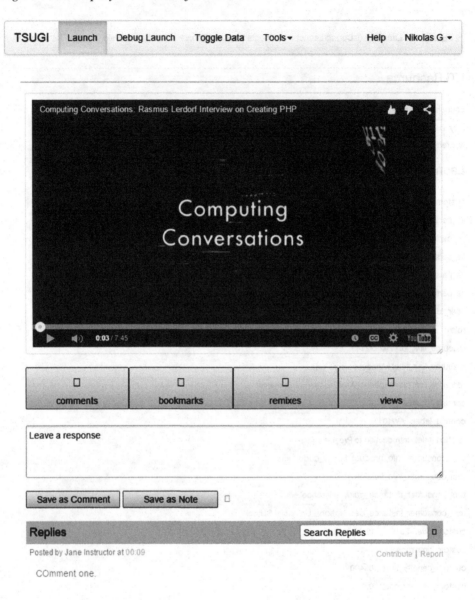

same window, an iframe or in a new window. The function builds a form containing all the launch parameters (signed by OAuth) of the target tool and the viewing preferences (window, iframe, etc.) and then posts it and returns the result which is in turn printed on the screen.

Figure 8. Sample code for launching an LTI tool

```
1   public static function postLaunchHTML($newparms, $endpoint, $iframeattr=false) {
2       global $LastOAuthBodyBaseString;
3       $r = "<div id=\"ltiLaunchFormSubmitArea\">\n";
4       if ( $iframeattr =="_blank" ) {
5           $r = "<form action=\"".$endpoint.
6               "\" name=\"ltiLaunchForm\" id=\"ltiLaunchForm\" method=\"post\"".
7               " target=\"_blank\" encType=\"application/x-www-form-urlencoded\">\n" ;
8       } else if ( $iframeattr ) {
9           $r = "<form action=\"".$endpoint.
10              "\" name=\"ltiLaunchForm\" id=\"ltiLaunchForm\" method=\"post\"".
11              " target=\"basicltiLaunchFrame\" encType=\"application/x-www-form-urlencoded\">\n" ;
12      } else {
13          $r = "<form action=\"".$endpoint.
14              "\" name=\"ltiLaunchForm\" id=\"ltiLaunchForm\" method=\"post\"".
15              " encType=\"application/x-www-form-urlencoded\">\n" ;
16      }
17      $submit_text = $newparms['ext_submit'];
18      foreach($newparms as $key => $value ) {
19          $key = htmlspec_utf8($key);
20          $value = htmlspec_utf8($value);
21          if ( $key == "ext_submit" ) {
22              $r .= "<input type=\"submit\" name=\"";
23          } else {
24              $r .= "<input type=\"hidden\" name=\"";
25          }
26          $r .= $key;
27          $r .= "\" value=\"";
28          $r .= $value;
29          $r .= "\"/>\n";
30      }
31      $r .= "</form>\n";
32      if ( $iframeattr && $iframeattr != '_blank' ) {
33          $r .= "<iframe name=\"basicltiLaunchFrame\"  id=\"basicltiLaunchFrame\" src=\"\"\n";
34          $r .= $iframeattr . ">\n<p>".self::get_string("frames_required","basiclti")."</p>\n</iframe>\n";
35      }
36
37      $ext_submit = "ext_submit";
38      $ext_submit_text = $submit_text;
39      $r .= " <script type=\"text/javascript\"> \n" .
40          " //<![CDATA[ \n" .
41          "    document.getElementById(\"ltiLaunchForm\").style.display = \"none\";\n" .
42          "    nei = document.createElement('input');\n" .
43          "    nei.setAttribute('type', 'hidden');\n" .
44          "    nei.setAttribute('name', '".$ext_submit."');\n" .
45          "    nei.setAttribute('value', '".$ext_submit_text."');\n" .
46          "    document.getElementById(\"ltiLaunchForm\").appendChild(nei);\n" .
47          "    document.ltiLaunchForm.submit(); \n" .
48          " //]]> \n" .
49          " </script> \n";
50      $r .= "</div>\n";
51      return $r;
52  }
```

5. CONCLUSION

The number of educational tools available is increasingly large and keeps evolving. New ones are constantly introduced and more and more teachers want to incorporate these tools in their teaching.

But it is not always easy or possible to add these educational tools into LMS, the main administrative software used by educational institutions worldwide. Besides every time that a new LMS version is created the educational tool must be adapted. Due to all these compatibility concerns, many big installations avoid installing un-official extensions or tools (even the ones developed within the organization), and teachers and students have to deal with a stock version of the LMS.

In this scenario a number of organizations have recently proposed interoperability standards to be implemented and followed by LMSs and content creators alike. These standards define ways that LMSs can interface with external learning tools in order to make them accessible from within the learning platform in an intuitive and concise way.

This chapter focuses on the service-oriented approach to interoperability and present two approaches: the OKI and the IMS approach. Details are provided for the IMS LTI approach because it allows integrating educational tools into an LMS so that the difference between an LMS native-activity and an external-activity is not visible.

Finally, the TSUGI framework is presented. It is a learning tool hosting environment, that makes it as simple as possible to write IMS Learning Tools Interoperability™ (LTI)™ tools supporting LTI 1.x and 2.x (soon). The main contribution of this framework is that neither LMSs nor educational tools need to keep updating their code to comply with the latest LTI specification version or subversion. An example of how an external learning tool is installed and launched in TSUGI is presented in this chapter.

As future work, TSUGI faces similar challenges to the ones faced by IMS when promoting LTI. Namely, developers are seemingly very attached and used to work with particular LMSs that they usually forget the prospect of interoperability of their tools and develop them specifically for the LMS of their choice. Strategies to promote TSUGI world wide must be defined.

REFERENCES

Alier, M., Casany, M. J., Mayol, E., Piguillem, J., & Galanis, N. (2012). Docs-4Learning: Getting Google Docs to Work within the LMS with IMS BLTI. *Journal of Universal Computer Science*, *18*(11), 1483–1500.

Berger, P. L., & Luckmann, T. (1991). *The social construction of reality: A treatise in the sociology of knowledge*. Penguin.

CeLTIc Project Wiki. (2014). *LTI/Best Practice/Introduction*. Retrieved February 13, 2015, from http://celtic.lti.tools/wiki/LTI/Best_Practice/Introduction

Galanis, N., Alier, M., Casany, M. J., Mayol, E., & Severance, C. (2014, October). TSUGI: a framework for building PHP-based learning tools. In *Proceedings of the Second International Conference on Technological Ecosystems for Enhancing Multiculturality* (pp. 409-413). ACM. doi:10.1145/2669711.2669932

IMS AF. (2003). *IMS Abstract Framework Specification*. Retrieved February 13, 2015, from http://imsglobal.org/af/index.html

IMS LTI. (2010). *IMS Learning Tools Interoperability*. Retrieved February 13, 2015, from http://www.imsglobal.org/lti/index.html

IMS LTI 2.0. (2015). *IMS Learning Tools Interoperability 2.0*. Retrieved February 13, 2015, from http://www.imsglobal.org/lti/#lti2.0

IMS Tutorials. (2015). *The basic overview on how LTI works*. Retrieved February 13, 2015, from http://developers.imsglobal.org/tutorials.html

Kurz, S., Podwyszynski, M., & Schwab, A. (2008). A Dynamically Extensible, Service-Based Infrastructure for Mobile Applications. In *Proceedings of Advances in Conceptual Modeling – Challenges and Opportunities*. Springer. Retrieved February 13, 2015, from http://luisa.atosorigin.es

Merriman, J. (2003). *Redefining interoperability. The Open Knowledge Initiative (OKI)*. Retrieved February 13, 2015, from http://www.okiproject.org/view/html/node/2916

Oauth 2.0. (n.d.). *Oauth 2.0 Security Protocol*. Retrieved February 13, 2015, from http://www.oauth.net

Pätzold, S., Rathmayer, S., & Graf, S. (2008). Proposal for the Design and Implementation of a Modern System Architecture and integration infrastructure in context of e-learning and exchange of relevant data. In *ILearning Forum* (pp. 82–90). European Institute For E-Learning.

Prensky, M. (2001). *Digital Game-Based Learning*. New York, NY: McGraw-Hill.

Vickers, S. P., & Booth, S. (2014). Learning Tools Interoperability (LTI): a Best Practice Guide. CeLTIc developers Project.

Chapter 3
Technological Ecosystem Maps for IT Governance:
Application to a Higher Education Institution

Rafael Molina-Carmona
Universidad de Alicante, Spain

Carlos J. Villagrá-Arnedo
Universidad de Alicante, Spain

Patricia Compañ-Rosique
Universidad de Alicante, Spain

Francisco J. Gallego-Durán
Universidad de Alicante, Spain

Rosana Satorre-Cuerda
Universidad de Alicante, Spain

Faraon Llorens-Largo
Universidad de Alicante, Spain

ABSTRACT

Technological ecosystems are a widespread solution to address the challenges of the information technologies in organizations. It is important to have tools to correctly and quickly evaluate them. The Technological Ecosystem Map (TEmap) is a tool to intuitively interpret complex information maintaining both a global and a detailed vision of the technologies. It is a polygonal and structured representation of the main elements of the ecosystem. Each element is evaluated according to its maturity level, indicating how it contributes to fulfil the organization objectives. Each maturity level is represented by a colour, so that the TEmap takes the form of a heat map. The particular case of the University of Alicante is chosen to illustrate its construction. The TEmap is a simple but powerful way to identify the strengths and weaknesses of a technological ecosystem and the possible actions to improve the solution to the strategic questions of the organization.

DOI: 10.4018/978-1-5225-0905-9.ch003

INTRODUCTION

The information technology governance (IT governance) is one of the main processes to be implemented in an organization to respond to the technological challenges of current times. IT governance is a high level process in which decision-making has become very critical since decisions that can lead to the whole organization success or failure. A reasoned and informed decision-making is based on the ability of the organization to anticipate events, collect and analyse internal and external data, and transform them into complete and useful information and knowledge. In this context, powerful information representation tools can help organizations to better know their internal situation and their environment. The key question is how to represent the huge quantity of information in an agile and intuitive way so that decisions can be made maintaining both a global and a detailed vision of the organization.

The current trend in organizations to address the IT problems is conceiving the technological solutions as an ecosystem. By analogy with natural ecosystems, a technological ecosystem is a community of methods, policies, regulations, applications, and people teams that coexist in the organization, so that their processes are interrelated and their implementation is based on the physical factors of the technological environment. All the elements and their relations make up together a very complex heterogeneous system, very difficult to manage and evaluate as a whole. The complicated nature of ecosystems makes them affordable from many levels so that it is particularly difficult to know where the organization is in the process of the ecosystem development.

In this chapter, the question to be answered is whether it is possible to evaluate the situation of the technological ecosystem of an organization at a glance, by representing the information in a simple and intuitive manner but maintaining the richness of the original information. To respond this question, the Technological Ecosystem Maps (TEmaps) are presented. A TEmap is a polygonal representation of the main elements of a technological ecosystem. It is divided into levels (levels of abstraction from which to study the ecosystem), facets (basic principles that guide the organization and are transferred to the technological ecosystem) and components (specific aspects that are affected by the technological ecosystem). Each component, at each facet, studied from each level, is evaluated according to its maturity level. To do so, a maturity model is required so that it can be measured how good the element of the ecosystem is to fulfil the required objectives. Each maturity level is represented by a colour, so that the TEmap finally takes the form of a heat map.

To illustrate the construction of the TEmap of an organization, the process is applied to a particular institution. The case of the University of Alicante is selected since the authors are university professors and responsible of the IT services of this university during the definition of its technological ecosystem. As an example, a whole facet, Open Knowledge, is built, including the assignment of maturity levels and the identification of the main strategies, operational decisions and projects.

TEmaps are an easy-to-build tool that gives a global vision and a diagnosis about the situation of the technological ecosystem of the organization. They allow the detection of colour patterns that provide global information about the organization situation and the strengths and weaknesses of its ecosystem.

BACKGROUND

Learning Society and Intelligent Organizations

Current world has evolved from the Industrial Society to the Information, Knowledge and Learning Society. The growth of living standards nowadays is due more to the way people have learned to learn than to the accumulation of capital and resources (Stiglitz & Greenwald, 2014). This continuous learning for the society as a whole to move forward should be transferred to organizations. Some the most important aspects that have led to this new society are the internationalization of organizations, economy globalization, technological dynamism and, motivated by the previous ones, the growing importance of knowledge and learning.

If there is agreement on something right now, it is that present times are times of change and transformation. Digitization and globalization have paved and levelled the field in which organizations play (Friedman, 2005). Competition is global, representing a threat but also an opportunity. In this complex world, the solutions are not simple. It is a time of dualities: global versus local, technology versus humanism, innovation versus status quo. In short, change is unstoppable and inevitable and forces organizations to transform. And this transformation must be the result of learning.

Knowledge and learning are the cornerstones of this transformation as they are the key concepts to reduce the complexity and uncertainty that characterizes the organizational environment. The change implies the need for a review of the other processes linked to the traditional organization in order to adapt them to the new approach. These processes include, due to its relationship with the knowledge and its use for the strategic management, the processes of Organizational Learning and Strategic Planning (Dalmau Espert, 2016). Thus, knowledge and learning are the main pillars of a new organizational model: the intelligent organization (Zara, 2008).

Learning in organizations involves good practices and productivity improvements. Thus, good practices need to be part of the organization ecosystem and the productivity improvement becomes the ultimate goal of the intelligent organization. According to Stiglitz and Greenwald (2014) there are three factors that may lead to a productivity increment: benchmarking, total quality and reengineering.

Nonaka and Takeuchi (1995) define organizational learning as the process by which the knowledge created by individuals is amplified in an organized way and crystallized as part of the knowledge system of the organization. Based on this, it can be stated that organizations cannot create knowledge without individuals and without them sharing their individual knowledge with other people and groups. The main issue to address in the process of organizational learning is how to accomplish the creation and management of a shared understanding within the organization. This shared understanding is defined by Bittner and Leimeister (2014) as the agreement to which people come on the value of the properties, the interpretation of concepts and the mental models of cause and effect with respect to an object of understanding. This shared understanding is essential to enable the sharing of information, knowledge and experiences between people involved in the process of organizational learning.

In this context the organization is understood as a set of connected entities driven by social interactions between independent actors with the aim of achieving a common goal (Bonjour, Belkadi, Troussier, & Dulmet, 2009). This is how the concept of ecosystem arises. An ecosystem is a community of living things whose vital processes are interrelated, and whose development depends on the physical characteristics of the environment. The definition of a technological ecosystem may vary from one author to another, but they all agree on one point: there is an evident relationship between the characteristics of a natural ecosystem and the characteristics of a technological ecosystem (Chang & West, 2006). Establishing an analogy with the definition of natural ecosystems, a technological ecosystem is a community of methods, policies, rules, applications and work teams that coexist in such a way that the processes are interrelated and their application is based on the characteristics of the technological environment (Llorens, Molina, Compañ, & Satorre, 2014). The architecture of the digital ecosystem is based on hardware and software components that combine to work together to support the gradual evolution of the system through the contribution of ideas and new components from the community (European Commission, 2006). A crucial property for a technological ecosystem to be durable is its ability to evolve and to assimilate new members in the community, which may or not consolidate. In fact, relatively few technological innovations achieve a sufficient level of maturity for them to be considered established, while the rest disappear more or less prematurely. There are other technologies that emerge with an aura of fashion and fascination, and their use leads to unsystematized practices (most frequently ad-hoc practices) that have no plans for extended relevance, and which in most cases are quickly abandoned because they fail to live up expectations and are absolutely abandoned in a short time (García-Peñalvo et al., 2015). This vertiginous rhythm of change and evolution should not affect to the core structure and principles of the technological ecosystem.

Governance and Information Technologies

Juiz and Toomey (2015) consider that Information Technology governance (IT governance) is no longer a choice for any organization. IT is a major instrument of business change in organizations of any nature. Without good governance, organizations face loss of opportunity and potential failure. The need to govern IT follows from two strategic factors: business necessity and enterprise maturity. According to Toomey (2009), one of the two fundamental equations that must be taken into consideration to understand IT governance is:

Business Systems = (People + Process + Structure + Technology)

It states that information technology is useless if it is not combined with the three other vital ingredients to make a business system.

The publication of ISO 38500 in 2008 (ISO/IEC, 2008), was a great support for the recognition of the importance of IT governance and has become a benchmark and an excellent starting point for the implementation of IT systems. The objective of this International Standard is to provide principles, definitions, and a model for governing boards to use when evaluating, directing, and monitoring the use of information technology (IT) in their organizations (ISO/IEC, 2015).

Aware of this reality, the Conference of Rectors of Spanish Universities (CRUE, from Spanish *Conferencia de Rectores de las Universidades Españolas*) launched a project for the Spanish universities to have available the necessary tools to address implementation processes of IT governance systems: IT Governance for Universities (ITG4U) (Fernández Martínez & Llorens Largo, 2011). In UNIVERSITIC 2010 (UNIVERSITIC is the annual report of CRUE about the IT in the Spanish universities) it was stated that IT should not be a goal itself but a means to help generate value to universities (Uceda Antolín & Barro Ameneiro, 2010). If universities do not get their IT create value, they will be ineffective and will lose an important competitive advantage. From that moment, UNIVERSITIC reports have evolved to collect features belonging to innovative models of IT governance that were already successfully applied in other organizations. Thus, complementing the detailed inventory of IT implanted in Spanish universities best practices in management of IT in operation are analysed (IT resources, IT projects, IT services, IT management, IT standards, quality, regulatory and collaboration) (Píriz Duran, 2015).

IT governance is a responsibility of the highest management level and is at the top of a pyramid that would be based on IT operations and IT management (Figure 1). Therefore the success of the IT governance is linked to the understanding and support of the university management committees (Fernández Martínez, 2009).

Figure 1. IT governance pyramid
Obtained from (Fernández Martínez & Llorens Largo, 2009).

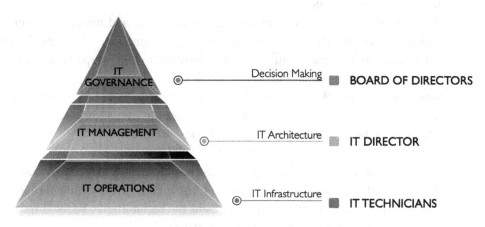

The ITG4U Framework proposed by CRUE has been very useful in establishing improvement actions that may be implemented in each university to achieve a higher IT governance maturity level (Fernández Martínez & Llorens Largo, 2009).

Information Evolution and Maturity Levels

Organizations need to have mechanisms that allow appropriate measurements to assess IT as a whole and make decisions about their governance, so that the governing boards can know how their organization is evolving toward its strategic goals.

It is important to differentiate between information and knowledge (Maruta, 2014). Organizational Learning as a process involves the transformation of information into knowledge, dissemination and exploitation thereof in order to increase the innovative and competitive capacity of the organization. It is based on a broad set of disciplines, technologies and tools focused on information and knowledge.

To establish a full development in information management of organizations, the model of information evolution establishes five phases (Davis, Miller, & Russell, 2006):

1. **Operational Phase:** Characterized by the "ownership" and control of individual data, which is applied to address functional issues of everyday life.
2. **Consolidation Phase:** Where individual perspective is replaced by standards, measurement units and perspectives on all dimensions at the departmental or functional level.

3.   **Integration Phase:** It extends the consolidation phase to the perspective of the company as a whole.
4.   **Optimization Phase:** The company can better know and understand their markets and constantly adapt to remain optimally aligned with these markets and achieve market leadership by applying new prediction perspectives about customers, suppliers and partners.
5.   **Innovation Phase:** A significant percentage of incomes are obtained from ideas and projects that are less than three years old and where sustainable growth is stimulated by the creativity and constant renewal.

Information evolution must be supported by the development of the corresponding technologies. Similarly, Nolan (1982) considers that organizations evolve through six states in their IT implementation processes as the technologies become more sophisticated and the interest in IT governance grows:

- **Initiation:** In organizations that are in this situation, IT is only used to automate repetitive processes seeking to reduce costs, so the focus is purely operational and the interest in IT governance is very low.
- **Contagion:** During this stage, a rapid growth cycle is produced, caused by the constant demands of users, who perceive the potential of technology occurs. Since the interest among the governing board is still small, the expansion is carried out in an uncontrolled manner.
- **Control:** The governing board starts getting interested in IT and it expects that the investments involve a visible benefit. At this stage, upgrade plans are produced and developing standards are defined. However, the first complaints from users appear since they do not see their needs met.
- **Integration:** The integration of the various systems is tackled, through the use of corporate databases. The goal is to create information systems that provide service to users.
- **Data Administration:** The concept of information is applied to the organization, instead of limiting IT to only process data. Databases are really taken advantage and exploited.
- **Maturity:** An actual alignment between corporate and IT strategic planning is carried out.

The maturity model concept was initially developed for the processes regarding the development and implementation of software by the Software Engineering Institute (SEI) at Carnegie-Mellon University and later extended to the evaluation of any other organizational process. A maturity model tries to measure how good the processes, practices and behaviours of an organization are to produce the required outcomes. The measures are structured in predefined levels so that the organization state can be understood and compared with others.

There are several adaptations of the maturity model concept to different environments or fields: software, project management, quality management, strategy, human resources, and so on. Although they manage different elements, the main concept is common: measuring the level of maturity of an organization in a particular field. The maturity models in the Control Objectives for Information and Related Technology (COBIT) framework for IT management and governance, were first created in 2000 and at that time were designed based on the original SEI Capability Maturity Model (CMM) (Paulk, Curtis, Chrissis, & Weber, 1993) scale with the addition of an extra level (0) as shown below:

Level 0: Non-existent.
Level 1: Initial/ad hoc.
Level 2: Repeatable but Intuitive.
Level 3: Defined Process.
Level 4: Managed and Measurable.
Level 5: Optimized.

The CMM, suitable for information technology, can be easily adapted to evaluate the maturity level of a technological ecosystem.

Decision Making and Information Representation

IT governance is a high level process that enables an organization to make decisions to ensure that its IT sustains and extends its strategies and objectives (Cater-Steel, 2009). More concretely, the organization must evaluate and direct the use of IT to support the organization, monitor the use of IT to achieve plans, use the IT strategy and policies to accomplish its purpose and align the IT strategy with the organization goals.

To perform these tasks and make correct decisions, it is crucial to clearly understand the strategic goals and objectives and the state of the organization. However, the number of variables to be considered is usually too high to base the decision on the analysis of the raw data. In this context, graphical tools can provide the decision maker a meaningful way to analyse variables and select good solutions from a global perspective without losing the important details. The visual presentation of information in the form of maps, globes, charts, tables, and so on, has a strong tradition in the social studies. Graphic representations can help the human brain understand the world by identifying the important elements individually, but also the relationships among them and the clusters and structures that emerge from the whole system. Furthermore, graphical information visualization improves the response time and enables the individuals to extract knowledge from this information more quickly. In addition, graphical visualization increases the degree of reliability (Keim, 2002).

TECHNOLOGICAL ECOSYSTEMS MAPS

One of the central elements in nowadays organizations is their technological ecosystem. All the elements of the ecosystem and their relations make up together a very complex heterogeneous system, very difficult to manage and evaluate as a whole. An initial hypothesis is stated as germ of this work: It is possible to evaluate the situation of the technological ecosystem of an organization at a glance, by representing the information in a simple and intuitive manner but maintaining the richness of the original information. The proposed solution is the Technological Ecosystem Map (TEmap).

A TEmap is a graphical representation of the components of the ecosystem. It provides an underlying structure that facilitates the understanding of the elements of the ecosystem and their relationships. The addition of a colour code to represent the level of maturity of every element allows the construction of heat map so that, besides the structure given by the TEmaps, it also provides a visual representation of the state of the ecosystem.

TEmaps are powerful representation tools that have the following main objectives:

- Providing a systematic way to structure the components of the technological ecosystem of the organization.
- Evaluating the technological ecosystem of the organization.
- Identifying the aspects to improve in the technological ecosystem.

To achieve these objectives, the TEmaps are structured in the following elements:

- **Levels:** Levels of abstraction from which to study the problem.
- **Facets:** Basic principles that guide the organization and are transferred to the technological ecosystem.
- **Components:** Concrete aspects that are affected by the technological ecosystem.

These elements are represented in a pyramid. The pyramid has as many faces as facets, with at least three facets so that the pyramid can be constructed. Each face, for its part, is divided horizontally in levels and vertically in components. Pyramid in Figure 2 has six dimensions, four levels and three components (but in the highest level, with only one component)

The TEmap is the projection of the pyramid in a plane, from a zenith view (Figure 3). The result is a regular polygon with as many faces as facets are considered in the model.

As the number of facets increases, the polygonal map approaches a circle, which is the generalized form of the map. Nevertheless, when building the map, a decision about the appropriate number of faces is needed, since too many faces may imply difficulties to understand the whole map.

The TEmap can be completed by introducing a colour scale to indicate how deeply every element is developed in the ecosystem, that is, how mature the ecosystem is in every particular aspect. As a consequence, some kind of heat maps are obtained. Figure 4, represents a complete TEmap, where the colour scale indicates the maturity level (in a range of five levels).

The identification of every element in the map depends on the particular case of every organization. Nevertheless, a good starting point to build the TEmap is the IT strategic plan of the organization, since it can give some of the clues to identify

Figure 2. Elements of a TEmap, structured in a pyramid, with levels, facets and components

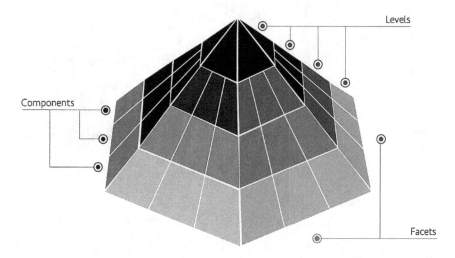

Figure 3. TEmap, projection of the pyramid

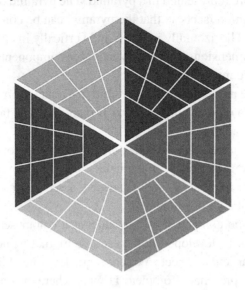

Figure 4. TEmap, considering five possible levels of maturity

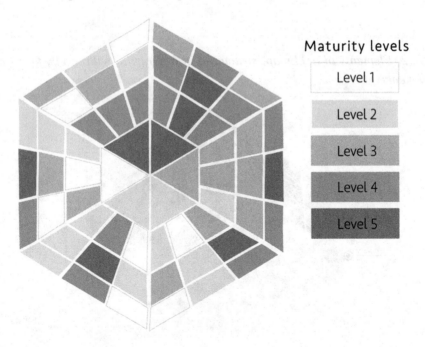

the different elements in the map. In the following sections, each element in the TEmap and the way to design are deeply explained.

Designing the Levels

The levels represent different levels of abstraction. The apex represents the concepts of a higher level of abstraction, that guide the definition of the general objectives of the TE in the organization, while the base represents the particular tools, methods and procedures that are implemented to achieve the general objective.

Each organization must decide how many levels to distinguish in its technological ecosystem. Nevertheless, a set of four possible levels is a good starting point for most organizations. The proposed model considers a decomposition in the following levels, although this division is up to the concrete organization:

- **Philosophical Level:** The higher level of abstraction represents the principles in which the technological ecosystem of the organization in based. The mission values of the IT strategic plan should be considered to establish the principles of the philosophical level, since they express the way the organization must conduct itself, what the key elements of the organization and the main features of the organization to achieve its mission are.
- **Strategic Level:** Based on the philosophical level, the strategic level is made of the set of strategies, policies and high-level decisions that favour the achievement of the corresponding principle. The strategic level may be defined from the set of the strategic objectives of the IT strategic plan. They are therefore long-term objectives that establish a bridge from the philosophical principles to the specific services of the operational level.
- **Operational Level:** Services that are offered and units that perform each task, how to get them involved, and how to integrate them, so that each objective in the strategic level is achieved.
- **Technical Level:** This is a set of specific actions, tools, methods and interconnections that pursue the development of the services in the operational level.

There must be some measure criteria and indicators for every objective in every level that allow the measurement of its achievement.

Designing the Facets

Each facet is a basic principle identified in the philosophical level. The facets will depend on the organization characteristics and mission values.

It is not possible to define a set of desirable principles, since they can be very different from one organization to another. Nevertheless, some aspects should be considered:

- To obtain a pyramid (and therefore a valid polygonal map) at least three facets or principles are needed. In addition to geometrical reasons, there are other reasons to propose at least three facets: fewer facets give a very partial vision of the ecosystem.
- The number of principles can be as high as desired but a deep study of every possible principle could be too complex and, moreover, it could make difficult the comprehension of the whole ecosystem diagnosis. Therefore, although there is no limitation on the maximum number of facets, it is advisable to maintain it limited. Empirically, it is determined that a maximum of six or seven facets is optimal to allow a correct interpretation of the map.

Designing the Components

The components are the specific aspects which solutions are aimed at. Of course, the components, as the facets, are very dependent on the features of the organization. Nevertheless, the IT strategic plan is again a source of elements to help in the design of the components. Specifically, it is possible to make use of the following elements of the IT strategic plan:

- The strategic axes, since they are the dimensions, fields or areas where the efforts are concentrated. They are defining the areas of organizational intervention and the programs or projects that are planned to run as a priority.
- The involved groups, that is, individuals, groups of individuals and institutions whose actions can positively or negatively influence the fulfilment of the objectives. They are important because they are both participants in the ecosystem development and users of the ecosystem.

In general, the components are the same for every facet, since it is important to study every component from the point of view of every facet. However, it is possible to introduce some specific components that are only suitable to be studied from only some facets.

Measuring the Maturity Level

As stated before, a maturity model allows the structuration of the development degree of any studied aspect in predefined levels, so that the organization state can be understood and compared with others. This proposal is based on the Capability Madurity Model (CMM) (Paulk et al., 1993), suitable for Information Technology and therefore for evaluating the Technological Ecosystem. The CMM introduces five levels defined along the continuum of the model. Each level comprises a set of process goals that, when satisfied, stabilize an important component of the process. These levels, adapted to the technological ecosystem case, are:

- **Initial:** The technological solutions are characterized as ad hoc, and occasionally even chaotic. Few processes are defined, and success depends on individual effort.
- **Repeatable:** Basic technological ecosystem management processes are established to track cost, schedule, and functionality. The technological ecosystem process is at least documented sufficiently such that repeating the same steps may be attempted.
- **Defined:** The technological ecosystem for both management and elements is documented, standardized, and integrated into a standard process for the organization. All technological solutions follow an approved standard process to be developed and maintained.
- **Managed:** Detailed measures of the technological ecosystem process and quality are collected. Both the technological ecosystem organization and its elements are quantitatively understood and controlled.
- **Optimizing:** Continuous technological ecosystem improvement is enabled by quantitative feedback from the technological ecosystem evolution and from piloting innovative ideas and technologies.

The five maturity levels define an ordinal scale for measuring the maturity of an organization's technological ecosystem. A TEmap (Figure 4) is built by assigning a colour to each maturity level: from white (level 1) to red (level 5). The heat map is a fast way of identifying the strengths and weaknesses of the technological ecosystem, so that a general diagnosis could be made. Some colour patterns can be detected in the heat map.

THE UNIVERSITY CASE

To illustrate the construction of the TEmap of an organization, the process is applied to a particular institution. The authors are university professors and responsible of the IT services of the University of Alicante (UA) during the definition of the technological ecosystem of the university, so the example of this institution is used. The master lines of the IT Strategic Plan of the UA that guided the definition of the technological ecosystem in its initial stages are first introduced, then the evolution and current state of the UA ecosystem, and finally the construction of the TEmap and the evaluation of the technological ecosystem state.

The IT Strategic Plan of the UA (2007-2012)

The first IT Strategic Plan of the University of Alicante was developed to give a response to the challenges that the UA should face in the period 2007-2012 in the field of IT, as part of the whole Strategic Plan of the UA (Llorens-Largo, 2007). As a consequence of the plan, several strategic and operational objectives were identified. Some of these objectives were to be fulfilled by designing a developing a technological ecosystem that could be easily adapted and evolved in an environment of uncertainty.

The IT strategic plan is based in the model proposed by Llorens-Largo (2007), presented in Figure 5. This diagram represents both the main elements of the strategic plan (the boxes) and their dependencies (the arrows).

The initial element that guides the organization is the mission. In this case, the mission of the UA was defined as (Llorens-Largo, 2007):

The University of Alicante is a public, dynamic and innovative institution, with international projection and a campus of reference, whose mission is the education of their students and the commitment to the advance and improvement of society through the creation and transmission of knowledge and cultural, scientific and technological development.

Although very general, it sets some elements that will guide the development of the strategic plan and the technological ecosystem: dynamic, innovative, international, integral education, compromise, progress, improvement, knowledge creation and transmission and cultural, scientific and technological development.

The strategic values are more concrete and can help to build the technological ecosystem (Llorens-Largo, 2007):

Figure 5. Model of the strategic plan, used in the UA

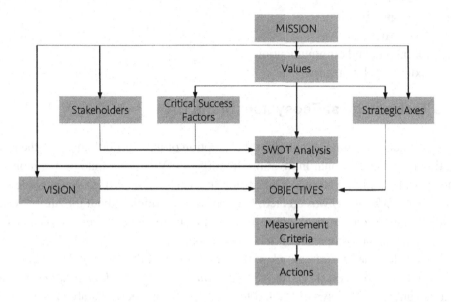

Quality, social commitment, environmental awareness, development cooperation, equality, inclusion, participation, critical thinking, tolerance and transparency. Moreover, regarding IT aspects: Ethical behaviour when using ICT, mentality to change, innovation and creativity, and digital inclusion of people, formats and technologies.

The strategic values are too general to directly define the facets of the technological ecosystem pyramid, but they are a source of inspiration.

While the strategic values are very useful to identify the facets of the technological ecosystem pyramid, the implied groups and the strategic axes can help to define the components of each facet. In the case of the UA, the main implied groups are:

- Students,
- Staff,
- Other external groups such as suppliers, other universities, schools, public institutions, companies and so on.

The strategic axes, for their part, are:

- Human component,
- Teaching-learning,

- R+D+I,
- Strategic direction,
- Infrastructures,
- Marketing and communication,
- External relationships.

The Technological Ecosystem of the UA

Since its inception, the UA opted for the adoption of new technologies and the promotion of the educational innovation. In 2005, the Vice-Rectorate of Technology and Educational Innovation (VrTIE, from Spanish *Vicerrectorado de Tecnología e Innovación Educativa)* was created, to integrate the policies about the digital technologies and the educational innovation, and the university services responsible for these policies: the computer services and the library.

To develop the IT strategic plan, the VrTIE created the Area of Technological Educational Innovation (ITE, from Spanish *Innovación Tecnológica Educativa*) to take advantage of the synergies and to develop all the decisions about the use of technology for education. The task of the ITE was to give response to the needs of the students, faculty and staff in a context of rapid development, expansion and transformation of technologies. The challenge was to achieve a double objective: on the one hand, to propose and develop a calm, thoughtful, visionary and ambitious strategic plan about the use of technology for education. This objective would allow the university to get ready for the future, beyond the fashions of every moment. On the other hand, it was necessary to quickly respond to the needs of different user groups of the university, allowing and facilitating the adoption of technologies, as users demanded them. The aim was joining the mainstream of technological evolution while a reflection about the long-term strategies is done.

To give a response to the users' needs, the solution was to propose a technological ecosystem, that is, a community of open and interrelated educational methods, policies, regulations, applications, and people teams coexisting in a complex technological environment. The proposal was not a monolithic application, neither multiple applications on a single device, nor even a computer system platform, but a framework that integrated information and a set of different methods, applications, tools and teams. All the elements of the framework were related so that they made up together a single heterogeneous group with a common purpose: to create a technological ecosystem where the students had access to the contents from multiple devices and platforms and where the teachers could create the contents using multiple tools too. The main features of the UA technological ecosystem are:

- The technological ecosystem is a community of organisms (of educational methods, policies, regulations, technical tools, and people teams), since the organisms are independent (they have their own features and their own life cycle), but they live together and they complement one another.
- The organisms of the community are living, that is, they are changing and evolving. The technological ecosystem is ready to adapt to the changes as the available technologies and the educational needs progress, since the educational and technological environment is changing dramatically over time.
- The organisms are interrelated, so inputs and outputs are shared and reused.
- The technological ecosystem is adapted to the physical factors of the environment, so different frameworks are proposed for different needs.

The Levels

Four levels for the implementation of the ecosystem are adopted, as proposed before:

- **Philosophical Level:** The principles to base the technological ecosystem on.
- **Strategic Level:** The university policies that favour the technological ecosystem development and implementation.
- **Operational Level:** Services that allow the achievement of the objectives determined by the policies and units that perform each task.
- **Technical Level:** Tools and methods to provide the services.

The Facets

The facets make up the set of features that guide the technological ecosystem. They are inspired in the general strategic values of the IT strategic plan of the UA. Six facets have been selected to be evaluated:

- **Open Knowledge:** The principle of open knowledge is the base for the knowledge progress.
- **Collaboration:** Collaboration is the way to generate and share the knowledge.
- **Adaption:** The ecosystem must adapt to the means, in a general sense, so that every participant must be able to find the correct adaptation of the technological ecosystem to his or her needs.
- **Evolution:** The ecosystem is in constant growth an evolution, so it must be prepared to evolve and integrate new elements.
- **Integration:** Although made up of several heterogeneous components, the ecosystem must act as a whole, integrating each element and connecting it

with the others. This way, the addition of all the components is much more than the mere sum up of the individual components.

- **Security:** Every element of the ecosystem must provide security to the users in the broader sense.

The Components

The implied groups and the strategic axes inspire the definition of the components. In the case of the UA the following components are proposed:

- **Work Teams:** The human component is the central element of the ecosystem, particularly students and staff. Besides the attention to individual users and the research groups, that have traditionally been paid a central attention in the universities, one of the strategic objectives of the IT strategic plan is the promotion of the collaborative work, specially the transversal teams working on educational innovation.
- **Places:** Another strategic objective is providing collaborative and interactive environments to aid in the teaching-learning process. The physical places are, therefore, essential. The work teams must be supported by suitable infrastructure (rooms, devices, software…) for developing its work.
- **Training:** The definition and implementation of a training plan in IT is detected as a need and, therefore, stated as a strategic objective. Most users (staff and students) probably need some training to carry out their tasks using the technological tools at their disposal.
- **Institutional Support:** A determined institutional support is needed to foster the use of the most suitable technological tools, to establish the priority in the research and development lines in IT or to guarantee a robust reliable secure infrastructure, for instance. Establishing grants, incentives and the right standards and regulations is crucial to succeed in the implementation of the ecosystem.
- **Diffusion:** Another strategic objective is providing a permanent and effective channel to fulfil the informative demand of the society. Some actions to achieve this objective is the implementation of marketing tools and the creation of segmented and specialised channels that the audience can adapt to its needs.

TEmap Construction

To illustrate the construction of the map, one facet has been selected. The process should be repeated with the other facets. In the following paragraphs, the process is done for the Open Knowledge principle facet, including the different components, describing the decisions made for each one, and evaluating the level of maturity for each component at each level.

Philosophical Level

The principle to be evaluated in this facet is Open Knowledge. It has been selected because the University of Alicante has made a firm commitment with the open knowledge movement. It is also a not so structured principle as other (such as security, easier to define and measure), therefore it can help to illustrate some aspects.

Strategic Level

This level establishes the strategic decisions taken to achieve the principle of Open Knowledge, from the point of view of each component. These decisions are:

- **Work Teams:** Foster the creation of heterogeneous groups to work on Educational Innovation using open technology, giving them some kind of recognition so that they become a stable working group and they have the possibility of access to grants and incentives.
- **Places:** Create physical spaces with technological equipment to produce and distribute open contents.
- **Training:** Provide training for the use of open technology to both teachers (as material developers) and students (as end users).
- **Institutional Support:** Offering an open institutional platform that complements third party tools. Another strategic decision is establishing a system of aids and grants to groups. This support contributes to the perception that this task has the same importance as other more traditional institution actions, such as scientific research.
- **Diffusion:** Provide different open channels to diffuse contents, and a mechanism to integrate them in the habitual workflow of the teachers.

Operational Level

This level identifies the services that allow the fulfilment of the strategic objectives, as well as the units or departments that offer these services. The set of services and units are:

- **Work Teams:** Support services for educational innovation groups: an official registry of groups, a web portal for the groups, etc. These services are offered by the ITE
- **Places:** Services to create and convert video and audio contents: a multimedia factory and associated software and hardware to record, store and diffuse the contents. These services are offered by the Library.
- **Training:** Personalized training plans for teachers and students, in the form of short courses. These courses are offered by the ITE and the Institute of Education Sciences (ICE, from Spanish *Instituto de Ciencias de la Educación*).
- **Institutional Support:** Integration of the open tools in the technological ecosystem, providing the corresponding integration or gateways with the institutional platform gateways. These services are offered by the university Data Center. Other institutional services are the call for grants and incentives for educational innovation groups. These services are offered by the ITE.
- **Diffusion:** Diffusion services in the main open platforms, institutional websites, repositories, open educational resources platforms, multimedia websites, and websites of general use, to facilitate a multiple and heterogeneous access, adapted to the features and taste of each user. These services are offered by the Data Center and the Library

Technical Level

This level identifies the specific tools, regulations, services or projects that implement the services identified in the operational level. The main projects, divided into the corresponding components, are:

- **Work Teams:** Two projects related with work teams have been developed: Groups of Technological Educational Innovation (GITE, from Spanish *Grupos de Innovación Tecnológica Educativa*) (ITE-UA, 2016), established in 2009, which are groups of teachers with common educational interests. One of the main activities of the GITEs is to generate open multimedia materials with noticeable educational contents. The other project is Open Knowledge and Free Software at the University of Alicante (COPLA, from Catalan *Coneixement Obert i Programari Lliure a la Universitat d'Alacant*) (COPLA,

2016), a good sample of the integration of services and policies, based on the shared principles of open knowledge and free software movement. In 2006, the University of Alicante signed the Berlin Declaration on Open Access to Knowledge in Sciences and Humanities (Max Planck Society, 2003).

- **Places:** Once the teams are defined, the infrastructure is also needed. Physical spaces with technological equipment to produce them are mandatory. This physical space is located in the Library of the University of Alicante in what is called the fragUA (from Spanish *fragua*, forge) (fragUA, 2016), in reference to where these multimedia materials are forged. Typically, in the fragUA the users record UA Training Pills (pUAs, from Spanish *Píldoras Formativas UA*), which are short video and audio pieces to present a subject. This type of presentation must be short and incisive, aimed at a very specific subject and meaningful by itself. Thus, several related pUAs can make up a complete course, and a single pUA can be reused in different courses. Finally the contents should be disseminated, providing the university community and the whole world with the technological ecosystem that allows the users to spread their production. The starting point of this technological ecosystem is the Campus Virtual platform (UA learning management system), and in particular the Vértice application. Vértice allows the teachers to upload videos and audiovisual materials to the different websites (SI-UA, 2016).

- **Training:** Training in technology for teachers, students and other members of the staff is structured in three main elements: Tutorials (short online training tutorials about some specific technologies, such as Moodle, Wimba Create, …), Microtraining (short on-order training actions for individuals or a short groups, up to 2 hours, to fulfil very specific learning objectives related to particular tools) and Workshops (training actions for short groups, around 20 hours, to fulfil more general and wider learning objectives related to tools o methodologies).

- **Institutional Support:** The central element of the technological ecosystem of the UA is Campus Virtual. It was first conceived as an institutional closed platform, but it has been evolved to a general platform where open and closed applications coexist. A great effort has been made to integrate the different tools, allowing the interoperability but maintaining the own character of every tool and allowing the incorporation of new tools. Open tools and services are now available, such as an institutional repository (RUA, from Spanish *Repositorio de la Universidad de Alicante*), the OpenCourseWare platform (OCW-UA), Moodle, and others. Lately, a cloud model has been adopted, giving birth to the UACloud platform, the evolution of Campus Virtual, and integrating other services such as the cloud tools of Google and Microsoft. The other important elements of the institutional supports are the call for grants and incentives. They are particularly important to encourage the participation of new users, so they have been changing along the years. In the first years, there were grants for the creation of GITEs, for the creation of courses in the OCW-UA and for the storing of the documents in the RUA. Now, with the consolidation of groups and the routines of the results archive, the policies about grants have changed, now oriented to Massive On-Line Open Courses (MOOCs).

- **Diffusion:** The university community and the whole world are provided with the technological ecosystem that allows the spread of their production. The starting point of this technological ecosystem is the Campus Virtual platform, and in particular the Vértice application. Vértice allows the teachers to upload videos and audiovisual materials to the different websites. Once these materials are stored, they can be made available in Campus Virtual so that they can only be accessed by regular students. If these materials are considered to have enough quality, they can also be made public through the RUA, so that any person can have open access to them. When enough loose material is published in RUA, a comprehensive teaching proposal can be created to be published through the University OpenCourseWare. Another option is to place them in the audiovisual website (*Portal Audiovisual*) (SI-UA, 2016), which hosts institutional and research materials, and that opened their educational collection in 2011, as the way to disseminate teaching materials created by the faculty of the University of Alicante. Finally, there is the possibility of getting a link with external visibility that the teacher can use in other websites, blogs, etc. All these are portals of the University of Alicante and they are hosted on its servers. But other open spaces in the Internet have also been launched. This way, the audiovisual materials are available in cloud platforms, networks and the Internet. Two very popular points of access have been enabled by the University of Alicante: YouTube EDU and iTunes U. Another example is blogsUA (blogs.ua.es), a blogs platform that can be used by any member of the university community.

Maturity Level Evaluation

Estimating the maturity level of the elements is one of the main tasks when constructing a TEmap. It is not simple since it is very dependent on the concrete elements considered in the map. The first task is identifying the particular measures and indicators that can be used to evaluate the elements, bearing in mind that the goal of the maturity model is measuring how good the process, practice, behaviour or action is to reach the objectives of the organization at this level. Indicators can be of different types:

- Yes/No indicators, to indicate is a particular attribute is present or not.
- Quantitative indicators, to measure the attribute as a quantity.
- Qualitative indicators, to select the value of the attribute among a series of possible answers.

The structured and systematic way of obtaining the maturity level is defining some kind of rubric, that is, a scoring guide that splits each evaluation item into small criteria at particular levels of achievement. Table 1 presents an example of rubric, for the particular case of the UA, for the facet about open knowledge.

This rubric has being used to evaluate the maturity levels of the open knowledge facet for the UA case and to build the TEmap (Figure 6). It must be considered as an academic exercise to illustrate the map construction. A more exhaustive study is needed to configure a complete and valid TEmap with practical utility.

Table 1. Rubric to evaluate the maturity level of the open knowledge facet at the UA

Level	Indicator	Measurement
Philosophical level	Does the principle of open knowledge appear in the statutes of the UA?	Yes/No
	Does the principle of open knowledge appear in the UA strategic plan?	Yes/No
	Have the UA signed the Berlin Declaration?	Yes/No
Strategic level	Has any policy about open knowledge been approved?	Yes/No
	Are there strategic objectives in the UA strategic plan that refer to the open knowledge?	Yes/No
	Do the UA regulations about research include some reference on open knowledge?	Yes/No
	Is there any guideline that encourages open publication of teaching materials?	Yes/No
Operational level	Are there multi-year plans that reference open knowledge?	Yes/No
	Does the UA have platforms for open publication?	Yes/No
	Are there calls for publishing open teaching and researching materials?	Yes/No
	Are there grants and incentives for publishing open teaching and researching materials?	Yes/No
Technical level	To what extend is each tool/project/action developed?	Incomplete/Performed/ Managed/Defined
	To what extend is each tool/project/action accepted by the users?	Unaccepted/ Accepted by a minority/ Accepted by the majority/ Completely accepted

Figure 6. Open knowledge facet of the TEmap of the University of Alicante

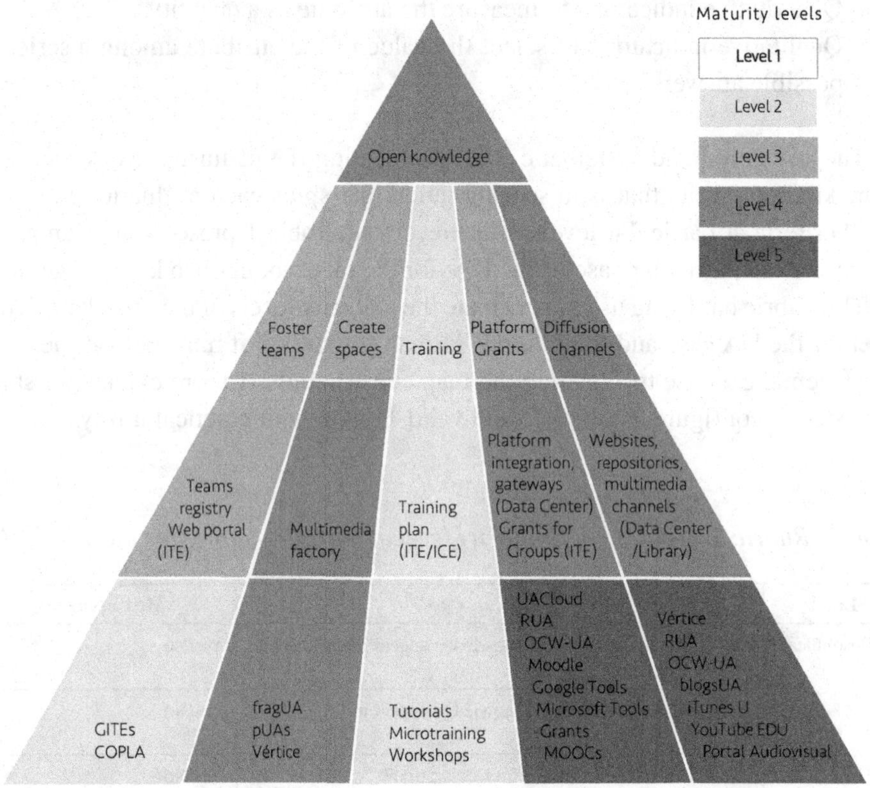

EVALUATION PATTERNS

The TEmaps allow the study and evaluation of the TE at a simple sight. Some colour patterns can be detected, so that a quick evaluation can be done. Although in most cases the colour distribution is not so clear and most TEmaps have characteristics of several patterns, it is possible to distinguish different cases. In the following paragraphs the main patterns are shown and explained.

A typical pattern in the one in which the red colour is mainly concentrated in the centre of the heat map (Figure 7). An organization with this colour distribution has a very developed strategic behaviour, but it is not able to transform the strategic lines into concrete services and tools.

Just the opposite case is when the red colour is mainly concentrated in the periphery of the heat map (Figure 8). These organizations put a lot of services and tools into practice but in a chaotic way. They are not guided by a consolidated strategy.

Figure 7. TEmap of an organization that is not able to transform IT strategic lines into actions

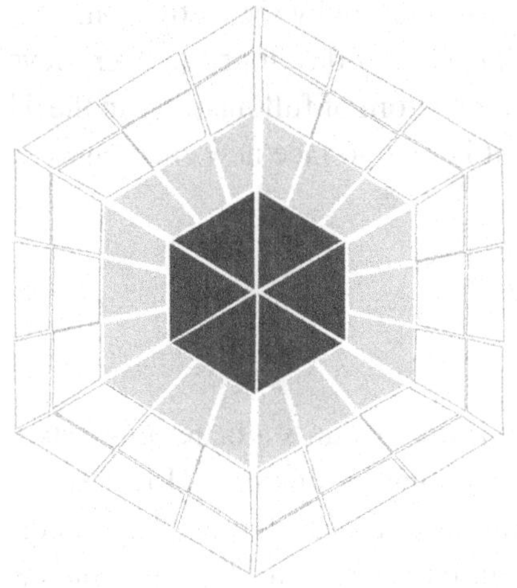

Figure 8. TEmap of an organization whose actions are not supported by a consolidate IT strategy

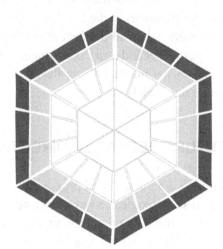

Figure 9. TEmap of an organization with a very unbalanced development of IT

Figure 10. TEmap of an organization with a chaotic management of IT

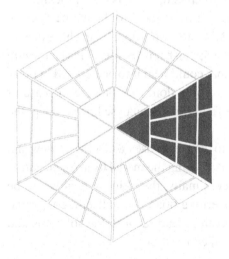

Another typical case is when the red colour is mainly concentrated in few facets of the heat map (Figure 9). In this case, the organization has developed all the levels in the map (from philosophical to technical) but in for few facets, so the development of the TE is quite unbalanced.

Another possibility is when there is no pattern, that is, the red colour is randomly distributed in the heat map (Figure 10). There is not a clear model in the organization, so that the strategic decisions are seldom spread to the low-level units, and the initiatives in the low-level units are not supported by the institution.

Finally, when all the heat map is red, the TE is fully developed in every level, for every facet and every component. This is a symptom of full maturity in the TE. Since, by definition, a TE is always evolving, it is time to face new challenges and revise the model.

FUTURE RESEARCH DIRECTIONS

TEmaps are not a closed proposal. They open a way towards a better understanding of technological ecosystems and a useful evaluation of them. However, it is an emerging field of study, endorsed by the current interest of researchers on data representation and information. Concretely, future research on TEmaps is planned to deal with two main aspects: the application of TEmaps to different cases and the improvement of the model by adding new features and developing new tools.

The application of the model to the UA case still has a way to go. The UA is continuously evolving its technological ecosystem and it has recently developed a new strategic plan, so the evolution of the TEmap is the first issue on the agenda. Moreover, there is a possibility of spreading out this model to the whole Spanish university system, taking advantage of the UNIVERSITIC reports, that have deeply impacted on the culture of IT governance in the Spanish universities. This fact would suppose an important support to the model that could lead it to be adopted in other organizations. An important research work is to be done, to compare the case of different organizations belonging to diverse fields and to analyse how to adapt the model to various situations.

The experience gained in the application to different cases will allow review and complete the model. Furthermore, a guide for applying the model to an organization could be developed thanks to this experience. Finally, the ultimate goal would be to develop computer tools that assist the governing boards to collect the information, elaborate the TEmaps, help to interpret them and identify the solutions and improvements to be done on the technological ecosystem.

CONCLUSION

An interesting research line is exploiting the expressiveness of data. The use of charts, maps, tables or graphics of several types may help to provide a deeper and wider representation of the situation in any aspect of life. TEmaps model is a step forward to help interpreting the situation of an organization, particularly its technological ecosystem.

TEmaps have several features that make them powerful to evaluate the situation of the technological ecosystem of the organization. First, the information is presented in a graphical way. Graphic representations is proven to help humans understand the situation at a glance. Although simple to interpret, TEmaps include a complete and exhaustive information about the technological ecosystem, so that important elements can be identified individually, as well as their relationships and underlying configurations.

TEmaps also provide a way to structure the information about the ecosystem and to systematize its evaluation. Some organizations find difficult to convert strategic decisions into concrete actions. Moreover, other organizations have plans to implement actions but they do not follow any particular strategy. TEmaps propose a structure based on levels, facets and components that can help to concretize general strategies (top-down development) or to make up strategies from particular actions (bottom-up development).

Colour patterns that can be detected in the TEmaps are also an interesting feature, since they provide global information about the organization situation. It is a fast way to identify the strengths and weaknesses of the ecosystem and to compare the ecosystems of different organizations.

In summary, TEmaps enables the individuals to extract complex knowledge from the information in a simple way. As a consequence, it will be easier to determine the features of the organization and the state of its technological ecosystem, and to identify possible improvement actions so that the technological ecosystem could give solution to the strategic questions of the organization.

REFERENCES

Bittner, E. A. C., & Leimeister, J. M. (2014). Creating Shared Understanding in Heterogeneous Work Groups: Why It Matters and How to Achieve It. *Journal of Management Information Systems*, *31*(1), 111–144. doi:10.2753/MIS0742-1222310106

Bonjour, E., Belkadi, F., Troussier, N., & Dulmet, M. (2009). Modelling interactions to support and manage collaborative decision-making processes in design situations. *International Journal of Computer Applications in Technology*, *36*(3/4), 259. doi:10.1504/IJCAT.2009.028048

Cater-Steel, A. (Ed.). (2009). *Information technology governance and service management: frameworks and adaptations*. Hershey, PA: Information Science Reference. doi:10.4018/978-1-60566-008-0

Chang, E., & West, M. (2006). *Digital Ecosystems A Next Generation of the Collaborative Environment*. Presented at the 8th International Conference on Information Integration and Web-based Application & Services, Yogyakarta, Indonesia.

COPLA. (2016). *Coneixement Obert i Programari Lliure a la Universitat d'Alacant*. Retrieved from http://blogs.ua.es/copla/

Dalmau Espert, J. L. (2016). *Sistema multiagente para el diseño, ejecución y seguimiento del proceso de planificación estratégica ágil en las organizaciones inteligentes*. (Tesis Doctoral). Universidad de Alicante, Alicante. Retrieved from http://hdl.handle.net/10045/54217

Davis, J., Miller, G. J., & Russell, A. (2006). *Information revolution: using the information evolution model to grow your business*. Hoboken, NJ: John Wiley.

European Commission. (2006). *Digital Ecosystems: The New Global Commons for SMEs and local growth*. European Commission.

Fernández Martínez, A. (2009). *Análisis, planificación y gobierno de las tecnologías de la información en las universidades*. Universidad de Almería, Almería: Tesis Doctoral.

Fernández Martínez, A., & Llorens Largo, F. (2009). *An IT Governance framework for universities in Spain*. Academic Press.

Fernández Martínez, A., & Llorens Largo, F. (2011). *Gobierno de las TI para universidades*. Madrid: CRUE TIC.

fragUA. (2016). *La fragUA*. Retrieved from http://biblioteca.ua.es/fragua

Friedman, T. L. (2005). *The world is flat: a brief history of the twenty-first century* (1st ed.). New York: Farrar, Straus and Giroux.

García-Peñalvo, F. J., Hernández-García, Á., Conde, M. Á., Fidalgo-Blanco, Á., Sein-Echaluce, M. L., Alier, M., … Iglesias-Pradas, S. (2015). *Learning services-based technological ecosystems*. ACM Press. http://doi.org/10.1145/2808580.2808650

ISO/IEC. (2008). *ISO/IEC 38500:2008 Corporate governance of information technology*. Retrieved from http://www.iso.org/iso/catalogue_detail?csnumber=51639

ISO/IEC. (2015). *ISO/IEC 3850 Information technology — Governance of IT for the organization. Second Edition*. Retrieved from https://www.iso.org/obp/ui/#iso:std:62816:en

ITE-UA. (2016). *Servicio de Informática*. Grupos de Innovación Tecnológico-Educativa. Retrieved from http://si.ua.es/ite/gite

Juiz, C., & Toomey, M. (2015). To govern IT, or not to govern IT? *Communications of the ACM, 58*(2), 58–64. doi:10.1145/2656385

Keim, D. A. (2002). Information visualization and visual data mining. *IEEE Transactions on Visualization and Computer Graphics, 8*(1), 1–8. doi:10.1109/2945.981847

Llorens, F., Molina, R., Compañ, P., & Satorre, R. (2014). Technological Ecosystem for Open Education. Smart Digital Futures, 262, 706–715.

Llorens-Largo, F. (2007). *Strategic Plan of the University of Alicante (Horizon 2012)*. Retrieved from http://web.ua.es/en/peua/horizon-2012.html

Maruta, R. (2014). The creation and management of organizational knowledge. *Knowledge-Based Systems, 67*, 26–34. doi:10.1016/j.knosys.2014.06.012

Max Planck Society. (2003). *Berlin Declaration on Open Access to Scientic Knowledge*. Retrieved from http://oa.mpg.de/lang/en-uk/berlin-prozess/berliner-erklarung

Nolan, R. L. (1982). *Managing the Data Resource Function* (2nd ed.). St. Paul, MN: West Publishing Company.

Nonaka, I., & Takeuchi, H. (1995). *The knowledge-creating company: how Japanese companies create the dynamics of innovation*. New York: Oxford University Press.

Paulk, M. C., Curtis, B., Chrissis, M. B., & Weber, C. V. (1993). *Capability Maturity Model for Software, Version 1.1* (No. CMU/SEI-93-TR-024, ESC-TR-93-177). Pittsburgh, PA: Software Engineering Institute, Carnegie Mellon University. Retrieved from http://www.sei.cmu.edu/reports/93tr024.pdf

Píriz Duran, S. (2015). *UNIVERSITIC 2015: Análisis de las TIC en las Universidades Españolas*. Madrid: Conferencia de Rectores de las Universidades Españolas.

SI-UA. (2016). *Servicio de Informática*. Retrieved from http://si.ua.es/vertice/

Stiglitz, J. E., & Greenwald, B. C. (2014). *Creating a learning society: a new approach to growth, development, and social progress.* New York: Columbia University Press. doi:10.7312/columbia/9780231152143.001.0001

Toomey, M. (2009). *Waltzing with the elephant: a comprehensive guide to directing and controlling information technology.* Belgrave South, Australia: Infonomics.

Uceda Antolín, J., & Barro Ameneiro, S. (2010). *UNIVERSITIC 2010: Evolución de Las TIC en el Sistema Universitario Español 2006-2010.* Madrid: Conferencia de Rectores de las Universidades Españolas.

Zara, O. (2008). Le management de l'intelligence collective: vers une nouvelle gouvernance (2nd ed.). Paris: M21 Editions.

Chapter 4
Gamification Ecosystems:
Current State and Perspectives

Velimir Štavljanin
University of Belgrade, Serbia

Miroslav Minović
University of Belgrade, Serbia

ABSTRACT

Gamification is hot topic today. Many organizations consider the application of gamification in their processes. Therefore, to implement gamification, it's necessary to know all elements and their relationships that comprise gamification ecosystem. The aim of this chapter is to clarify all details related to that ecosystem. At the beginning we defined gamification and similar concepts. Next, we introduced different types of gamification. One of the key parts of the chapter describes various game elements taxonomies and most used game elements or building blocks of gamification. Player as an inseparable part of that ecosystem is described through player identification, player types and player life cycle. It's clear now that there is lot of different approaches available for application of games in non-leisure context. Rather than to talk about one kind of game or game system, we decided to use term ecosystem in order to be clearer and more consistent with our approach. That is to integrate different approaches and orchestrate different tools in order to make them work together.

DOI: 10.4018/978-1-5225-0905-9.ch004

INTRODUCTION

Games are something that is related to the earliest development of the human community. It should be noted that the play in part is responsible for the survival of the human species, given that they through the play the people improved their hunting skills or learn the importance of following the rules (Bergeron, 2006, p. xv). Koster (2014, p. 64) agrees that games teach us the survival skills. The play is important in the modern era as clearly emphasizes Jane McGonigal (2011, pp. 3-4) in his book "Reality is Broken," stating that "Reality is not engineered to maximize our potential. ... The truth is this: in today's society, computer and video games are fulfilling genuine human needs the real world is currently unable to satisfy". The projects that have emerged in recent years as Nike +, Volkswagen initiative The Fun Theory (The World's Deepest Bin, Piano Staircase, the Speed Camera Lottery), Microsoft Language Quality game, Foursquare location service, Club Psych the fan site of television series, Samsung Nation program, ReserchGate site, as well as many others include elements of the game, but are not a play in the true sense of the words in order to engage users. The term gamification is bonded for previous projects, which experienced its real expansion in 2010 (Deterding et al. 2011; Werbach & Hunter 2012, p. 25). Although a relatively new concept, he quickly gained a large number of fans in different disciplines. Overall, the planet spends more than 3 billion hours per week playing games (McGonigal, 2011, p. 6).

BACKGROUND

The term gamification is not easy to define, given that gamification to different people means different things (Zichermann & Cunningham, 2011, p. xiv). Difficulties in defining came in because of the different disciplines in which the gamification is defined, such as education, information technology, business and marketing. Another source of the definition problem is mixing of this issue with the game, serious game, as well as some other terms.

Deterding et al. (2011) define the gamification as the use of design elements characteristic for games in non-game contexts.

Zichermann i Cunningham (2011, p. xiv) has defined gamification as the process of game-thinking and game mechanics to engage users and solve problems.

In an interview that Richard Bartle held with Andrzej Marczewski (2012) on gamification, the modern use of gamification is defined as taking techniques from games and applying them to non-games.

Werbach and Hunter (2012, p. 26) has defined gamification as use of game elements and game-design techniques in non-game contexts.

According to Kapp (2012, p. 10) gamification is using game-based mechanics, aesthetics and game thinking to engage people, motivate action, promote learning, and solve problems.

Gamification from the perspective of marketing services (Huotari and Hamari 2012) is defined as the process of enhancing a service with affordances for gameful experiences in order to support user's overall value creation.

Gamification (Koster, 2014, p. 50) attempts to use the trappings of games (reward structures, points, etc.) to make people engage with more product offerings.

Asked whether gamification involves creating game, the authors Werbach and Hunter (2012, p. 25) said that the result of the gamification might not be game; it is a process which has game elements, but has no gameplay. When gamification process has gameplay too, then that game is called a "serious game" or "game with a purpose". The same opinion is shared by Richard Bartle (Marczewski, 2012). Deterding et al. (2011) noted that the difference between serious game and gamification is that the game represents a serious full-fledged game that is used for non-entertainment purposes, while gamification represents the incorporation of elements of the game. The authors note that the line between serious game and gamification is often blurry.

GAMIFICATION IN DETAILS

Gamification of similar concepts can be separated by observation in relation to the two dimensions - playing/gaming, and parts/whole (Detering et al., 2011). Playing refers to freeform, expressive, improvisational recombination of behaviors and meanings, and gaming refers to playing by the rules and structured pursuit of the objective. Figure 1. is the matrix with similar concepts in relation to gamification.

Otherwise, the different elements of gamification surround us daily, but we are not even aware of it. Table 1 (Werbach & Hunter, 2012, p. 32) show examples of gamification concepts facing daily in our lives.

Given that gamification relates to the use of game elements, games techniques, or game thinking in solving problems, it can be assumed that it is suitable for every problem. However, Werbach and Hunter (2012, p. 44) note that gamification is not suitable for every problem and propose four key questions that should be taken into consideration in order to determine whether the gamification meets the needs of:

- **Motivation:** Where would you derive value from encouraging behavior?
- **Meaningful Choices:** Are your target activities sufficiently interesting?

Figure 1. Gamification and similar concepts
Detering et al., 2011.

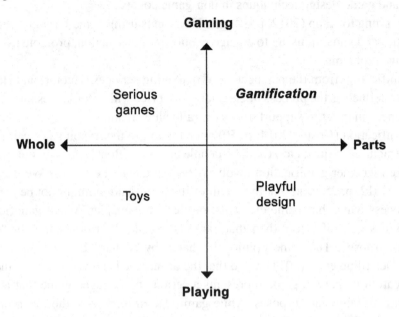

Table 1. Concepts of game in real world

Real World Activities	Game Concept
Monthly sales competition	Challenge
Frequent flyer program tiers	Level
Weight Watchers group	Team
Free coffee after ten purchase at Starbucks	Reward
American Express platinum card	Badge

Werbach & Hunter, 2012, p. 32.

- **Structure:** Can the desired behaviors be modeled through a set of algorithms?
- **Potential Conflicts:** Can the game avoid conflicts with existing motivational structures?

Some processes will have more benefits of gamification than others. Gamification motivates specific behavior and if the motivation is important for the problem to be solved, then the process will have major benefits from gamification. Three types of activities important for gamification are (Werbach & Hunter, 2012, p. 45): creative work, mundane tasks, and behavior change. Gamified system must provide the user the options that offer choice and noticeable consequence arising out of there. This ensures users with a sense of autonomy, essential for not making a user feeling bored. Gamification also means that it is possible by algorithms to measure and react to the action and easily monitor user activity. If there is no structure that will enable it, gamification is not the way to improve the system. Gamification should not be in contradiction with existing systems to motivate the user. If this is the case, a conflict occurs that would prevent the full efficiency of the system. As can be concluded from the above, the ideal candidate for gamification is a process that depends on the motivation, offers interesting challenges to be easily encoded in rules and reinforce the existing system of rewards (Werbach & Hunter, 2012, p. 48).

Types of Gamification

The approach to gamification can be applied in different circumstances, taking in consideration several categories of gamification. Figure 2. (Werbach & Hunter, 2012, p. 21) represents the categories of gamification in relation to the level of benefits that can vary from individual to organizational and whoever is involved in gamification, from the employees internally, to the individuals externally.

- **Internal Gamification:** The initiative of gamification in this context is a way to improve productivity within the organization in order to achieve positive business results. Internal gamification benefits already created community

Figure 2. Categories of gamification
Werbach & Hunter, 2012, p. 21.

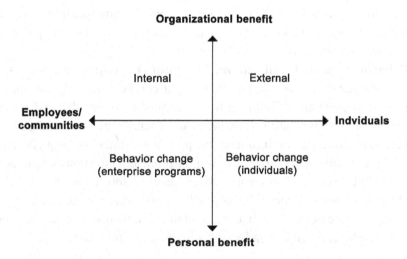

within the company in which employees already interact with each other and share a common culture and values. In addition, the motivational element can be connected with the existing management structure and remuneration. Microsoft created a game "Windows Language Quality Game" to address the problem of errors in dialogs with the localization of the operating system Windows 7, which employees solved faster and more cost efficiently. Game "Idea Street" Department for Work and Pension (DWP), of the United Kingdom is used to gather ideas from employees and their implementation in order to improve business DWP. Sun Microsystems has created a game "Rise of the Shadow Specters" for the training of new employees in order to get a basic knowledge of business units San, and technologies that are used.

- **External Gamification:** Gamification in this sense is driven by marketing goals representing way to improve relations between the company and the consumer, in order to increase engagement, identification with the product, higher loyalty and ultimately more profit. Gamification can be used as a mean of motivating consumers. Nevertheless, in order to apply gamification as a form of marketing activity, it is essential that behavior can be modeled, by using modern data driven practice. There are many successful examples of external gamification. Website "My Starbucks Idea" of the company Starbucks benefits gamification to collect good ideas for products and services from consumers. Application "Samsung Nation" has used gamification to engaged visitors of the site Samsun.com on social media and build community. *Club Psych* fan loyalty program of the known television series Psych NBC Universal's USA Network benefits the gamification in order to improve the relationship with customers. "Nike +" concept uses sensors integrated into the sports equipment and mobile applications, aiming to gamify users community on exercise and sports activities, which may be the example of gamification in function of changing behavior.

- **Behavior Change Gamification:** This form of gamification refers to creating new habits among the population that can be externally and internally looking organization. Changing behavior must be motivated, and games are one of the best motivators. New behavior generally creates socially desirable behavior. Given the results among the population, the most frequent sponsors of these gamification programs are non-profit organizations or the government, but programs can create private benefits, too. Examples of behavior change are *Keas* application designed for corporate use, which in gemified environment can monitor changing malnutrition habits of the employees and how employees lose weight by switching to a healthier diet.

Zichermann and Linden (2013, p. 7) define six basic types of gamification approaches aiming to driving engagement and problem solving:

- **Grand Challenge:** These are competitions that involve a cash prize and the most suitable for solving the problem of large or medium complexity.
- **Rapid Feedback System:** This is a system in which feedback shapes the behavior in real time.
- **Simulation Discovery:** These games allow exploration of new ideas, models or scenarios.
- **Status Marathon:** These are long-arc games that use ladders status and rewards.
- **Commercial/Negotiation:** These games are based on the virtual sphere, or economy from real world including markets and auctions.
- **Expressive:** These ones are designed to facilitate creativity, individuality and users' emotional satisfaction.

Previous approaches can be used individually or in combination, to stakeholders within and outside the company.

GAME ELEMENTS

Simply put, game elements are built in gamified system to create a gamified experience. Should be noted that these elements are similar to those of games, but they are more focused and optimized for gamification (Zichermann & Cunningham, 2011, p. 35). Given the fact that there are different sets of game elements, the authors Detring et al. (2011) even ask the question, what are the elements that make up a collection of game elements? Their interpretation is that the game elements are the "elements that are characteristics to games - elements that are found in most games, readily associated with games, and found to play a significant role to the gameplay." These elements are usually displayed as a group of elements or presented in the form of a framework. One of the most common framework for the design of games MDA (Zichermann & Cunningham, 2011, p. 35), initially developed by Hunicke LeBlanc and Zubek (2004), consist of the following group of elements:

- Mechanics,
- Dynamics,
- Aesthetics.

Game Mechanics

Game mechanics make functioning elements of the game (Zichermann & Cunning-ham, 2011, p. 36). More specifically, mechanics describes particular components of the game (Hunicke, LeBlanc, & Zubek 2004). These are the tools which if properly used create meaningful response. Game mechanics consist of the following elements (Zichermann & Cunningham, 2011, p. 36):

- Points,
- Levels,
- Leaderboards,
- Badges,
- Challenges/quests,
- On-boarding, and
- Engagement loops.

Dynamics

Dynamics are user's interaction with game mechanics (Zichermann & Cunningham, 2011, p. 36). According to Hunicke et al. (2004) dynamics describes the run-time behavior of the mechanics acting on player inputs and each other's' outputs over time. They determine how users will react to the system mechanics, both on an in-dividual level, and compared to other players. Zichermann and Cunningham (2011, p. 80) presented twelve game dynamics that are commonly used in gamification:

- Pattern recognition,
- Collecting,
- Surprise and Unexpected Delight,
- Organizing and Creating Order,
- Gifting,
- Flirtation and Romance,
- Recognition for Achievement,
- Leading Others,
- Fame, Getting Attention,
- Being the Hero,
- Gaining Status,
- Nurturing, Growing.

Authors emphasize that mechanics could combine in order to create dynamics.

Game Esthetics

Game esthetics affects the player trying to provoke his/her feelings during the interaction. Aesthetics are a composite outcome of the mechanics and dynamics (Zichermann & Cunningham, 2011, p. 36). Hunicke, LeBlanc and Zubek (2004) note that aesthetics comprises the desirable emotional responses created in the player, when interacting with the system. Taxonomy of aesthetics includes (Hunicke, LeBlanc and Zubek 2004):

- Sensations,
- Fantasy,
- Narrative,
- Challenge,
- Followship,
- Discovery,
- Expression,
- Submission.

A slightly different approach was proposed by Werbach and Hunter (2012, p. 78), which also represent the three categories of game elements, organized in descending order by abstraction. The elements are:

1. Dynamics,
2. Mechanics,
3. Components.

As seen, mechanics with previous authors represents the lowest level of abstraction, while in Werbach and Hunter at the lowest level are represented components, while mechanics are at higher level of abstraction. Elements can be visually displayed in the form of a pyramid (Figure 3) to create a sense of hierarchy among the elements.

Game Dynamics

Game dynamics represent the highest level of abstraction of the game elements. They can be seen as a big picture, as well as elements that will never be directly found in the game. The most important dynamics are (Werbach & Hunter, 2012, p. 78):

- Constraints,
- Emotions,
- Narrative,

Figure 3. Games' component pyramid
Werbach & Hunter, 2012, p. 82.

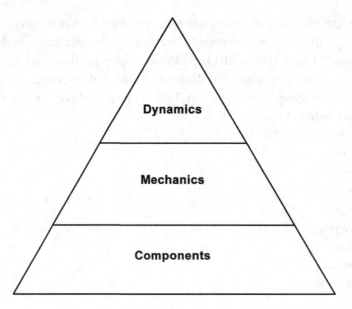

- Progression,
- Relationships.

Game Mechanics

Game mechanics are on the lower abstraction level relative to the dynamics and every mechanic ties to one or more dynamics. They are the elements that drive the action forward and generate player engagement. Ten important game mechanics are (Werbach & Hunter, 2012, p. 79):

- Challenges,
- Chance,
- Competition,
- Cooperation,
- Feedback,
- Resource Acquisition,
- Rewards,
- Transactions,
- Turns,
- Win States.

Game Components

Game components are the most specific forms that mechanics or dynamics can take. Every components tie to one or more elements of a higher abstraction level. Fifteen important components are (Werbach & Hunter, 2012, p. 79):

- Achievements,
- Avatars,
- Badges,
- Boss Fights,
- Collections,
- Combat,
- Content Unlocking,
- Gifting,
- Leaderboards,
- Levels,
- Points,
- Quests,
- Social Graphs,
- Teams,
- Virtual Goods.

Authors Blohm and Leimeister (2013) present two groups of game elements:

- Mechanics,
- Dynamics.

Mechanics

Mechanics include a variety of building blocks to gemify basic offer. The most important mechanics they indentify are (Blohm & Leimeister, 2013):

- Documentation of behavior,
- Scoring systems, badges, trophies,
- Rankings,
- Ranks, levels, reputation points,
- Group tasks,
- Time pressure, tasks, quests,
- Avatars, virtual worlds, virtual trade.

Dynamics

Dynamics describe the effects that mechanics have on the subjective experience of users over time, which correspond to certain users' motifs. The most important dynamics are (Blohm &T Leimeister, 2013):

- Exploration,
- Collection,
- Competition,
- Acquisition of status,
- Collaboration,
- Challenge,
- Development/organization.

However, the issue is whether there is a minimum number of elements necessary to achieve gamification? Werbach and Hunter (2012, p. 71) based on research analyzing over 100 gamification implementations, identified that the vast majority comprise three elements. These elements are PBL - points, badges, and leaderboards. Authors immediately give an explanation that these elements do not make gamification, but are an excellent starting point. Other authors (Zichermann & Cunningham, 2011, p. 36) agree that there are elements which are a prerequisite for each gemified system comprising points, levels and leaderboards. Zichermann and Linder (2013, p. 18) consider the basic game mechanics: points, badges (achievements), levels, leaderboards, and rewards.

Points

Simply described, points are systems used to monitor the behavior, keep score, and provide feedback (Zichermann & Linder, 2013, p. 19). Points can be important for players, for exchanging them with other players, and definitely, for exchange with games designers (Zichermann & Cunningham, 2011, p. 36). Users are encouraged to certain activities by collecting points, assuming the harder way or use of particular services in exchange for points. They represent a good basis for users dealing with collecting the points, or those who strive to prove themselves in front of others. There are multiple ways to incorporate the points into the system (Werbach & Hunter, 2012, pp. 72-73):

1. Points effectively keep score, and, through them, you can easily see how the player progresses. They can indicate how many points are necessary for the next level. The points simply define the progress of the game till its end.

2. Points may determine the win state of gamed process, by defining a point's level that verifies a winning situation.

3. Points create a connection between progression in the game and extrinsic rewards. Systems can offer a real reward for a certain level of points or for redeeming virtual points.

4. Points provide feedback. As stated above, the feedback is an important component of good gamification. Points are a very nice feedback mechanism pointing to progress in the game.

5. Points can be an external display of progress. When users are involved in the community, points can show the gamer's progress, ie. they can be status indicators.

6. Points provide data for the game designer. The points which can be easily traced, my provide data on the system functioning indicating how to make some improvement.

The gamification can implement one of the five point systems (Zichermann & Cunningham, 2011, p. 36; Zichermann & Linder, 2013, p. 19):

- **Experience Points:** Authors pointed them as one of the most important points system, which enable monitoring the progress of players, giving a point during each activity in the system. Their value is always growing and cannot be replaced. In some implementations, points can eventually expire.
- **Redeemable Points:** Can substitute certain things within the system. They form the basis of the virtual economy.
- **Skill Points:** Assigned to specific activities in the system and are bonus points that a player can earn in addition to the basic points.
- **Karma Points:** A unique system that rarely occurs. The role of these points is to be shared, because only then the player has an advantage.
- **Reputation Points:** The most complex point system, which includes when the trust between two or more parties to the system cannot be not explicitly guaranteed. They are used as a proxy for trust.

All gemified systems should implement the experience points first (Zichermann and Linder, 2013, p. 19).

Badges

Badges are most closely connected with the points. So far, they may be defined as a visual representation of some of achievement within the gamified process (Werbach & Hunter, 2012, p. 74). Certainly, the achievement is provided by a number of points. However, there are badges not associated with points, but with the activities of the user. For example, one can get a badge for the most goals scored or badge for possession of certain skills. Zichermann and Linder (2013, p. 20) state that there are generic points, achievements and trophies, and other symbols of accomplishment. Otherwise, the badges are very flexible element not limited neither by a number, nor the aim.

Gamified design may deliver different functions to the badges, but mostly they are used to display the status and progress of the players. They may be linear or variable. The main idea is to allow the player a sense of fulfillment that otherwise would not be easy to achieve. Sometimes badges can have features that are difficult to express, because they represent a form of privileged status and they are known as reputation badges. Badges can be organized also as a collection accumulated by users (Zichermann & Linder, 2013 p. 20).

Well-designed badges system has five motivational characteristics (Werbach & Hunter, 2012, p. 74):

- Badges can provide the goals to which users can aspire to, having a positive effect on motivation.
- Badges provide guidance what is possible within a certain system and generate a shortcut on what can be expected from the system.
- Badges are a sign of what the user cares about and what the user has already done, and they represent a sign of someone's reputation.
- Badges are a status symbol and affirmation how the user navigates through gemified system.
- Badges have the functions of origin, when in possession of a badge which have other users too, creating a feeling of affiliation to a group.

Leaderboards

Leaderboard is an ordered list that shows the score for the players and represents a system of ranking in games. Although widely used, it is one of the most complex elements that can provide motivation, or distraction (Werbach & Hunter, 2012, p. 76). It motivates by a presentation of progression, so the user can see where he/she is in relation to the others, and the same ranking the others can see, as well, what can be an additional motivation factor. However, if the user is far from the leaders, it can slow down or stop the progress, and may convert the game into the struggle for a better place, which is not the goal. There are two types of leaderboards used nowadays (Zichermann & Cunningham, 2011, p. 50): no-disincentive leaderboards and infinite leaderboards. No-disincentive leaderboards should create incentive, not to discourage players. Regardless of the actual score the player is placed in the middle, instead regarding his/her absolute leaderboards rank. This is implemented through percentage scale of a certain criteria fulfillment. But if a player is already in the top 10 or 20 players, it should be directly displayed. Infinite leaderboards is a kind of leaderboards that allows players to exist forever. In order to achieve this, some games represent limited views only, providing the player to be included on the list. Examples are to display players locally, globally or socially.

GAMERS

In each game the player takes a role. Understanding the role of players is important for the creation of games, but also to understand how users interact with the business. Player person is a fictional character who is trying to grasp the personality, attitudes and attributes of real life (Radoff 2011, p. 63). The process of creating a person includes following steps (Radoff 2011, p. 63):

1. Identifying your best customers
2. Collecting information about customers through research and interviews
3. Organizing information into descriptions, motivations and goals
4. Repeating as necessary based on what you learn, or to fill-in gaps in your knowledge

The process of building a player persona, necessary requires selecting a person's name easy to remember.

Gamers' Types

Richard Bartle (Bartle 1996) the inventor of multiuser dungeon (MUD) games tried to understand the motivations for their playing. He found that some players emphasize "world" in the game, while other are interested in players of the game. In addition to these differences, he identified that some players are more interested in the interaction or "acting with", while others were interested in "acting on". Players can be sorted into various categories on the graph shown in Figure 4. Although the types are developed in the context of MUDs, the author notes that MUDs can be of great importance to non-game applications or "serious" application, which implies the use in gamification projects. Based on the previous categories, four groups of players are identified (Bartle 1996):

Figure 4. Bartle's interest graph
Bartle 1996.

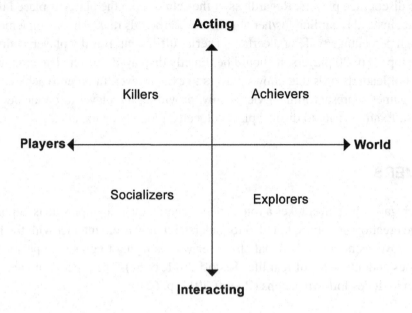

- **Achievers:** Players who impose game-related objectives to be achieved and subordinate all to these goals. Objectives are usually related to points-gathering and rising in levels. This is the type of player interested in acting on the world in the game.
- **Explorers:** Players who try to discover more about the world in the game. They like to try progressively esoteric actions in wild, out-of-the-way places, looking for interesting features (i.e., bugs) and figuring out how things work. Explorers are interested in interacting with the world of game. For the other players are not interested, unless they are part of the game.
- **Socializers:** Players interested in other players and what they have to say. Socializers are interested in interacting with other players. Usually they converse with others and explore other people trying to understand them better.
- **Killers:** Players who cause harassment of other players. This type of player is interested in acting on other players. This, of course, not with consent of the other players. But they do not care for it, and they just want to demonstrate their superiority over others.

Obviously, the previous groups are intertwined and players will, depending on their mood and the current style of play, switch to another group. However, the author notes that players usually have one primary style, although applying other styles as a means to advance their main interest.

Bartle has introduced an improved model which engages eight types of players (Bartle 2004, pp. 165-170). In order to segment better the customers it is introduced another dimension implicit / explicit. Implicit and explicit refers to how players deal with certain activities, both explicitly or implicitly. Explicit manner refers to the fact that the players do not leave anything to chance, all is planned in advance. Implicit refers to the response of players when something happens. Analyzing on that way the previous model with four types of players, identified are eight types of players:

- **Opportunists:** Implicit achievers directed where fancy takes them.
- **Planners:** Organized achievers planning what to do and how to reach it.
- **Politicians:** Players who directly act on other players
- **Grievers:** Players who are ready to seize power or other inconveniences to be observed.
- **Hackers:** Implicit explorers who highly know the virtual world and they are able to investigate it by using intuition only.
- **Scientists:** Explicit explorers who experiment according to plan in an orderly way.
- **Networkers:** Players that directly interact with other players
- **Friends:** Players who interact with already known players and with those having deep bonds.

The categorization of the four types in some cases cannot be applied and it is difficult to identify easily explorers and killers, resulted the development of new approaches. One approach that should overcome all shortcomings is Radoff's access to social gameplay motivations (Radoff 2011, p.82). Access has a dimension of motivation focused on single-player experience or multiuser experience and dimension to consider motivation as a quantitative or qualitative (Figure 5). With this approach it is possible to identify different motivations that can be captured by four quadrants (Radoff 2011, pp. 82-83):

- **Achievement (Single, Quantitative):** Any possibility that gives the player a sense of progress, and can be measured in, for example, the collection and ownership issues, gaining levels or badges, or earning prestige.
- **Immersion (Single, Qualitative):** The sense of forming an enduring emotional connection to a game by feeling as if you're actually part of something, and is satisfied by exploring game content, unraveling game stories, and learning about secrets.

Figure 5. Social gameplay motivations
Radoff 2011, p.82.

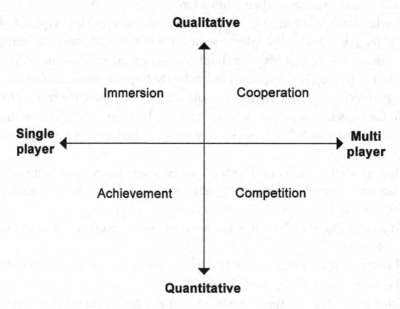

- **Competition (Multi, Quantitative):** Associated with a special sense of victory over real people in game. Victory over competitors can be enhanced with leaderboards, which affects the prestige. Competition includes the struggle for limited resources.
- **Cooperation (Multi, Qualitative):** When the player interacts with other players in the noncompetitive way and includes establishing teams to solve problems that are impossible to solve alone, leading and forming groups, helping each other with information or gifts, or simply getting to know other players.

Gamers' Motivation

Aim of gamification is to provide an environment that is both fun and simultaneously, enables the achievement of defined goals. Authors (Malone 1981; Malone & Lepper, 1987) have identified four motivational factors in gamers:

1. **Challenge:** The structure of the game must be neither too simple nor too complicated;
2. **Control:** A player must have a sense of manageability that may affect the outcome of the game;

3. **Curiosity:** For example, opportunities to explore the world in the game can lead to unexpected outcomes;
4. **Fantasy:** The perception of participation in the imagined world.

The main challenge when designing gamified system is the realization of a balance between factors that stimulate the motivation to play in a way that does not harm the defined process (e.g. Learning, problem solving, attitudes,...). Games or simulations can easily distract players in the way that is counterproductive for defined aims. For example, games that have a fast logic do not leave time for reflection. Games or simulations that have a very detailed and realistic visualization and audio effects can lead to memory overload of the players. Also, games or simulations with rich worlds, can lead to significant activities of the players, but with very little learning. The solution lies in the careful selection of motivational elements in the game in a way that they support and not interfere with the basic psychological mechanism of learning. Nicole Lazzaro has conducted research looking at people when they play games, based on which he has found four groups of emotions that the players show in their facial expression: hard to have fun, easy entertaining, altered state, and human factors (Lazzaro 2004). When we successfully resolve the issue given to us, we stimulate the brain with a dose of satisfaction (Koster 2005). If the inflow of new problems slows down, pleasure will disappear and can induce boredom. If the inflow of new problems increases above our capacity, we will not feel the satisfaction, as we will be unable to make progress.

State of Flow

It represents the time that most of the players are referring to as "being in the zone". One of mostly cited academic definitions is one given as Csikszentmihalyi's concept of 'flow', where flow - is a condition in which the player enters when experiencing an absolute concentration on the task (physical, mental or both), so he loses sense of time and the outside world (Csíkszentmihályi 1996). Lazzaro (Lazzaro 2004) calls this phenomenon 'hard fun' (hard fun). This condition is not achieved very often, but when it happens it is a great experience. The problem is to precisely match the challenges and the capabilities of the player, which is a very difficult task. If they had been in this kind of situation, the players usually ascertained "This was really fun." If it was not the case, they would say: "... it was fun" but with less enthusiasm. It does not mean that there is no fun if there is no entry into this condition. So the fun is not a state of flow. The state of flow can also be experienced in many situations that are not fun.

Creativity

Creativity is another important component of playing games (Zichermann & Linder, 2010). Today, the people are increasingly required to be creative, from primary education, to their daily business activities. Creativity is closely related to the selection. The increasing choices possibilities encourage users to be more creative in their choice. There are three forms of creativity (Radoff, 2011):

- **Unstructured Creativity:** There are some restrictions, but they are beyond the imagination of users and are the hereditary characteristics of the medium.
- **Structured Creativity:** Includes the existence of significant constraints in choice, but there are certain elements that can be combined and provide uniqueness that reflects the uniqueness of a person.
- **Extraordinary Creativity:** Creativity that is poorly structured, but very dependent on the platform provided by someone.

The structured creativity is the most important for playing games and it is associated with a limited selection, but still allows users to select, individualize and express themselves in a structured process.

Players' Life Cycle

The player usually has a life cycle in relation to the game. The life cycle consists of several stages, through which the player is overcoming. In case the player does not master one stage he/she loses the game. The game is more ineffective in retaining players when the number of players is decreasing during the game.

A player's life cycle of can be represented through the experiences he/she has in applying a specific system. In this way we can define three categories (Werbach & Hunter, 2012, pp. 93-94):

- **Novice:** Basic category, when the user learns the first steps and is in need of help due to not knowing the system.
- **Regular:** Novice is becoming a regular user who is expecting that a play offers him something new and never used previously.
- **Expert:** User who has experienced all, he/she requires higher challenges to maintain his/hers engagement.

Bartle (Bartle 2004, pp. 150-151), in his book "Designing Virtual Worlds" shows six circles presented by "Ultima Online" player *Hedron*, which describe how players advance through different states of maturity. Players are organized into six concentric circles and start from the outer to the inner circles:

- **First Circle – Survival:** The player starts as newbies and his main interest is to acquire basic skills, stats and items needed to survive.
- **Second Circle – Competence:** Gained experience, the player will start moving forward and virtual world will become more fun.
- **Third Circle – Excel:** How getting better he/she tends to greater challenges to overcome them.
- **Fourth Circle – Prove Master:** Once acquired technical mastery, he/she wants to show it to others, and it works by helping, mentoring or leading and now he/she can attack other players.
- **Fifth Circle – Seek New Challenges:** The player feels that he has exhausted all that virtual world can offer and the only fun is the interaction with other players.
- **Sixth Circle – Everything Is One:** The player recognizes the ways in which others play virtual world and has a full understanding of the merits of all of them.

Player life cycle (in social games) can be represented through three phases shown in Figure 6, like a funnel (Radoff, 2011, pp. 167-168):

Figure 6. Player's life cycle in a social game
Radoff, 2011, p. 168.

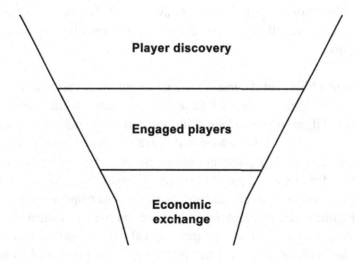

1. **Player Discovery:** Through advertising or through communication with other players through messages about news, statuses updates, or direct messages.
2. **Engaged Player:** Player engages through experience in which they will enjoy. If the game is fun and engaging, players will progress through the game towards the end of her.
3. **Economic Exchange:** Performed by the players in order to start an event, unlock special content or customize experience.

GAME VS. GAMIFICATION

Game is a formal rule-based system with variety and measurable outcomes, where different outcomes receive different levels, player invests effort to influence the outcome, the player recognizes the connection of its acting with the outcome, and consequences of the activities are optional and variable (Koster, 2005).

This chapter presents the most important games' classification. The classification aims to shed light on the basic factors linking groups games, and to highlight the critical differences between groups and members of the group games. A well designed classification will discover the principles that underlie the development of games.

However, the classification represents only a way to organize a large number of related objects. Since the field of games is too young, and that the pattern is small, it is not easy to find good criteria for the division. Games existing nowadays are more the product of chance, and not the inevitable result of well-organized forces (Crawford, 1982).

By type of game we decided to quote the classification given by Chris Crawford, in his book 'The art of computer games' (Crawford, 1982), printed for the first time in 1970. It is a classification by type of game, and essentially covers actually, the up-to date games.

1. **Games of Skills and Actions:** They represent the largest and most popular group of computer games. Most people associate all the games with this category. All arcade games are skills and actions games; also almost all the games for the Atari 2600 belong to this group. Characteristics are playing in real time, relying on graphics and sound effects, and use of joystick rather than keyboard. Players are required to possess the basic such as to coordinate the movements of the hand and the eye, as well as fast response time.
    a. **Fighting Games:** Fighting games present a direct violent conflict. The player has to shoot and destroy the bad guys controlled by a computer. The challenge lies in the fact that the player is positioned so as to avoid the enemy's attack and shots. This is a very popular group games, and

there are plenty of variations on the theme, the environment in which to play, and the types of weapons used.

b. **Labyrinth:** The second sub-group of the skills and actions games classification are games with labyrinth. PAC-MAN is the most successful representative of this group. The basic characteristic is the existence of a maze, with the path that the player must pass in order to successfully master the game. Some of it has a way out where is necessary to arrive.

c. **Sport Games:** These games model popular sports. The basic idea is to design games that simulate sports games in the real world. Since the players are already familiar with these games in the real world, the electronic versions more easily find their way to them. For example, there are games based on basketball, football, baseball, American football, tennis, boxing and other sports. Each of them neglects certain aspects of the real sport adapting it to be played on a computer.

d. **Paddle Games:** We use the term paddle games to describe games based on PONG game. PONG is certainly one of the most successful games, with even more successful clones and sequels. The main characteristic of this class of games is the interception and diversion of a moving object. The original version was made for two players, as the electronic version of the table tennis (ping-pong), of which derives its name. Version which brought the greatest popularity was created for one player who has the task by retrieving the ball to destroy brick wall.

e. **Racing Games:** Some video games include classic racing. Most of these games allow the player to move at a constant speed, and requests the players to skillfully avoid obstacles and steer the vehicle. For example, a player in the game of skiing must avoid trees and rocks; the result is based on the time it takes for a player to finish the race. MATCH RACER is a car race with obstacles on the road such as oil stains. NIGHT DRIVER is also a race car with a view of the road from the cabin. The problem with this class of games is that they are not real games, but mostly a puzzle type games, because there is no real interaction between the player and the enemy. Indeed, it is difficult to identify the enemy in these games.

f. Various other games.

2. **Strategic Games:** Strategy games are another large group of computer games. These games favor the thinking before manipulation. This does not mean that some of the games of skills and actions group do not have strategic content. The main factor that distinguishes the strategic game of the skills and action games is whether they require certain motor capabilities. Strategic games does not require it, are essential for while skills and action type games Playing in

real time is very rare at the strategy, although in recent years appears more strategies in real time. Strategy games usually require more time to play than games such as skills and actions. Strategy games are rare on gaming consoles like the Atari 2600; they are more common in version of a home computer.

a.   **Adventure:** This group of games is derived from one of the oldest computer games, which was called the 'Adventure'. For adventure player moves through a complex world, collecting objects and preys to overcome every obstacle, until the final goal is reached.

b.   **D&D (Dungeons & Dragons) Games:** Fully independent direction of games' development started based on the D & D game. The first game of this type, was on the board game, without a computer, Dungeons and Dragons by Gary Gygax, containing research, cooperation and conflict, and is set in a fairy-tale world of castles, dragons and wizards. The group of players led by leader of the game, the so-called 'dungeonmaster''s, goes in search of treasure. The game is played with very little equipment. Players gather around the table and use a block of papers. The leader of the game applies rules of the game and controls the players. He has the authority to rule on all events during the games. In this way we can create very complex systems without burdening complex rules. The atmosphere is very relaxed and informal. For these reasons, the D & D has become a very popular game, with unlimited number of variations and successor.

c.   **War Games:** War games are the third subclass of strategy games, and are the most complex and most demanding games available to the public. Books with the rules seem contracts for company's acquisition, while playing time often exceeds three hours.

d.   **Games of Chance:** Games of chance are playing in the last few thousand years, and it was expected to be realized as a computer game. They are quite simple to program, so there are many versions of these games. Despite the great offer, this game did not prove so popular, primarily because they do not take advantage of the computer. They are simply transferred games from one medium to another.

e.   **Educational and Children's Games:** The next category is the educational games. While all games are educational in its own way, the games in this group are designed with an explicit educational goal. Group of these games is not yet popular, probably because people in the field of education have not yet paid enough attention to creating games.

f.   **Interpersonal Games:** We were investigating a group of games which focus on human relations. One such game is investigating the group for gossip. Player exchange gossip with seven computer-controlled characters.

The topic of conversation is always feelings, positive or negative, of one participant to another. A wise choice results in increasing popularity. Similar games can realize the subject of corporate policy, the situation of opera, gothic romance, as well as international diplomacy and espionage. Although this category of games is still undeveloped, we believe it is important because it deals with fantasies of great important to people. Many other forms of art devote a great deal of attention to interpersonal relations. It is only a matter of time before computer games will take the same path.

Hereby we listed a classification of the serious games according to its destination, given in the book Serious Games (Clark A. C., 1970), and the field of application:

- For military,
- For a government and civil services,
- For education,
- For corporations,
- For health,
- For politics, religion and art.

Social Games

Board games are the type of games that people play among each other (Zicherman & Linder, 2010). These games have been around for millennia. However, in recent years the concept of social games is linked to a special category of online games on social networks. The concept of social game is, otherwise, much wider than the games on social networks. Board games first included only two players, as in the case of the Backgammon, chess or cards (Radoff, 2011). At a later stage, games included multiple players, which can be divided into two opposing teams, like the forerunner of football, today the football itself, and some sports games, or the games played individually. All previous games require players to be in one location. But back in the 9th century, chess was played through correspondence, too while in the 60s of the last century emerged games that could be played through the mail. One such game is *Diplomacy*. The arrival of e-mail enabled playing this game through the new electronic media. A large number of these games are strategic, and games that include stunning motifs and figures. The next evolution was in relation to the inclusion of BBSs through which they played these games. The user interface of these games was the textual and in the 90s, these games acquired a graphical interface. These first multiplayer online role games were two-dimensional, developing in three-dimensional lately. The World of Warcraft was one of the most popular, still occupying a multimillion playground. Further evolution included games in the community on social media, among which the most popular are the ones on social networks, primarily Facebook.

Game industry on social media in a short time attracted millions of users. In 2008, the Pew Research explored the teenagers in America and came to the conclusion that more than 97% of them play games. Today games are even created for those populations that never play them as women, families and pensioners. The result is a market of online social games, which is the fastest growing market.

Games apply some basic rules whether they are in a traditional in the online environment, or an environment of social media. When creating a game, it is necessary to limit the choice and thus, provide a fun experience (Radoff, 2011; Zicherman & Linder, 2010). Today people are exposed on a daily basis on a large number of decisions to make. When it comes to games, designers must simplify the matter, so that games were fun. When the decisions in games were as in real life, complex games would not be fun (Radoff, 2011). It is necessary for designers to identify several entertaining outcomes and to focus the user's attention to them. When the choice is well-balanced the product is always successful, such as the example of the company Apple with the iPhone or iPad, which have those options required by most users. For additional options required by users, it is necessary to install new applications. Professor Barry Schwartz in his book "The Paradox of Choices" concluded that the growing number of facing choices make the consumer unhappy. He argues that the growing number of choices becomes tyranny of choice. A good game should have implemented this principle in its design. It needs to grow in complexity with the knowledge of the user. As the iPhone may be made more complex by using additional applications, so the game should allow more intricate elections. In game design, this growth of complexity from a simple to a more composite system is called pop complexity, as opposed to inherited complexity, in which things are complex at the beginning.

GAMIFICATION IMPLEMENTATION

Gamification implementation should not start with elements of the game and how to implement them in a specific system. As will be seen in a process presented by the author Werbach and Hunter (2012, p. 86), the elements of the game are the last step of implementation. Gamification can be implemented through six steps:

1. Define business objectives,
2. Delineate target behaviors,
3. Describe your players,

4.   Devise activity cycles,
5.   Don't forget the fun!
6.   Deploy the appropriate tools.

The first step to be defined is the goals that gemified system should achieve. It is suggested to make a list of all potential targets, ranked by relevance, expel those objectives that are a means to achieve something, and finally describe how each objective will contribute to the organization. Once the objectives are defined; it is necessary to determine what users should do and how to measure it. It should provide a customer choice through the different options. When the behavior is defined, it is necessary to define metrics. The next step involves defining the user, his relationship with the company and what motivates them. Users should be segmented considering that the system will be used by multiple user groups and that the systems offer more options for different users. The next step is to model the activities of gemified system. This can be achieved by using activity cycles that may be (Werbach & Hunter, 2012, p. 94): engagement loops and progression stairs. Engagement loops describe what happens at the micro level, and progression stairs gives a macro view of the user journey. The next step is the installation aspect of fun in the system. Fun can be classified in different ways, but it is necessary to ensure the collection of entertainment that will suit the context. The final phase is the implementation. It is necessary to implement the elements of the game in accordance with pre-defined stages. This is an iterative process aimed at refining the project.

CONCLUSION

The paper gives an overview of the gamification topics, as well as definitions of the most important terms of that domain. From all this follows our proposal to develop an integrated framework for gamification, including methods, techniques and tools for development of gamified ecosystems as well as game elements alone.

Developing such a framework involves a multidisciplinary approach and cooperation between scientific disciplines, such as psychology, computer science, and human-computer interaction.

The main objectives that should achieve the development of integrated gamification framework are as follows:

•   Defining ontology of gamification, which will allow further development of this domain and greatly facilitate communication between all participants in the process of research and development.

- Defining the methodology of gamification, which will facilitate the development and monitoring of projects related to this issue.
- Defining the model of gamification, based on the standard models for software development, but expanded with semantics necessary for modeling all the specifics of the various application areas (e.g. marketing, medicine, teaching, ...).
- Defining patterns for solving certain classes of known problems of the gamification domain.
- Defining development tools and usage.

The integrated development framework should resolve most of identified problems, as well as to define a systematic approach to gamification, which would reconcile the different roles of the participants of this process. The development method should define the process of gamification to consolidate the creation of multimedia content, design and logic of a game, as well as the development of software systems, using the experience gained in each of these areas independently. This will enable creation of effective gamified systems.

REFERENCES

Adams, E. (2010). *Fundamentals of Game Design* (2nd ed.). Berkeley, CA: New Riders.

Bartle, R. (1996). *Hearts, Clubs, Diamonds, Spades: Players Who Suit MUDs.* Retrieved from http://www.mud.co.uk/richard/hcds.htm

Bartle, R. (2004). *Designing Virtual Worlds*. New Riders Publishing.

BBVA Innovation Centre. (2012). *The fun way to engage*. Retrieved from https://www.centrodeinnovacionbbva.com/en/innovation-edge/gamification/gamification-fun-way-engage

Bergeron, B. P. (2006). *Developing Serious Games*. Charles River Media.

Blohm, I., & Leimeister, J. M. (2013). Gamification - Design of IT-Based Enhancing Services for Motivational Support and Behavioral Change. *Business & Information Systems Engineering, 5*(4), 275–278. doi:10.1007/s12599-013-0273-5

Clark, A. C. (1970). *Serious Games*. Viking Press.

Crawford, C. (1982). *The art of computer game design*. Academic Press.

Csíkszentmihályi, M. (1996). *Creativity: Flow and the Psychology of Discovery and Invention*. New York: Harper Perennial.

Deterding, S., Dixon, D., Khaled, R., & Nacke, L. (2011). From game design elements to gamefulness: defining "gamification". In *Proceedings of the 15th International Academic MindTrek Conference: Envisioning Future Media Environments (MindTrek '11)*. ACM. doi:10.1145/2181037.2181040

Edery, D., & Mollick, E. (2009). *Changing the Game - How Video Games Are Transforming the Future of Business*. Upper Saddle River, NJ: FT Press.

Hugos, M. (2012). *Enterprise Games: Using Game Mechanics to Build a Better Business*. O'Reilly Media Incorporated.

Hunicke, R., Leblanc, M., & Zubek, R. (2004). MDA: A Formal Approach to Game Design and Game Research. In *Proceedings of the 19th National Conference of Artificial Intelligence*. Retrieved from http://www.cs.northwestern.edu/~hunicke/MDA.pdf

Huotari, K., & Hamari, J. (2012). Defining gamification – a service marketing perspective. In *Proc 15th MindTrek conference*.

Kapp, M. K. (2012). *The gamification of learning and instruction: game-based methods and strategies for training and education*. Pfeiffer - John Wiley & Sons, Inc.

Koster, R. (2005). *A theory of fun for game design*. Scottsdale, AZ: Paraglyph Press.

Koster, R. (2014). *Theory of Fun for Game Design* (2nd ed.). O'Reilly Media, Inc.

Lazzaro, N. (2004). *Why We Play Games: Four Keys to More Emotion Without Story*. XEODesign,® Inc.

Malone, T. W. (1981). Towards a theory of intrinsically motivating instruction. *Cognitive Science*, 4(4), 333–369. doi:10.1207/s15516709cog0504_2

Malone, T. W., & Lepper, M. R. (1987). Making Learning Fun: A Taxonomy of Intrinsic Motivations for Learning. Aptitude, Learning and Instruction: III. Cognitive and affective process analyses. Academic Press.

Marczewski, A. (2012). *An Interview with Richard Bartle about Gamification*. Retrieved from http://www.gamified.uk/2012/12/31/an-interview-with-richard-bartle-about-gamification/

McGonigal, J. (2011). *Reality Is Broken: Why Games Make Us Better and How They Can Change the World*. New York: The Penguin Press.

Radoff, J. (2011). *Game On: Energize Your Business with Social Media Games.* Indianapolis, IN: Wiley Publishing Inc.

Shuen, A. (2008). *Web 2.0: A Strategy Guide*. Sebastopol, CA: O'Reilly Media Inc.

Werbach, K., & Hunter, D. (2012). *For the Win: How Game Thinking Can Revolutionize Your Business*. Wharton Digital Press.

Zicherman, G., & Linder, J. (2010). *Game-based Marketing – Inspire Customer Loyalty Through Rewards, Challenges, and Contest*. Hoboken, NJ: John Wiley & Sons Inc.

Zichermann, G., & Cunningham, C. (2011). *Gamification by Design Implementing Game Mechanics in Web and Mobile Apps*. Sebastopol, CA: O'Reilly Media.

Zichermann, G., & Linder, J. (2013). *The Gamification Revolution - How Leaders Leverage Game Mechanics to Crush the Competition*. McGraw-Hill Education.

KEY TERMS AND DEFINITIONS

Ecosystems: System that integrate different approaches and orchestrate different tools in order to make them work together.

Game: Activity defined using game elements, mechanic and dynamic, with specific rules, goals and actions available to users.

Game Dynamics: Dynamic aspect of the game, specifying gaming process and logic.

Game Elements: Structure parts of game, which game is consisted of.

Game Mechanics: Structure aspect of game, defining rules of game.

Gamer: User involved in playing game.

Gamification: Approach where one or elements of game are used in order to achieve specific goals.

Chapter 5
Long–Term Analysis of the Development of the Open ACS Community Framework

Michael Aram
Vienna University of Economics and Business, Italy

Stefan Koch
Bogazici University, Turkey

Gustaf Neumann
Vienna University of Economics and Business, Italy

ABSTRACT

The OpenACS community framework is a mature software toolkit for developing online community platforms. Originally invented at a university, it has prospered due to a high commercial demand and major investments, and subsequently settled as an open source project. In this chapter, the authors extend a previous analysis of the evolution of this software framework and its surrounding community. This long-term analysis of fourteen years of the project's evolution considers the commercial background of the members of the developer community (for-profit or non-profit), investigates the changing contribution and collaboration structures and the geographical distribution of the user community. The results reveal a continuous shift from new product development work by commercial developers to maintenance work by the open community and a relatively uniform and growing global distribution of users over the years.

DOI: 10.4018/978-1-5225-0905-9.ch005

INTRODUCTION

OpenACS (Hernández & Grumet, 2005) is a high-level community framework designed for developing collaborative Internet sites. It started from a university project at the Massachusetts Institute of Technology (MIT), got momentum from the ArsDigita Foundation, and split up into a commercial and an open source version. After the end of ArsDigita the development of OpenACS was driven by a collection of independent consultants and small companies implementing diverse and complex large-scale mostly commercial Web solutions. The background from a development based on commercial applications shifted over the years, especially after .LRN (Blesius, Moreno-Ger, Neumann, Raffenne, Boticario, & Kloos, 2007), a course management and e-learning solution was developed. Being primarily designed as a web development framework, OpenACS serves as a basis for various successful, large-scale applications, which are substantially tailored to their domain-specific needs. Examples are Project Open (http://www.project-open.com), Learn@WU (Neumann, Sobernig, & Aram, 2014), LMS.at (https://lms.at), or the e-learning systems at Galileo.edu (http://www.galileo.edu) or UNED (Santos, Boticario, Raffenne, & Pastor, 2007), which follow different development goals but share a common core of software artifacts. The ERP software Project Open is used by about 6,000 companies worldwide, including some Fortune 5,000 companies (Huger & Bergmann, 2013). Learn@WU, which is based on .LRN, is one of the most-intensively used university e-learning systems (160,000 learning resources, up to 4 million page impressions per day, up to 2,500 concurrent users). As of today the framework's code base contains about 3.6 million lines of code, which were developed with an estimated effort based on the COCOMO model of over 1,000 person years (Open HUB, 2015).

In this paper, we extend the previous work (Demetriou, Koch, & Neumann, 2006) on this technological ecosystem into two directions. While the original study covered the years 1995 to 2006, we will extend the analysis until present time, covering in total nearly 20 years of development. Secondly, we approach the analysis with different methods by focusing on contributions and collaborations, which are analyzed using social network analysis. Our social network analysis approach not only covers contributions to the code base, but also sheds light on more informational contributions, which extends the view from the software artifacts to the community structures that can be observed to user groups in the business domain. Based on these instruments we can visualize a comprehensive picture of the complex characteristics of the framework and how these structures have changed in the different phases of the life of the project.

The paper is structured as follows. The next section provides an overview of relevant literature on open source development communities from three different perspectives, i.e. their size and structure, the geographic origin of the developers, and their embedded social networks. Following this literature review there is a section that recapitulates the history of the OpenACS project. Thereafter, the section "Analysis of the OpenACS Community", which presents the core contribution of this chapter, provides extensive details about both the evolution of the OpenACS community and the evolution of the source code. Before ending with the conclusion, the chapter reflects on solutions and recommendations and sketches future research directions.

LITERATURE REVIEW: OPEN SOURCE DEVELOPMENT COMMUNITIES

Size and Structure

Often, the open source style of development is hypothesized to be a new production mode, lacking collocation of members as well as any centralized management. While there is one seminal description of the bazaar style of development by Raymond (1999) enforcing this view, it should be noted that open source projects do differ significantly in the processes they employ (Scacchi et al., 2006), and that reality has been found to differ from this very theoretical description. For example, there are strict release processes in place in several open source projects (Jorgensen, 2001; Holck & Jorgensen, 2004), and a considerable level of commercial involvement in several areas (Henkel, 2006; Roberts et al., 2006; O'Mahony & Bechky, 2008). Governance structures in general do exist, and O'Mahony and Ferraro (2007) specifically focused on the emergence of governance, finding that members develop a shared basis of formal authority but limit it with democratic mechanisms that enabled experimentation with shifting conceptions of authority over time. Barcellini et al. (2008b) report on a study of the design dynamics in open source projects using an analysis of electronic discussions. They find community consensus as well as implicit rules to govern some of these exchanges, as well as specific participants ("top hierarchy") active in framing. In a second, related study (Barcellini et al., 2008a), the authors find several key participants acting as boundary spanners between user and developer communities (and mailing lists). They therefore argue that OSS design may be considered as a form of "role emerging design", i.e. design organized and pushed through emerging roles and through a balance between these roles, with the communities providing a suitable socio-technical environment to enable such role emergence.

Several ways have been discussed to describe different open source development processes, e.g. Crowston et al. (2006) operationalize a process characteristic based on the speed of bug fixing, Michlmayr (2005) used a construct of process maturity, while also concentration indices have been used to characterize development forms (Koch & Neumann, 2008). We find that there is considerable variance in the practices actually employed, as well as the technical infrastructure. Numerous quantitative studies of development projects and communities (Dempsey et al., 2002; Dinh-Trong & Bieman, 2005; Ghosh & Prakash, 2000; Koch & Schneider, 2002; Koch, 2004; Krishnamurthy, 2002; Mockus et al., 2002) have proposed process metrics like the commit, which refers to a single change of a file by a single programmer, or the number of distinct programmers involved in writing and maintaining a file or project to study open source work practices. One of the most consistent results coming out of this research is a heavily skewed distribution of effort between participants (Koch, 2004; Mockus et al., 2002; Ghosh & Prakash, 2000; Dinh-Trong & Bieman, 2005). Several studies have adopted the normalized Gini coefficient (Robles et al., 2004), a measure of concentration, for this. The Gini coefficient is a number between 0 and 1, where 0 is an indicator for perfect equality and 1 for total inequality or concentration, and can be based both on commits or lines-of-code contributed, with studies showing no major difference. For example, Mockus et al. (2002) have shown that the top 15 of nearly 400 programmers in the Apache project added 88 per cent of the total lines-of-code. In the GNOME project, the top 15 out of 301 programmers were only responsible for 48 percent, while the top 52 persons were necessary to reach 80 per cent (Koch & Schneider 2002), with clustering hinting at the existence of a still smaller group of 11 programmers within this larger group. A similar distribution for the lines-of-code contributed to the project was found in a community of Linux kernel developers by Hertel et al. (2003). Also the results of the Orbiten Free Software survey (Ghosh & Prakash 2000) are similar, the first decile of programmers was responsible for 72 per cent, the second for 9 per cent of the total code.

A second major result regarding organization of work is a low number of people working together on file level. For example, Koch and Neumann (2008) have found that only 12.2% of the files have more than three distinct authors. Most of the files have one (24.0%) or two (56.1%) programmers and only 3% have more than five distinct authors, in accordance with other studies on file or project level (Koch, 2004; Krishnamurthy, 2002; Mockus et al., 2002; Ghosh and Prakash, 2000).

Another aspect that cannot be underestimated with regard to the implications for organization of work is the increased commercial interest in open source software. This has also lead to changes in many projects, which now include contributors who get paid for their contributions and others, who receive no direct payment. This can have repercussions on motivation and participation (Roberts et al., 2006), and is also reflected in several surveys: For example, Lakhani and Wolf (2005) found that 13% of respondents received direct payments, and 38% spent work hours on open source development with their supervisor being aware of the fact. Ghosh (2005) reports a group of 31.4% motivated by monetary or career (mostly for signaling competence) concerns in a sample of 2,280 responses. Hars and Ou (2001) found a share of 16% being directly paid, Hertel et al. (2003) report 20% of contributors receiving a salary for this work on a regular basis with an additional 23% at least sometimes in a survey of Linux kernel developers. Demetriou et al. (2006) have shown some implications of this fact in a case study of the OpenACS project: Historically, developers with a commercial interest dominated the project history and code base, but this fact might be slowly changing, with his large amount of commercial interest having led to a governance structure which puts great value on control and stability by requiring Technical Improvement Proposals for major changes. On the other hand, this rigidity seems to have affected the way of work, in that sideway developments might be established creating coexisting sub-frameworks. From an architectural viewpoint, this would be disadvantageous, and it might also have the effect of preventing true open source style development, as the code in these parts would tend to be more specific and only usable in a certain context. In the empirical data, there seem to be indications for this happening especially in conjunction with commercial developers: The authors found that packages being to a high degree dominated by commercial background tend to include less developers overall and less volunteers, and also tend to be changed less often and by the same group of people.

Geographic Origin

There is a limited number of studies that deal with the geographic origin of open source developers, and those mostly rely on survey methodologies. A comprehensive overview of results is provided by David and Shapiro (2008). Despite differences, most surveys show a majority of developers coming from (western) Europe with about 40-70%, followed by North America with about 15-50% of developers. Nevertheless the total number of countries is relatively high according to all results, ranging from 16 to 94, hinting at participation from other regions, although at smaller scale, as well. Tuomi (2004) presents a quantitative study based on Linux credit files, showing 154 contributors from the U.S., making this the single largest country, but below the EU with total 187 developers. Tuomi also clearly describes problems and uncertainties involved in using IP addresses for location. The most in-depth quantitative analysis was provided by Gonzalez-Barahona et al. (2008), who present an alternate approach in which databases are analyzed to create traces of information from which the geographical origin of developers can be inferred, including time-zone stamps. The authors apply this technique to the SourceForge (https://sourceforge.net) users database and the mailing lists archives from several large projects, and in total cover one million individuals. Again, the U.S. comes into first place, followed by Germany, UK and Canada. In terms of region ranking North America is ranked being slightly before Europe, followed by Asia, Oceania, South America and Africa.

Network Analysis

Numerous studies have adopted a network analysis perspective to analyze open source projects, as well as overall project ecologies. In these studies, networks have been built based on projects as nodes, with edges representing joint developers or re-use of code, as well as modules within a single project in the same role. Other studies have adopted developers as nodes with connections representing joint work or communication, mostly based on mailing list participation.

Ghosh (2003) has proposed to cluster based on collaborative authorship. One of the earliest examples focusing on a developer-project network, showing collaboration on joint projects within SourceForge, comes from Madey et al. (2005). They find one large cluster, and otherwise power law distributions on most aspects. Their analysis also highlights the importance of linchpin developers. Grewal et al. (2006) construct an affiliation network based on the joint developers between projects, similarly to Madey et al. (2005). They then try to relate the network embeddedness of the project manager to project success, and find that considerable heterogeneity exists in network embeddedness and that it has strong and significant effects on both technical and commercial success, but that those effects are quite complex. Similar data on project co-participation is used by Shen and Monge (2011) to understand network attachment.

Also Toral et al. (2010) take up the point of linchpin developers, but construct a directed valued graph based on the ARM Linux mailing list discussion threads. They find a centralized network around the core, which is responsible for the majority of interactions, and that the presence of enough brokers with an active mediation leads to less centralized topologies and more dynamic communities. Similarly, Oh and Jeon (2007) explore how different network characteristics (i.e., network size and connectivity) influence the stability of an OSS network, based on two project's mailing list archives and creating dyadic relationships using e-mail headers. Also Valverde and Sole (2007) base their work on e-mail archives. Their weighted network analysis suggests that a well-defined interplay between the overall goals of the community and the underlying hierarchical organization play a key role in shaping its dynamics, with OS communities being seen as elitarian clubs where strong hubs control the global flow of information generated by many peripheral individuals. Oezbek at al. (2010) again employ mailing list data, and using mostly visualizations argue for non-smooth transitions to the core of developers. Bird et al. (2008) also use data from mailing lists, but also check whether the sub-communities found in communication also collaborate on the code level more often, finding this behavior in four out of five inspected projects. Finally, Kidane and Gloor (2007) use the temporal aspects of communication networks based on mailing list data to explain productivity.

Lopez-Fernandez et al. (2004) show how a network of collaboration on modules can be generated from CVS data, showing both the module and the developer network. They also derive some basic measures like connection degree of clustering coefficient for Apache and GNOME. While MacCormack et al. (2006) do not use network analysis directly, their perspective of employing design structure matrices (DSMs) to map dependencies can be seen as similar. They define metrics that allow them to compare the structures of different designs, and use those to compare the architectures of two software products developed via contrasting modes of organization. Based on this, they find redesign activities aimed at enhancing the modularity.

Long and Siau (2007) use monthly data from the bug tracking systems in order to achieve a longitudinal view of the interaction pattern of three projects. Their findings suggest that the interaction pattern of OSS projects evolves from a single hub at the beginning to a core/periphery model as the projects progress.

As one of the latest studies published, Nan and Kumar (2013) use collaboration network as well as software structural interdependency together to check for joint effects on OSS development performance. They find that developer team structure and software architecture significantly moderate each others effect on OSS development performance, with larger teams tend to produce more favorable project performance when the project being developed has a high level of structural interdependency while projects with a low level of structural interdependency require smaller teams in order to achieve better project performance.

The OpenACS Project

As summarized in more detail in (Demetriou et al., 2006), the development of OpenACS was started by Philip Greenspun with his work on the site photo.net in 1995 (Greenspun, 1999b). The OpenACS project started out as a rapid prototyping framework for web-applications, based on the experiences of photo.net. The core elements of the framework were the highly scalable web-server NaviServer (https://bitbucket.org/naviserver/naviserver/) with a tight integration with relational databases (especially with Oracle and PostgreSQL), and the scripting language Tcl (Ousterhout, 1989). NaviServer was originally developed by the company NaviSoft. The server changed its name to AOLserver (Greenspun, 1999a) when AOL bought NaviSoft in 1995. AOL used AOLserver to run its busiest sites, such as digitalcity. com and aol.com. In 2005 the project forked into a pure webserver (AOLserver) and a version with broader functionality (such as multi protocol support) under the old name NaviServer. The server is implemented in C and achieves high scalability due to its multi-threaded architecture, extensive pooling support (such as e.g. for threads and database connections) and caching and monitoring support. NaviServer uses the built-in scripting language Tcl as primary extension language to provide a flexible means of composing systems from predefined components. This way, application specific hot spots can be quickly programmed and the server can be extended on the fly (without restarting) to provide continuous services.

Due to the positive experience with its short development cycles the company ArsDigita was founded in 1997 and attracted quickly high profile companies as customers. The company grew quickly backed by a nonprofit organization, the ArsDigita Foundation. With the rise of the Internet bubble on the stock market in 2000, the company attracted many investors, which did not share the mindset of the developers. In particular, the investors aimed for a Java-based enterprise collaboration software entailing a full reimplementation of the framework. These forces led into a split-up of the framework in 2001 into an open source version under then name OpenACS and a commercial version named ACS-Java. Partly due to the changes at the stock market the proprietary product was never launched. In 2002, ArsDigita was acquired by Red Hat that shelved a few years later silently the Java version.

The OpenACS system consists of a core system addressing the needs of most web applications such as user and community management (represent people and relationships between them), security management (authentication, rights management and data security), content management (content repository), and templating (representational building blocks, skins). The code base of ACS emphasizes collaboration and management of geographically distributed on-line communities. One of the key assets of OpenACS is its functionality as a community framework, which supports delegation of responsibilities to groups that can tailor and adapt the system for their needs (such as decide what kind of applications are offered to group members, tailor group appearance, offering internal and external services). OpenACS is based on a substantial and flexible relational data model. The data model of a full OpenACS installation with several application packages can reach easily 1,000 tables and views. The database middleware supports database abstractions like vendor abstraction (PostgreSQL and Oracle) and version abstraction (allows different SQL queries depending on the version of the Database). Most notably, the package manager supports version dependencies, data migration scripts and remote upgrading of packages from an app-store repository.

The application packages use the OpenACS core packages and provide application specific functionality such as forums, FAQ, bulk-mail, file-storage, calendar, web-shop, etc. Currently the OpenACS code repository contains 345 packages. This rich set of packages led to the adoption by developers and companies, and fueled the ongoing development of OpenACS without the strong former commercial backing. Since OpenACS was developed more as a framework than a product, companies and institutions could choose a set of packages matching their base needs and tailor the system with local specialties, like interfacing with preexisting systems or altering the appearance and interfaces.

While the most common requirements were well supported by the core framework, the more specific needs became addressed by the community. Two important sub-projects started to emerge, namely the learning management system .LRN and the ERP system Project Open, which is an ERP system with a focus on project and service management based on OpenACS, with currently 6,000 installations (Huger & Bergmann, 2013). We include in this study just the data of .LRN, since it shares the same code repository and website.

In 2002, the MIT Sloan School of Management contracted the company Open-Force to develop .LRN as a community and course management system for higher education. The primary goal was to address MIT Sloan's specific needs, but the project had a broader vision than internal deployment. This investment from MIT provided a strong impulse for the community after such a tumultuous period for the OpenACS project. However, the conflicting goals led to an inevitable governance plan discussion with lead institutions seeking formalized management structures to secure the investments of the funding organizations. The .LRN Consortium was founded, which is a non-profit organization with a clearly defined governance and membership structure. The consortium is guided by a board of directors and sees its mission in "creating and supporting a freely available suite of web based educational applications to support learning communities". This can be seen as a form of 'guarding the commons' (O'Mahony, 2003). Today, .LRN is one of the leading enterprise-class open source software for supporting e-learning and digital communities: according to the .LRN homepage (http://dotlrn.org), it is installed at a variety of universities like the JFK School of Government at Harvard University, or the Vienna University of Economics and Business in Vienna (Alberer et al., 2003), or the University of Valencia and the Open University of Spain (UNED, Universidad de Educacion a la Distancia with about 200.000 students), the JFK School of Government at Harvard University, UCLA, the Costa Rica Institute of Technology or Galileo University in Guatemala.

ANALYSIS OF THE OPENACS COMMUNITY

Analysis Method

To analyze the development structures of the OpenACS framework, we have applied an adapted version of an approach to multilayered analysis of continuous co-development of artifacts in business information systems (Aram & Neumann, 2015). Software development repositories contain a plethora of information on the underlying software and the associated development processes (Cook et al., 1998; Atkins et al., 1999). Studying software systems and development processes using these sources of data offers several advantages (Cook et al., 1998): This approach is very cost-effective, as no additional instrumentation is necessary, and it does not influence the software process under consideration. In addition, longitudinal data is available, allowing for analyses considering the whole project history (Kemerer & Slaughter, 1999). The approach applied here can be summarized as follows. First of all, we have gathered data from multiple sources, i.e. from the relevant source code repositories on the one hand (from the OpenACS CVS repository), and from the content repository of the community's website on the other hand. Secondly, an overall, aggregate analysis of the data was conducted. Thirdly, we investigated the data year by year to obtain a more fine-grained picture.

In the course of both the aggregate and the evolutionary analysis of the code base we studied contributions to software artifacts on the one hand, and – based on this contribution data – subsequently analyzed the underlying collaboration structures on the other hand. In particular, we have investigated difference between the commercial and non-profit contributors.

Contributions were visualized as directed, bipartite contribution graphs, where the size of contributor vertices is based on their (out) degree: the more artifacts an individual contributor contributed to, the larger the vertex. Degree-based metrics relate to the contribution behavior: a contributor who contributed to two artifacts has a degree of 2 (two "contribution relationships" represented as edges in the graph). Additional contributions by the same individual to the same artifacts increase the edge's weight. Network metrics such as the "average/median degree of contribution" represent the average/median degree of all contributor vertices in the bipartite graph; the degree values of artifact vertices are not taken into account. Therefore an average degree of contribution of 5 means that on average, each individual contributor has added/modified/deleted five artifacts within the respective time frame. All artifact vertices were deliberately drawn with equal size and in grey color, only those that are part of the OpenACS core are colored black.

Collaboration structures among contributors were visualized as unipartite collaboration graphs (comprising collaborators as vertices only). The graphs represent a one-mode projection of the bipartite graphs, i.e. these networks comprise only one type of vertices (people). Each contributor, who contributed to an artifact to which another person had contributed as well (within the respective time frame) counts as a collaborator. Such a collaboration results in a collaboration relationship (edge), the weight of which is increased in case of additional collaborations on other artifacts. In contrast to bipartite graphs, within the unipartite collaboration graphs the simple metric density provides a meaningful measure: complete collaboration, where everyone collaborated with everyone else, would result in a network density of 1.

All visualizations of both contribution and collaboration networks were rendered using the force-directed ForceAtlas2 algorithm using the Gephi software tool (Jacomy, Venturini, Heymann, & Bastian, 2014).

Moreover, we conducted an analysis of the geographical locations (based on IP addresses, visualized on a map) of the users of the openacs.org website, the downloaders of the OpenACS source code releases, the contributors to the openacs.org website, and the contributors to the source code repository.

Project Evolution and Commercial Participation

One of characteristics of OpenACS is that many of its components were originally developed by for-profit developers. We classify contributors as for-profit, when they were regularly (or at least on several occasions) receiving payment for contributions of code to the OpenACS project or were working for a company offering OpenACS support. All other contributors are classified as volunteer contributors, including employees of organizations that use OpenACS to provide their services (such as companies or universities).

Between 2001 and 2015 so far 126 distinct committers have contributed to the CVS repository. 71 contributors (56%) can be classified as volunteers (non-profit contributors), and 55 contributors (44%) have as well a commercial motivation. Figure 1 shows the contributions of the community members over time. The first y-axis of the diagram shows the number of contributions. A code contribution can be either a checkin (providing an initial version of a file) or a modification or a removal of a file. About 175,000 contributions have been added over the lifetime to the source code repository. The second y-axis on the right side shows the number of artifacts in the source code repository at the time of the x-axis.

The linear trend lines in Figure 1 show clearly that the commercial background of the project is vanishing. While around 2003 the vast majority of contributions were from commercial contributors, the situation in 2014 shows a majority of vol-

Figure 1. Timeline of contributions to the OpenACS source code repository with number of artifacts

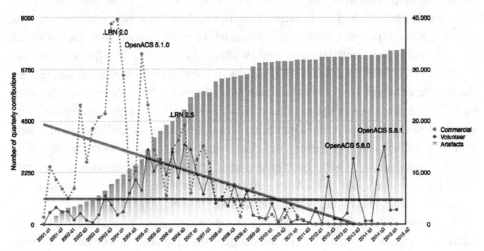

unteer contributions. Interestingly the trend line of the volunteer contributions is horizontal, meaning a constant number of contributions. The number of artifacts in the source code repository stabilized.

At visual inspection, the overall participation seems close to a Norden-Rayleigh curve. Based on the work of Norden (1960), any development project is modeled as a series of problem-solving efforts by the manpower involved to reach a set of objectives. The number of problems is assumed to be unknown but finite. Each solving of a problem removes one element from the list of unsolved problems. The occurrence of such an event is random and independent, it is assumed to follow a Poisson distribution. The number of people usefully employed at any given time is assumed to be approximately proportional to the number of problems ready for solution at that time. Therefore, the manpower usefully employed towards the end of a project becomes smaller as the problem space is exhausted.

As Putnam (1978) has shown, the time of peak manning is close to the time the software becomes operational, i.e. is released, while effort thereafter is expended for modification and maintenance. Koch (2008) has presented a large-scale study on the use of the Norden-Rayleigh model for open source development projects. It is a surprising result that the curve proposed for commercial projects decades before relatively well fits these projects. For many projects, the decrease after operation assumed is not visible though and alternative manpower functions incorporating additional requests from the user and developer community leading to the generation of new problems outperform the standard model (Koch, 2008).

For the case of the OpenACS community, drawing on both regular software evolution as well as the Norden-Rayleigh-model, the project has entered a more maintenance-oriented phase. The most striking result is that the rate of non-profit developer contribution is constant over all periods, while the profit-oriented developers seem to have abandoned the project altogether. This seems to indicate that these developers were involved in adding new functionality in more isolated projects, as also the findings before indicated (Demetriou et al., 2006), and afterwards shift the maintenance work to the open community. The implications of this are interesting, in that it might indicate the costs are socialized after the initial development.

Figure 2 blends the number of source code contributions from Figure 1 with site contributions on the second y-axis. A site contribution is a content contributions to the openacs.org website, which might be an entry in a forum, in the news package, in a wiki page, or e.g. an entry in the issue tracker. For every content item the OpenACS framework creates an object, which is saved in the database together with meta-data such as creator, creation date, and the IP address of the creator. Since the site OpenACS.org is built with the OpenACS framework, we can obtain detailed usage data from the database. Figure 2 shows that most of the site contributions seem to be code related: a very high correlation between the number of the source code contributions and the number of site contributions can be observed.

Aggregate Analysis of Co-Development of Source Code Artifacts

At first sight, an initial analysis of the aggregate data of the OpenACS source code repository suggests relatively intensive co-development structures. Overall, there were 126 contributors who contributed more than 175,000 times to a total of nearly

Figure 2. Timeline of contributions with site contributions

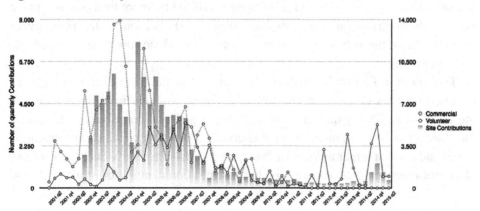

Table 1. Contributions to the OpenACS code repository from 2001 until 2014

	Total	Commercial	Volunteer
Contributors	126	55	71
Contribution Relationships	86,744	53,583	33,161
Contributions	175,022	110,882	64,140
Artifacts	41,852	32,037	20,626
Co-artifacts	18,520	11,341	7,691
Average Degree of Contribution (AD)	688.4	974.2	467.1
Median Degree of Contribution (MD)	144.5	211.0	111.0
Average Weighted Degree of Contribution (AWD)	1389.1	2016.0	903.4

42,000 artifacts (see Table 1). Each individual contributor contributed to nearly 700 files on average (AD); the median was at about 140 files (MD). The average weighted degree of contribution (AWD) means that each contributor on average performed about 1,400 actual contributions. Nearly half of all artifacts can be considered co-artifacts, because more than one person edited these.

An investigation of the contribution network with respect to the commercial background of the contributors reveals that the group of 55 for-profit contributors outperforms the larger group of 71 volunteers with respect to all contribution-related metrics listed in Table 1. Nearly two thirds, i.e. over 110,000 of the in total 175,000 contributions, were conducted by commercial actors. These contributions established over 53,000 contribution relationships (edges in the network) to over 32,000 artifacts, each further contribution thereby increasing the contribution intensity (edge weights) to on average over 2000 (AWD) for this group of contributors. The volunteers, on the other hand, although more in numbers, contributed "only" about half as much (AD, MD, AWD). They contributed nearly 65,000 times to about 20,000 artifacts; nearly 7,700 of these were modified by more than one volunteer. Overall, the contribution intensity of the commercial contributors has been higher than the one of the volunteers, showing that they work on more files (and update these more often).

The graph in Figure 3 visualizes this data set in the form of a bipartite contribution network comprising contributors who contributed to artifacts (files) in the code base. The visualization reveals heterogeneous contribution structures: there are about a dozen more noticeable contributors (four of which are strikingly large) and a much larger amount of averagely contributing individuals. The crowd of contributors (colored vertices) is divided into commercial/for-profit (red) and

Figure 3. Visualization of aggregate contributions to the OpenACS source code repository

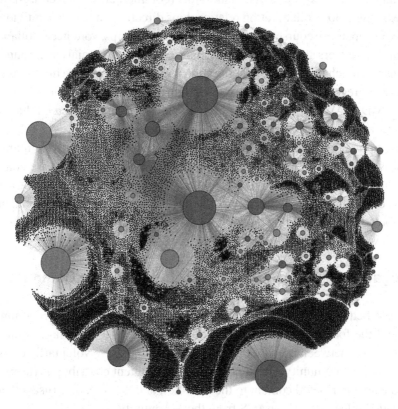

volunteer/non-profit (blue) contributors. The visualization reflects the dominance of commercial contributors despite their smaller number.

From this analysis of contributions to the OpenACS source code, collaboration structures in the OpenACS developer community can be derived in the form of a social network of collaborators. It shows that practically all of the contributors have collaborated on at least one artifact, only two actors contributed completely in isolation. There are in total more than 3,300 collaboration relationships (edges connecting two collaborator vertices in the network) within this community of developers, based on nearly 120,000 distinct collaborations. Both average and median degree of collaboration (CAD, CMD) show that each collaborator typically co-edits artifacts with about 50 others. The CAWD measure incorporates the number of different artifacts two collaborators have collaborated on as edge weights in the collaboration graph. It amounts to nearly 2000 for the aggregate collaboration data. The density metric of the overall collaboration network (CD) shows that 43% of all possible collaboration relationships exist.

Analogous to the analysis above, the collaboration network was deeper investigated in the light of the background of collaborators (commercial/volunteers). About 800 of the existing 3,302 collaboration relationships directly connect two individuals of the same group. In the course of these in-group relationships, volunteers collaborated with other volunteers about 21,000 times; people with commercial background more than twice as much. Analogously to the contribution-based degree measures (Table 2), in the aggregate data set the degree-based measures of collaboration intensity (CAD, CMD, CAWD, CD) all show higher values for the commercial than for the non-profit developers.

The graph in Figure 4 shows a one-mode projection of the graph in Figure 3, i.e. it consists of only one class of vertices, namely collaborators, who are connected only if they have collaborated on an artifact. In this aggregate view we see a homogeneous collaboration network among the developers; the degree of collaboration is distributed relatively uniformly among the collaborators (many individuals collaborated with a comparable amount of other people on artifacts.)

Aggregate Analysis of Global Distribution of the Community

In order to better understand the global distribution of the OpenACS community, we extend the focus from the source code development to the usage community. We distinguish between users of the website (users that have voluntarily created an account on the community website openacs.org), content contributors (users of the website who contributed content to the website), and downloaders (users that have downloaded releases of OpenACS from the community website).

Table 2. Collaborations on the OpenACS code repository from 2001 until 2014

	Total	Commercial	Volunteer
Collaborators	124	54	70
Collaboration Relationships	3,302	783	840
Collaborations	119,958	43,076	20,946
Average Degree of Collaboration (CAD)	53.3	60.1	48.0
Median Degree of Collaboration (CMD)	47.0	63.0	43.5
Average Weighted Degree of Collaboration (CAWD)	1934.8	2631.3	1397.5
Density of Collaboration (CD)	0.433	0.547	0.358

Figure 4. Visualization of aggregate collaboration structures around the OpenACS source code among actors with a commercial background (red) and volunteers (blue)

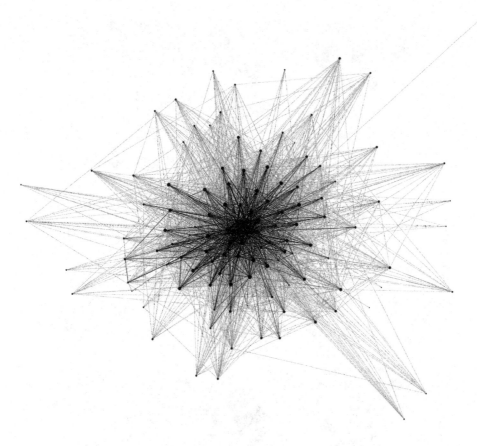

For each of these categories, we have determined the peer IP address of the corresponding activities and mapped these to its geographic origin. For this purpose, we have used the tool freegeoip (http://freegeoip.net/) to map IP addresses to geographic locations. The derived coordinates were visualized on a map using the maps module of the JavaScript charting library amCharts (http://www.amcharts. com/), the respective icons were taken from the Raphaël JavaScript library (http:// raphaeljs.com/icons/). Webkit2png (http://www.paulhammond.org/webkit2png/) was used to transform the JavaScript maps into image files.

Figure 5 shows separate maps for these three categories and additionally a map locating the developers. Since the source code repository does not contain information about peer addresses, we determined the IP address via the community account of the developer and used the location from where the account was created or from where the first contribution of the user came from.

Figure 5. *Global distribution of users, content-contributors, downloaders, and developers (2001 – 2014)*

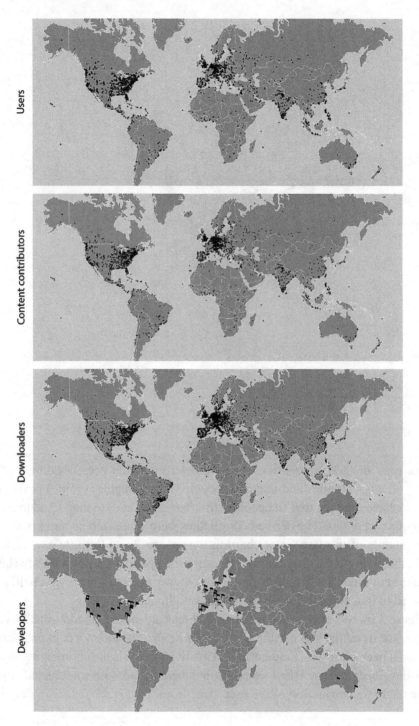

Our initial assumption was that there would be a strong observable prevalence of the US and Europe. Figure 5 provides evidence that the OpenACS community is a globally distributed community. It also shows that the three different views on the user community are very related, in that the geographical distribution is very similar.

Evolutionary Analysis of the Development of the OpenACS Community

A closer look at the history of the project reveals a more differentiated picture. In order to assess the changes over time of the project have analyzed every year from 2001 until 2014 with respect to source code contributions and the related collaboration structures (see Table 4). In the later sections we perform a deeper snapshot analysis of three significant years to provide a multi-dimensional picture of the developers and users.

Table 3 shows a decrease of the number of contributors within the most recent years: while there were over 50 individuals contributing in 2005, this number dropped to only four in 2014. While the commercial contributors dominated in the first years of the development of the open source version of the framework, the contributions

Table 3. Evolution of contributions to artifacts in the OpenACS source code repository from 2001 to 2014

Period	Contributors	Commercial Contributors	Non-Profit Contributors	Contribution Relationships	Contributions	Artifacts
2014	4	1	3	4636	6040	2925
2013	5	1	4	2790	4578	2674
2012	6	1	5	2884	3001	1221
2011	9	3	6	1368	1892	1310
2010	14	5	9	1479	2844	1250
2009	19	5	14	4652	6522	3484
2008	24	6	18	5429	9463	4334
2007	32	8	24	13626	19212	10658
2006	45	16	29	14899	23192	10720
2005	58	26	32	18026	28258	12209
2004	55	28	27	12723	23832	8052
2003	40	25	15	12014	24913	7629
2002	32	26	6	7352	11964	5061
2001	34	23	11	5508	8077	4594

Table 4. Evolution of collaboration on artifacts in the OpenACS source code repository

Period	Collaborators	Commercial Collaborators	Non-Profit Collaborators	Collaboration Relationships	Collaborations	Co-Artifacts
2014	4	1	3	6	1728	1695
2013	4	0	4	4	117	115
2012	4	1	3	4	2319	1007
2011	8	3	5	12	62	54
2010	12	4	8	26	248	214
2009	16	5	11	40	1239	1103
2008	24	6	18	73	1277	944
2007	29	8	21	145	3953	2301
2006	40	14	26	224	5796	2828
2005	55	25	30	480	9010	3823
2004	54	28	26	447	6878	3318
2003	39	25	14	281	6929	2877
2002	32	26	6	161	3552	1512
2001	31	21	10	72	1097	762

of 2014 came mostly from non-profit contributors. This is in line with our discussion of the evolution, and underlines the shift from initial development to a more maintenance-oriented phase. We do also see a continuous increase in the average degree of contributions of non-profit contributors (see Table 5, Appendix).

In the following sections we discuss both the user community and the developer community of the OpenACS project along three observable project phases by means of three sample years, namely 2002, 2005 and 2014.

The Initial Years of Framework Development

As mentioned earlier, the open source version of ACS, i.e. OpenACS, was forked in 2001 from its parent project, and in 2002 MIT's Sloan School of Management initialized the commercial development of the .LRN e-learning system.

The map in Figure 6 shows that while already in 2002 users and content contributors were already spread all over the world, the majority of the downloads came from the US and Europe.

In 2002 the developer community consisted of 32 different contributors contributing to about 5,000 different software artifacts, about 1,500 of which were developed collaboratively in the course of about 3,500 collaborations (Tables 3 and 4). The graphical visualizations of the social network underlying the developer community

Figure 6. Co-development of OpenACS in 2002

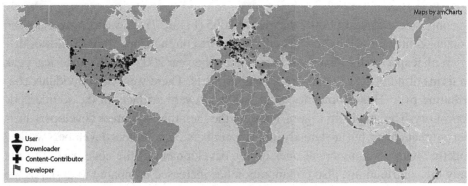

Users, Content Contributors, Downloaders, Developers

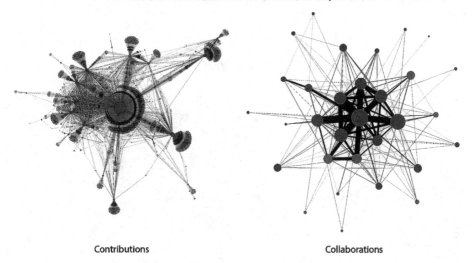

Contributions   Collaborations

(at the bottom of Figure 6) clearly show a strong dominance of the commercial developers (red vertices). In this year, 26 developers had a for-profit background and only 6 count as volunteers. The structure of the contribution graph hints at a division of labor (many artifacts assemble around an active developer) and shows a strong dominator: one remarkably large developer vertex at the center of the graph. The collaboration network fits into the picture: there is strongly collaborating group of mostly commercial developers. On average, every developer collaborated with about ten others (see Table 6, Appendix).

Peak Development

In contrast to the map of 2002, the map of 2005 (Figure 7) shows not only users and content contributors, but now also downloaders coming from all over the world.

With respect to the developer community, the year 2005 was the historical peak in terms of numbers of contributors and artifacts. There were 58 individuals contributing over 23,000 times to about 8,000 software artifacts in the source code repository. The graphs in Figure 7 reflect the fact, that volunteer developers have not only caught up, but are already more in numbers. 32 volunteer developers worked together with 26 commercial ones on the development of the code base. But not only the contributions, also collaboration has increased compared to 2002, as the degree-based measures (see Table 6, Appendix) and the visualization in Figure 7 evidence.

Figure 7. Co-development of OpenACS in 2005

Users, Content Contributors, Downloaders, Developers

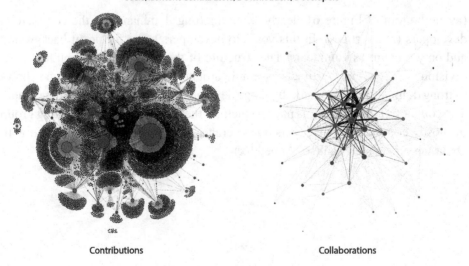

Contributions   Collaborations

Framework Stabilization

For the year 2014 the geographic map (Figure 8) shows a similar distribution of the user community compared to the map of 2005. However, contributions and collaborations at the source code layer differ completely: in 2014 there were close to 3,000 artifacts changed (which is more than in the years before), but by only four developers. Three of these are volunteers; only one has a commercial background. These developers alone contributed to about as many artifacts as e.g. the nineteen developers of 2009. The low amount of contributors and the very high number of contributions from two of them account for the highest degree-based contribution measures of all years (see Table 5, Appendix). The graph in Figure 8 on the left hand side visualizes this as a large cloud of co-artifacts between two large contributor vertices.

Figure 8. Co-development of OpenACS in 2014

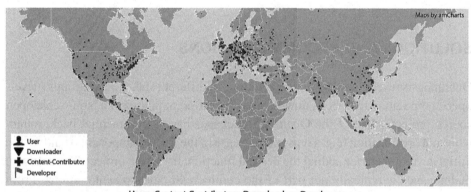

Users, Content Contributors, Downloaders, Developers

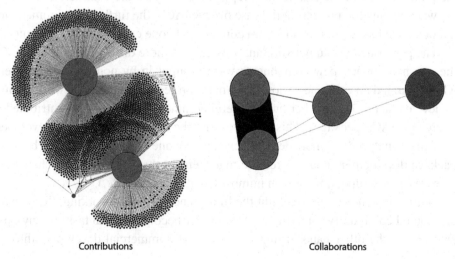

Contributions   Collaborations

Issues, Controversies, Problems

Our analysis relies on data from different sources (the source code repository and the database of the community website of the project), as well as a categorization in commercial versus non-profit contributors. The linkage of the source code data with the community data was based on a mapping of Unix user accounts to OpenACS website accounts. This mapping involved 126 developers and was therefore a moderate effort. In some cases we found users with multiple community accounts, which were folded together. In most cases, only one account was used actively. There might be certainly other community members with multiple community site accounts, but this does not bias the results. The mapping of the users to geo-locations was performed via IP addresses. In general, this does not lead to a precise location of the users (which is not a problem for this level of analysis) and it might lead to incorrect data through the use of VPN connections. We believe these effects to be negligible for our case, also due to the high project familiarity and knowledge of the community, but they need careful consideration in case of replication of the study.

SOLUTIONS AND RECOMMENDATIONS

Our analysis reveals some of the interactions of different stakeholder groups (developers, community members, downloaders) in different phases of a large-scale open source project. Most of the OpenACS packages have a commercial background, where an organization (e.g. a university in case of the .LRN components) paid for the initial development for adding the desired functionality to the project. The software maintenance is typically not part of the commercial development contract. From the point of view of the source code repository analysis, the commercial developers were leaving the project. In the case of OpenACS, the further development and maintenance has shifted mostly from commercial code contributors to volunteers.

The performed social network analysis gives a more differentiated picture. On the one hand, many new components were brought in by non-profit developers, who integrated for example various third party projects with the framework leading to new artifacts. On the other hand, several commercial developers contributed to many OpenACS packages. This indicates that the roles of commercial developers need to be analyzed at a more detailed level, where one should differentiate between package development and e.g. release management that often requires changes in many packages (updating version numbers, dependencies, etc.).

Our results once more highlight the importance of a well working, diverse and distributed community. Growing its community becomes a vital task for any open project. On the other hand, trying to counteract commercial developers through different means, although difficult, should gain importance. These means could revolve around governance structures, and maybe a boundary organization like a foundation, as well as creating more potential business and business models centered on services surrounding the project.

FUTURE RESEARCH DIRECTIONS

For future research, it would be important and necessary to reasses the findings of this extended case study in other settings, respectively other projects. This could take several directions: The geographic distribution of user community members could be influenced by several factors, including the distribution of contributors, as well as aspects like available language support. Moreover, the social network analysis could be extended to also cover the evolving co-development structures within the user community by investigating contributions to and collaboration on information/content objects in the content repository of the openacs.org website. For the collaboration structures, other research projects could provide more insights into the role of the architecture and design in shaping these structures. Finally, as we found a shift from commercial to non-profit contributors over time, and possibly over phases of the project, these findings are hinting at a socialization of maintenance work and therefore costs need further exploration. It is possible that again software architecture, but also governance structures can play a role in this shift. In this respect, future research efforts should strive for gaining a deeper understanding of the underlying mechanisms and reasons that can drive companies into the behavior of minimizing software maintenance costs by leaving maintenance work to the open source community, and in particular whether or not this proves advantageous (for one of the two, or even both sides). Recent efforts such as the VALS project (http://virtualalliances.eu/), for example, that engage in enabling the collaboration of non-profit developers (students) and for-profit developers (in companies) on open source software could provide a fruitful ground for further research on the interactions and potentials of this kind of co-development.

In general, emergence and evolution of social relationships between business organizations and open source projects should be revealed (e.g. hiring developers from the community, contributions to the open source project by former employees, et cetera). Moreover, the evolution of technical artifacts developed by the open source community and their adoption and adaptation within business information systems, as well as potential backflows originating from within these adopting organization back to the open source project, could be investigated.

The provided charts (e.g. Figure 1 and 2) and tables (e.g. 3 and 4) concerning the longitudinal development show significant periods of growth and decline of OpenACS, hinting at a rather moderate development in the recent years. These figures have to be treated with some caution and have to be put into relation with other projects. According to the data of Open HUB, more artifacts (files) and a similar number of changed lines could be observed in OpenACS compared with PostgreSQL over the last 12 months. This indicates, that in contrary to the decline, OpenACS is still an active project, stabilizing from a very active past. It would be interesting to develop metrics of liveliness and benchmarks of projects and to perform a deeper analysis with respect to other large software ecosystems. Some work has been done so far on defining and measuring the success of an open source project, including aspects like ability of the project to attract user and developer interest, release management, project activity, or development sustainability (Stewart et al., 2006; Ghapanchi, 2015), but it is yet unclear whether these approaches can be used to compare central characteristics of user and developer engagement in software ecosystems.

CONCLUSION

Based on previous work by Demetriou et al. (2006) this chapter presented an extended analysis of the evolution of the OpenACS software framework and its community of developers and users. Based on fourteen years of data from both the project's source code repository and content repository, the authors analyzed the long-term evolution of this open source project.

The analysis considered the background of community members (for-profit/non-profit), investigated the evolution of co-development (contribution and collaboration) structures by means of social network analysis techniques, and studied the global distribution of the community members (users, downloaders, content contributors, and developers).

The results revealed an underlying, continuous transformation process of the community's development structures, starting with commercially initialized product development in the beginning fading to mainly maintenance work by the open community nowadays, which may indicate a socialization of software maintenance costs. Overall, despite their smaller number, the contribution intensity and collaboration intensity of for-profit contributors was higher than for the non-profit contributors. Also, a high correlation between the number source code contributions (by software developers) and content contributions (by software developers and other community members) was observed.

The spatial distribution of the community members of the project, on the other hand, showed a fairly uniform picture over the years and revealed a truly global distribution of the OpenACS community.

REFERENCES

Alberer, G., Alberer, P., Enzi, T., Ernst, G., Mayrhofer, K., Neumann, G., et al. (2003). *The Learn@WU Learning Environment. In Proceedings of Wirtschaftsinformatik 2003*. 6th International Conference on Business Informatics, Dresden, Germany.

Aram, M., & Neumann, G. (2015). Multilayered Analysis of Co-Development of Business Information Systems. *Journal of Internet Services and Applications, 6*(1).

Atkins, D., Ball, T., Graves, T., & Mockus, A. (1999). Using Version Control Data to Evaluate the Impact of Software Tools. In *Proc. 21st International Conference on Software Engineering*. doi:10.1145/302405.302649

Barcellini, F., Detienne, F., & Burkhardt, J. M. (2008a). User and developer mediation in an Open Source Software community: Boundary spanning through cross participation in online discussions. *International Journal of Human-Computer Studies, 66*(7), 558–570. doi:10.1016/j.ijhcs.2007.10.008

Barcellini, F., Detienne, F., Burkhardt, J. M., & Sack, W. (2008b). A socio-cognitive analysis of online design discussions in an Open Source Software community. *Interacting with Computers, 20*(1), 141–165. doi:10.1016/j.intcom.2007.10.004

Bird, C., Pattison, D., D'Souza, R., Filkov, V., & Devanbu, P. (2008). Latent social structure in open source projects. In *Proceedings of the 16th ACM SIGSOFT International Symposium on Foundations of software engineering* (pp. 24-35). ACM. doi:10.1145/1453101.1453107

Blesius, C. R., Moreno-Ger, P., Neumann, G., Raffenne, E., Boticario, J. G., & Kloos, C. D. (2007). LRN: E-Learning Inside and Outside The Classroom. In B. Fernández-Manjón, J. M. Sánchez-Pérez, J. A. Gómez-Pulido, M. A. Vega-Rodríguez, & J. Bravo-Rodríguez (Eds.), *Computers and Education* (pp. 13–25). Springer. doi:10.1007/978-1-4020-4914-9_2

Cook, J. E., Votta, L. G., & Wolf, A. L. (1998). Cost-effective analysis of in-place software processes. *IEEE Transactions on Software Engineering, 24*(8), 650–663. doi:10.1109/32.707700

Crowston, K., Howison, J., & Annabi, H. (2006). Information systems success in free and open source software development: Theory and measures. *Software Process Improvement and Practice, 11*(2), 123–148. doi:10.1002/spip.259

David, P. A., & Shapiro, J. S. (2008). Community-based production of open-source software: What do we know about the developers who participate? *Information Economics and Policy, 20*(4), 364–398. doi:10.1016/j.infoecopol.2008.10.001

Demetriou, N., Koch, S., & Neumann, G. (2006). The Development of the OpenACS Community. In M. Lytras & A. Naeve (Eds.), *Open Source for Knowledge and Learning Management: Strategies Beyond Tools*. Hershey, PA: Idea Group.

Dempsey, B. J., Weiss, D., Jones, P., & Greenberg, J. (2002). Who is an open source software developer? *Communications of the ACM, 45*(2), 67–72. doi:10.1145/503124.503125

Dinh-Trong, T. T., & Bieman, J. M. (2005). The FreeBSD Project: A Replication Case Study of Open Source Development. *IEEE Transactions on Software Engineering, 31*(6), 481–494. doi:10.1109/TSE.2005.73

Ghapanchi, A. H. (2015). Investigating the Inter-relationships among Success Measures of OSS Projects. *Journal of Organizational Computing and Electronic Commerce, 25*(1), 28–46. doi:10.1080/10919392.2015.990775

Ghosh, R., & Prakash, V. V. (2000). The Orbiten Free Software Survey. *First Monday, 5*(7). doi:10.5210/fm.v5i7.769

Ghosh, R. A. (2003). Clustering and dependencies in free/open source software development: Methodology and tools. *First Monday, 8*(4). doi:10.5210/fm.v8i4.1041

Ghosh, R. A. (2005). Understanding Free Software Developers: Findings from the FLOSS Study. In J. Feller, B. Fitzgerald, S. A. Hissam, & K. R. Lakhani (Eds.), *Perspectives on Free and Open Source Software* (pp. 23–46). Cambridge, MA: MIT Press.

Gonzalez-Barahona, J. M., Robles, G., Andradas-Izquierdo, R., & Ghosh, R. A. (2008). Geographic origin of libre software developers. *Information Economics and Policy, 20*(4), 356–363. doi:10.1016/j.infoecopol.2008.07.001

Greenspun, P. (1999a). *Introduction to AOLserver*. LinuxWorld. Retrieved from http://philip.greenspun.com/wtr/aolserver/introduction-1.html

Greenspun, P. (1999b). *Philip and Alex's guide to Web publishing*. San Francisco, CA: Morgan Kaufmann Publishers Inc.

Grewal, R., Lilien, G. L., & Mallapragada, G. (2006). Location, location, location: How network embeddedness affects project success in open source systems. *Management Science, 52*(7), 1043–1056. doi:10.1287/mnsc.1060.0550

Hars, A., & Ou, S. (2001). Working for free? - Motivations for participating in Open Source projects. In *Proceedings of the 34th Hawaii International Conference on System Sciences*. Retrieved from http://dlib.computer.org/conferen/hicss/0981/pdf/09817014.pdf

Henkel, J. (2006). Selective Revealing in Open Innovation Processes: The Case of Embedded Linux. *Research Policy, 35*(7), 953–969. doi:10.1016/j.respol.2006.04.010

Hernández, R., & Grumet, A. (2005). OpenACS: robust web development framework. In *Proceedings of the Tcl/Tk 2005 Conference.*

Hertel, G., Niedner, S., & Hermann, S. (2003). Motivation of software developers in open source projects: An internet-based survey of contributors to the Linux kernel. *Research Policy, 32*(7), 1159–1177. doi:10.1016/S0048-7333(03)00047-7

Holck, J., & Jorgensen, N. (2004). Do not Check in on Red: Control Meets Anarchy in Two Open Source Projects. In S. Koch (Ed.), *Free/Open Source Software Development* (pp. 1–26). Hershey, PA: Idea Group Publishing.

Huger, J. W. (Interviewer) & Bergmann, F. (Interviewee). (2013). *Open source project management on the rise.* [Interview transcript]. Retrieved from the business section at the opensource.com website: http://opensource.com/business/13/5/open-project-interview

Jacomy, M., Venturini, T., Heymann, S., & Bastian, M. (2014). ForceAtlas2, a Continuous Graph Layout Algorithm for Handy Network Visualization Designed for the Gephi Software. *PLoS ONE, 9*(6), 1–12. doi:10.1371/journal.pone.0098679 PMID:24914678

Jorgensen, N. (2001). Putting it All in the Trunk: Incremental Software Engineering in the FreeBSD Open Source Project. *Information Systems Journal, 11*(4), 321–336. doi:10.1046/j.1365-2575.2001.00113.x

Kemerer, C. F., & Slaughter, S. (1999). An Empirical Approach to Studying Software Evolution. *IEEE Transactions on Software Engineering, 25*(4), 493–509. doi:10.1109/32.799945

Kidane, Y. H., & Gloor, P. A. (2007). Correlating temporal communication patterns of the Eclipse open source community with performance and creativity. *Computational & Mathematical Organization Theory, 13*(1), 17–27. doi:10.1007/s10588-006-9006-3

Koch, S. (2004). Profiling an open source project ecology and its programmers. *Electronic Markets, 14*(2), 77–88. doi:10.1080/10196780410001675031

Koch, S. (2008). Effort Modeling and Programmer Participation in Open Source Software Projects. *Information Economics and Policy, 20*(4), 345–355. doi:10.1016/j.infoecopol.2008.06.004

Koch, S., & Neumann, C. (2008). Exploring the Effects of Process Characteristics on Products Quality in Open Source Software Development. *Journal of Database Management, 19*(2), 31–57. doi:10.4018/jdm.2008040102

Koch, S., & Schneider, G. (2002). Effort, Cooperation and Coordination in an Open Source Software Project: Gnome. *Information Systems Journal, 12*(1), 27–42. doi:10.1046/j.1365-2575.2002.00110.x

Krishnamurthy, S. (2002). Cave or community? An empirical investigation of 100 mature open source projects. *First Monday, 7*(6). doi:10.5210/fm.v7i6.960

Lakhani, K. R., & Wolf, R. G. (2005). Why Hackers Do What They Do: Understanding Motivation and Effort in Free/Open Source Software Projects. In J. Feller, B. Fitzgerald, S. A. Hissam, & K. R. Lakhani (Eds.), *Perspectives on Free and Open Source Software* (pp. 3–22). Cambridge, MA: MIT Press.

Long, Y., & Siau, K. (2007). Social network structures in open source software development teams. *Journal of Database Management, 18*(2), 25–40. doi:10.4018/jdm.2007040102

Lopez-Fernandez, L., Robles, G., & Gonzalez-Barahona, J. M. (2004). Applying social network analysis to the information in CVS repositories. In *International Workshop on Mining Software Repositories* (pp. 101-105). doi:10.1049/ic:20040485

MacCormack, A., Rusnak, J., & Baldwin, C. Y. (2006). Exploring the structure of complex software designs: An empirical study of open source and proprietary code. *Management Science, 52*(7), 1015–1030. doi:10.1287/mnsc.1060.0552

Madey, G., Freeh, V., & Tynan, R. (2005). Modeling the Free/Open Source software community: A quantitative investigation. *Free/Open Source Software Development*, 203-221.

Michlmayr, M. (2005). Software Process Maturity and the Success of Free Software Projects. In K. Zielinski & T. Szmuc (Eds.), *Software Engineering: Evolution and Emerging Technologies* (pp. 3–14). Amsterdam, The Netherlands: IOS Press.

Mockus, A., Fielding, R., & Herbsleb, J. (2002). Two case studies of open source software development: Apache and Mozilla. *ACM Transactions on Software Engineering and Methodology, 11*(3), 309–346. doi:10.1145/567793.567795

Nan, N., & Kumar, S. (2013). Joint effect of team structure and software architecture in open source software development. *IEEE Transactions on Engineering Management, 60*(3), 592–603. doi:10.1109/TEM.2012.2232930

Neumann, G., Sobernig, S., & Aram, M. (2014). Evolutionary Business Information Systems. *Business & Information Systems Engineering*, 6(1), 33–38. doi:10.1007/s12599-013-0305-1

Norden, P. V. (1960). On the anatomy of development projects. *IRE Transactions on Engineering Management*, 7(1), 34–42. doi:10.1109/IRET-EM.1960.5007529

Nunamaker, J. F., Briggs, R. O., & Vreede, G. J. (2001). From Information Technology to Value Creation Technology. In G. W. Dickson & G. DeSanctis (Eds.), *Information Technology and the Future Enterprise*. Prentice Hall.

O'Mahony, S. (2003). Guarding the commons: How community managed software projects protect their work. *Research Policy*, 32(7), 1179–1198. doi:10.1016/S0048-7333(03)00048-9

O'Mahony, S., & Bechky, B. A. (2008). Boundary Organizations: Enabling Collaboration among Unexpected Allies. *Administrative Science Quarterly*, 53(3), 422–459. doi:10.2189/asqu.53.3.422

O'Mahony, S., & Ferraro, F. (2007). The Emergence of Governance in an Open Source Community. *Academy of Management Journal*, 50(5), 1079–1106. doi:10.5465/AMJ.2007.27169153

Oezbek, C., Prechelt, L., & Thiel, F. (2010). The onion has cancer: Some social network analysis visualizations of open source project communication. In *Proceedings of the 3rd International Workshop on Emerging Trends in Free/Libre/Open Source Software Research and Development* (pp. 5-10). ACM.

Oh, W., & Jeon, S. (2007). Membership herding and network stability in the open source community: The Ising perspective. *Management Science*, 53(7), 1086–1101. doi:10.1287/mnsc.1060.0623

Open H. U. B. (2015). *The OpenACS Open Source Project on Open Hub*. Retrieved May 8, 2015, from https://www.openhub.net/p/openacs

Ousterhout, J. K. (1989). *Tcl: An Embeddable Command Language (No. UCB/CSD-89-541)*. Berkeley, CA: EECS Department, University of California.

Putnam, L. H. (1978). A general empirical solution to the macro software sizing and estimating problem. *IEEE Transactions on Software Engineering*, 4(4), 345–361. doi:10.1109/TSE.1978.231521

Raymond, E. S. (1999). *The Cathedral and the Bazaar*. Cambridge, MA: O'Reilly & Associates.

Roberts, J. A., Hann, I.-H., & Slaughter, S. A. (2006). Understanding the Motivations, Participation, and Performance of Open Source Software Developers: A Longitudinal Study of the Apache Projects. *Management Science, 52*(7), 984–999. doi:10.1287/mnsc.1060.0554

Robles, G., Koch, S., & Gonzalez-Barahona, J. M. (2004). Remote analysis and measurement of libre software systems by means of the CVSanalY tool. In *ICSE 2004 - Proceedings of the Second International Workshop on Remote Analysis and Measurement of Software Systems* (RAMSS '04) (pp. 51–55). doi:10.1049/ic:20040351

Santos, O. C., Boticario, J. G., Raffenne, E., & Pastor, R. (2007). *Why using dotLRN? UNED use cases.* Paper presented at 1st International Conference on FLOSS: Free/Libre/Open Source Systems.

Scacchi, W., Feller, J., Fitzgerald, B., Hissam, S., & Lakhani, K. (2006). Understanding Free/Open Source Software Development Processes. *Software Process Improvement and Practice, 11*(2), 95–105. doi:10.1002/spip.255

Shen, C., & Monge, P. (2011). Who connects with whom? A social network analysis of an online open source software community. *First Monday, 16*(6). doi:10.5210/fm.v16i6.3551

Stewart, K. J., Ammeter, A. P., & Maruping, L. M. (2006). Impacts of license choice and organizational sponsorship on user interest and development activity in open source software projects. *Information Systems Research, 17*(2), 126–144. doi:10.1287/isre.1060.0082

Toral, S. L., Martínez-Torres, M. R., & Barrero, F. (2010). Analysis of virtual communities supporting OSS projects using social network analysis. *Information and Software Technology, 52*(3), 296–303. doi:10.1016/j.infsof.2009.10.007

Tuomi, I. (2004). Evolution of the Linux credits file: Methodological challenges and reference data for open source research. *First Monday, 9*(6). doi:10.5210/fm.v9i6.1151

Valverde, S., & Solé, R. V. (2007). Self-organization versus hierarchy in open-source social networks. *Physical Review E: Statistical, Nonlinear, and Soft Matter Physics, 76*(4), 046118. doi:10.1103/PhysRevE.76.046118 PMID:17995071

KEY TERMS AND DEFINITIONS

Collaboration: Collaboration occurs when individuals work towards a common goal. According to Nunamaker, Briggs, & Vreede (2001), who distinguish three levels of collaboration, this broad definition would refer to "collective collaboration". A more carefully "coordinated" collaboration of individual work becomes necessary, as soon as dependencies of work increase. "Concerted collaboration" would be required when any breaks in work synchronization endanger the common undertaking.

Contribution: We use the term contribution in the narrow sense of direct contributions to the source code repository that manifests itself as an initial addition (check-in), modification or removal of a file.

APPENDIX

Table 5. Evolution of contributions to artifacts in the OpenACS source code repository since 2001 – degree based metrics

Period	AD	Commercial AD	Non-Profit AD	MD	Commercial MD	Non-Profit MD	AWD	Commercial AWD	Non-Profit AWD
2014	1159.0	9.0	1542.3	1038.5	9.0	2054.0	1510.0	10.0	2010.0
2013	558.0	1.0	697.2	10.0	1.0	95.0	915.6	1.0	1144.2
2012	480.7	11.0	574.6	430.0	11.0	849.0	500.2	11.0	598.0
2011	152.0	346.7	54.7	66.0	280.0	50.0	210.2	467.3	81.7
2010	105.6	92.2	113.1	17.5	21.0	14.0	203.1	199.8	205.0
2009	244.8	543.2	138.3	27.0	396.0	14.0	343.3	727.0	206.2
2008	226.2	511.0	131.3	26.5	310.0	17.5	394.3	809.8	255.8
2007	425.8	1054.5	216.2	35.0	251.5	24.0	600.4	1278.6	374.3
2006	331.1	553.1	208.6	59.0	38.0	62.0	515.4	778.8	370.0
2005	310.8	463.4	186.8	94.5	131.0	61.0	487.2	708.9	307.1
2004	231.3	366.4	91.3	85.0	155.0	54.0	433.3	700.8	155.9
2003	300.4	403.8	128.0	77.0	84.0	68.0	622.8	894.1	170.7
2002	229.8	252.8	129.8	44.0	51.5	33.0	373.9	406.3	233.2
2001	162.0	185.2	113.5	60.5	59.0	62.0	237.6	273.8	161.7

Table 6. Evolution of collaboration on artifacts in the OpenACS source code repository since 2001 – degree based metrics

Period	CAD	Commercial CAD	Non-Profit CAD	CMD	Commercial CMD	Non-Profit CMD	CAWD	Commercial CAWD	Non-Profit CAWD	Density
2014	3.0	3.0	3.0	3.0	3.0	3.0	864.0	18.0	1146.0	1.000
2013	2.0	-	2.0	2.0	NA	2.0	58.5	-	58.5	0.667
2012	2.0	1.0	2.3	2.0	1.0	2.0	1159.5	2.0	1545.3	0.667
2011	3.0	3.7	2.6	3.0	3.0	3.0	15.5	16.7	14.8	0.429
2010	4.3	5.5	3.8	4.5	5.5	3.5	41.3	58.8	32.6	0.394
2009	5.0	7.2	4.0	4.0	7.0	4.0	154.9	263.6	105.5	0.333
2008	6.1	9.0	5.1	4.5	6.0	4.0	106.4	186.5	79.7	0.264
2007	10.0	12.4	9.1	8.0	9.0	8.0	272.6	492.4	188.9	0.357
2006	11.2	13.4	10.0	9.0	10.5	8.5	289.8	392.3	234.6	0.287
2005	17.5	19.9	15.4	16.0	21.0	15.0	327.6	494.2	188.9	0.323
2004	16.6	21.1	11.7	13.5	19.5	10.0	254.7	411.3	86.1	0.312
2003	14.4	16.0	11.5	11.0	14.0	10.0	355.3	485.3	123.3	0.379
2002	10.1	10.2	9.3	8.5	8.5	9.5	222.0	241.0	139.8	0.325
2001	4.6	4.7	4.6	2.0	2.0	3.5	70.8	79.6	52.3	0.155

Chapter 6

Need of the Research Community:
Open Source Solution for Research Knowledge Management

Dhananjay S. Deshpande
Symbiosis Institute of Computer Studies and Research (SICSR), India

Pradeep R. Kulkarni
Kholeshwar Mahavidyalaya, India

Pravin S. Metkewar
Symbiosis Institute of Computer Studies and Research (SICSR), India

ABSTRACT

Universities are playing main role in research and socio-economic development of the country. The University research generates lot of research information and it is physically added in to libraries. The Research information should be easily available to new Researchers. Every research is generating new knowledge, and it's just kept in the form of thesis, dissertations, research papers, articles, etc. The enormous amount of research data exists in different geographical locations, which could not be investigated by researchers because research data is not available in a central location. The research community is facing lot of problems in sharing, searching and collecting required information and knowledge for their research.

DOI: 10.4018/978-1-5225-0905-9.ch006

Due to these issues, researchers may do work of 'reinventing a wheel'. This chapter puts a conceptual study for open source community to develop a Knowledge Management System for researchers. This study specifically focuses on Knowledge management approach and proposes the OS_KMS model for research community as an open source software.

1. INTRODUCTION

Academic programs like Ph. D., M. Phil. and Master Degrees provided by various universities, are research oriented programs for motivating students for research. The research scholars are doing work on their research as an academic requirement of their degree course. Now days, lot of students are attracted towards research, and competition for these courses is increased. This leads to increase in the number of researchers in the research community. The academic research is a continuous process, which is going on from hundreds of years. The research work creates lot of research knowledge and information. It is physically added in to libraries. It should be easily available to new Researchers. In this Information Age, this Research information is awaiting for being open to all for further use and research purpose. Every research is generating new knowledge. This knowledge is just kept in the form of thesis, dissertations, research papers, articles and etc. research community is facing lot of challenges and problems in research. The researchers could not search huge amount of research data because research data is not available in centralized accessible form. Researchers could not reach to the old research data effectively. Hence researchers could do work of reinventing the wheel again and again. Researchers may not know that the topic selected is already used by any other researchers in any other University. There is lack of appropriate tools for information and knowledge sharing in academic research. Which is the major problem faced by research scholars (Deshpande, Kulkarni, & Metkewar 2015).

In the current era of Information & Communication Technology, research scholars have different tools like research repositories, research publication databases, open source solutions and free ware desktops software's like Research Gate, Mendeley, ShodhGanga, IEEE Explore, Scopus, Google Scholar and many more, but these are not sufficient tools to meet the need of the research community. The authors think that there is a need of open source solution, which must be more customized and improved research tool for the knowledge management of the research community at University or Institute level. For design the proper tools there is need of studying the problems, challenges, issues and requirements of research community. Also the major shortcomings of the free ware/web solutions available should be studied. As the implications of this study, authors are trying to mention about the required features for benefits for research community (Deshpande, Kulkarni, Metkewar, 2015).

Objectives of this chapter:

- To study research process with Knowledge Management approach.
- To study problems, challenges and requirements of research community.
- To study the required features in proposed open source solution for research community.

2. BACKGROUND

Tian, J., Nakamori, Y., & Wierzbicki, A. P. (2009) (p.76-92) found that the authors have done research work on Knowledge management and knowledge creation in academia a survey based study in a Japanese research university. The authors have given the purpose that to pose one major research question, i.e. why and how to use knowledge management methods in order to enhance knowledge creation in academia – at universities and research institutes? They have mentioned that, the first survey was focused on knowledge management in academia and investigated the current KM situations, special and diverse requirements from researchers. The second survey was concentrated on supporting the creative processes of academic research and investigated which aspects of knowledge creation processes should be supported in particular. The author have given findings based on survey that the first survey showed that the KM obstacles reflected on various aspects that was technological support, the people involved in creation activities, laboratory cultural, and so on. The seven most critical questions and three most important questions were evaluated by responders with respect to academic knowledge creation process in the second survey.

The authors have suggested with respect to the survey results that a creative environment in academia should be enhanced from both ''soft'' and ''hard'' aspects under the guidelines of a systems thinking framework for KM in scientific labs. From the soft side, by using personalization strategies, a knowledge-sharing culture has to be built in labs to facilitate scientific communication, debate and team work. From the hard side, by using technology strategies, it is hoped that the research can launch further debate and prompt practical steps to help research institutes or universities improve their management and increase the research efficiency. The authors have given the importance of KM in the university through this research at Japanese Research University. There is scope of more study in this area to actually implement KM for the academic research community.

Smokotin, V. M., Petrova, G. I., & Gural, S. K. (2014) (p.229-232) found that the authors have worked on their research topic that is Theoretical Principles for Knowledge Management in the Research University, the authors have considered the specificity of the contemporary university administration, when the University is losing its classical unity and acquires plural forms of existence. They have given particular attention to the research university, which transforms the classical university's ideas in its adaptation to the conditions of the information society. They have further mentioned that cognitive management in the research university is a form of governance that increases its competitiveness in the globalized educational area. They have brought most important factor about cognitive management based on the transformation of knowledge into information, which can increase the student's cognitive competence.

The authors have finally concluded that the knowledge management is the answer in the transformation to informational society within the sphere of education. They have also proposed practical recommendations that are the main task of knowledge management is shaping cognitive competence. Prorector (provost) of educational work is the main manager for the Research University. He provides expertise in development of curricula and may adjust them if their content is not aimed at the formation of student ability to generate new knowledge. The theory of communicative action by J. Habermas, shifted onto education, is the theoretical basis for knowledge management. The authors have clearly mentioned through this research paper that for the Research University Knowledge Management is the answer in this information society. Here is scope of study to implement Knowledge Management in different areas and scopes of the university that means from administration, E-learning, examinations and so on. Main important area of university is research community.

Razak, N. A. (2009) has found this research article to explain the objectives, needs and uses of university portal at the Rakan University in significance to the bridging Knowledge and digital divide among the varsity and the community. The author has mentioned that, the objective of E-Rakan University Portal was to develop a common platform for communication between the members of varsity and the community off-campus. The university is the rich source of knowledge and housed the best brain and experts in different areas, the community off-campus should be given opportunities to tap this information and reach the experts without many barriers. He has further mentioned that, E-Rakan University Portal provides services and information related to e-counseling, which contain topics such as education, career, lifestyle, health and religion. It also provides information based on user-generated content and based on the needs of the communities.

The author finally proposed that the impact of this portal was to help and to bridge the knowledge and digital divide between the communities; and the success of the portal would depend on aggressive promotional campaign. The author has explained the university portals purpose, objectives and how it would be helpful for the community; but not mentioned the exact university portal's structure and design; and is it in true sense knowledge management portal?

Toral, S. L., Bessis, N., Martinez-Torres, M. R., Franc, F., Barrero, F., & Xhafa, F. (2011) found that the authors have done an exploratory analysis of Social Network of Academic Research Networks. The authors have been analyzed joint article publications data using an automated tool. The authors have analyzed data using factors and noted the results such as collaboration intensity, scope of collaboration, absence of collaboration among the university in England. They have attempted to highlight and demonstrate how these collaborative networks are developing in practice. In this case study, they have limited data from works published in 2010 by England academic and research institutions.

The authors finally stated that, the outcomes of this work can help policy makers in realising the current status of research collaborative networks in England. But there is scope of study to know why universities are lacking behind in collaboration of research work? What are the main points due to which the collaboration is not happening? And what is exact solution for it.

Kidwell, J. J., Vander Linde, K., & Johnson, S. L. (2000) found that the authors have written article on higher education, focusing corporate knowledge Management practice in higher education. They have mentioned that, colleges and universities have significant opportunities to apply knowledge management practices in higher education to support every part of their mission. They have mentioned knowledge management system with various application and benefits for different areas of higher education like, research, curriculum development, alumni services, etc. The authors have focused on application view of Knowledge Management in higher education, but there is scope to study for, studying about actual needs of users, knowledge & Knowledge Management model, Knowledge Management System and its implementation related issues.

Oakley, A. (2003) found that the author has given his ideas about the Knowledge and Knowledge Management in educational practice using study of reviews in education research. The Author has mentioned with his huge experience in higher education field that the education system is about the production and dissemination of knowledge and what happens within it is itself knowledge-based. But again he explained that education is not 'simply' about the transfer of knowledge: it is about many other processes and outcomes as well. What is knowledge? Who is knowledge for? Who defines what we want to know about and why? How is knowledge used, and who benefits from (or is damaged by) these uses? Perhaps most problematic of all are the two questions: how does anyone know what they know? And, how do we get from knowledge to wisdom? They have finally concluded with the manag- ing knowledge a lesson for all, giving a importance of knowledge management in education and education research.

The author has given overall picture of knowledge and its management, but there is scope of study to know importance of Knowledge management in education systems different entities in their point of view as researchers, faculties, students and so on.

García, V. H. M., & Torres, D. A. S. (2012) found that the authors have studied the Graduate - Master degree programme; to propose the Knowledge Management Model for Research Projects Master's Program. The authors have focused on effective use of knowledge management in Higher Education and Academic Research. They have presented the adaptation of the knowledge management model and intellectual capital measurement NOVA model. They have finally proposed the final model that shows the strong responsibility that has an organization to support research by supporting their research groups and researchers. It is the responsibility of the researcher and the research group published results. They have mentioned that the model allows to express and communicate the roles involved in the research process and responsibilities of each, to complement classic methodologies for monitoring projects, as these methods do not have a way to express the process of knowledge.

The authors have proposed a Knowledge Management Model for Research Proj- ects of a graduate master's programme that means KM for higher education and Research; there is more scope of study, to use this knowledge management model for the academic research like M. Phil., Ph.D. and Post Ph.D. degree courses or propose the new knowledge management model.

F.M. Ross Armbretcht, t.Al., have done research work on 19 leading companies, to study the knowledge flow and Knowledge Management of R&D process of these companies. The authors have arranged group sessions, personal interviews and questionnaire to collect data from different level knowledge workers. The survey was based on different aspects like industry, size, KM program specifics, KM driv- ers, KM implementation, KM metrics, organizational culture, environment and etc. focusing to the role of knowledge Management in research and development. They have mentioned that this study was specific to three points i.e. to identify the model of knowledge flow in R&D process, to highlight the aspects of knowledge management that are unique and important in R&D process, to catalog the better practices that are used by knowledge managers for knowledge flow and knowledge creation throughout organization. Finally, they have reported their findings in three parts that is, they describe the flow of knowledge in R&D and its opportunities and requirements in R&D process; the basic three culture enablers means Infrastructure,

Information Technology and KM applications, which affects the KM performance. And lastly they have suggested holistic approach to implement KM in R&D process.

The authors have done fruitful study of 19 leading companies for knowing the knowledge flow model and knowledge management aspects and organizational culture for the R&D process. Hence there is a scope of study to know the knowledge flow model and knowledge management applications and organizational culture view of the R&D process of corporate world and effective use of these all concepts in academic research environment for research community in different universities.

The literature review and as per the above knowledge references related to knowledge management in research centers and universities. We can conclude that the Knowledge Management is the important field, though there are different view on definition of KM and but its proved that the KM is playing very important role in the growth and development of every business organization. The organizations most important asset is knowledge of employees working in the organization. It is having power of innovation, to improve the results and make positive growth of the organization. The Knowledge should be managed in proper way to achieve the goal of organization that means there is need of Knowledge Management System, using ICT or without it, to manage it and deliver the highly desired output.

We have also studied that now from last few years' education institutes and universities are trying to implement the KM for the benefit of the students, faculties and research students. We have studied KM Models, KMS Architectures, KMS implementations for institute level for E-learning environment, distance learning and other related activities of the educational institutions. Also we have seen the use of KMS for research community, to share the research knowledge among researchers in particular institute or organization. But as per the study so far have done by the researcher, there is lack of proper OS- KMS for the research community, which should be properly designed for the research community. A KM model specifically designed specifically for the research community has not seen through this research study. There is need of OS-KMS for researchers, to solve the actual problems, issues and challenges during their day to day research activities. Hence, this research is a important effort to propose the OS-KMS model for the research community. The OS-KMS Model architecture designed here is specifically a overall view for the Open Source Community to develop and implement the same at institute level or University level considering the scope of integration. Due to which the research activity should became an interactive and collaborative work for the research community to get high quality results for the Socio – Economical Development of the country in the current age of the knowledge-based economy.

2.1 Academic Research

Academic research is typically conducted in educational institutions. Free from hindrance that may characterize research done in industry, government agencies, or think tanks, such as pressure to turn a profit, instruction to work on specific subjects or promote a certain ideology, and stricture to meet deadlines, academic research is a unique privilege and an extraordinary pursuit. A key to creating wealth of a nation is applied research, which, in turn, traces back to academic research. Developed nations have universities as powerhouse to country. Now developing countries are also trying to imitate.

Research is a sincere, comprehensive, intellectual searching for facts and their significance or inference with reference to the problem under study. Research is symmetric activity to achieve the truth. Research in common parlance refers to search for knowledge. The concept of research is elaborated here, by means of definitions of research from different author's point of views:

- *Research is a systematized effort to gain new knowledge.* – Redman and Mory
- *Research is essentially an investigation, a recording and analysis of evidence for the purpose of gaining knowledge.* – Robert Ross
- *In the broadest sense of the word, the definition of research includes any gathering of data, information and facts for the advancement of knowledge.* – Broad definition of research given by Martyn Shuttleworth
- *Research is systematic work to create new knowledge or devise new applications of knowledge.* – Wikipedia

According to these all definitions we can observe that research is mostly related to most important word that is knowledge. Research is systematized effort to gain new Knowledge, to create new knowledge, advancement of knowledge, to verify and to expand existing knowledge and so on. Consequently, research most significant harvest is knowledge.

2.2 Steps in Academic Research Process

The Research comprises a systematic method of exploring actual person and groups, focused primarily on their social words, inclusive of social attitudes and values and the modes of analysis of these experiences permits stating proposition in the specific form. In short the search knowledge through objective and systematic method of finding solutions to a problem is research. Research process consists of a number of closely related activities. But such activities overlap continuously and do not follow a strictly prescribed sequence. Various steps involved in a research process are not mutually exclusive; nor are the separate and distinct. The following figure with various steps provides a useful procedural guideline regarding the research process:

- Identification of research problem,
- Literature review,
- Specifying the purpose of research,
- Determine specific research questions or hypotheses,
- Data collection,
- Analyzing and interpreting the data
- Reporting and evaluating research,
- Communicating the research findings and, possibly, recommendations.

The rapid development in information technology and science changes the paradigm of the university, now day's universities are working on online systems. Universities have adopted online solutions for different processes like admission process, convocation process, exam applications, online exams, etc. The research projects and research work running in the university, has most important assets of the university. The researchers contributing in their research works are most important knowledge resources. Researchers having subject expertise and set of knowledge in the respective subjects, due to various research projects and research work experience. The new researchers are added in the list as research students, Research Fellows, and Research Project Assistants. These all researchers, research supervisors and related all individuals forms a Research Community (RC) in the university. They need help and expertise guidance in different tasks of research process. They initially rely on resources available in university like library, Internet & expert consultation. But the expertise knowledge with individuals will not able to communicate due to geographical distances, so the knowledge exists in the individuals and in the university should be managed. Problem arise in the university is knowledge of individuals is not documented and well organized, and even the university itself does not realize that the individuals have knowledge that can enhance competitive advantage among researchers. Hence, at university or institute level there is need of the system for research community, would be preferably an open source solution. This can help researchers to easily communicate among community, to get idea about the expertise and knowledge set of individuals. Also, they should be able to pass information, to share their knowledge, views and experiences through this system. This research knowledge can be managed by this open source solution. The implementation of KMS aims to increase the competitive advantage of university and can be one factor to improve the performance of the university. This KMS should be designed specifically for Researchers point of view, which can be used by RC.

3. RESEARCH COMMUNITY

A social, religious, occupational, or other groups sharing common characteristics or interests perceived or perceiving itself as distinct in some respect from the larger society within which it exists (usually preceded by the): the business community; the community of scholars.

A community is a social unit of any size that shares common values. Although embodied or face-to-face communities are usually small, larger or more extended communities such as a national community, international community and virtual community are also studied.

As the concept of community, the university and its related institutions, colleges and students, teachers and other staff, this can be named as academic community. In this academic community special and important community in the higher education perspective at university level is Research Community or Research Knowledge Community (RC). The RC is a community of research scholars, research facilitators and research staff as shown in the Figure 1. RC at university level includes different research institutions, research centers, university departments which are the controlling bodies for the researchers. The RC members can be distributed in two different types i.e. direct members and indirect members. The RC direct member means, who are directly related to the research work as individual – Research Students, Research Fellows, Research Assistants, Research Guides / Supervisors. The RC indirect member means, the members, who are not directly working on research but they are working as employee in the university departments, institutions and libraries. Also the other research experts and research scholars from other universities can be indirect members. (Deshpande, Kulkarni, Metkewar 2015).

Figure 1. Structure of Research Community (RC)

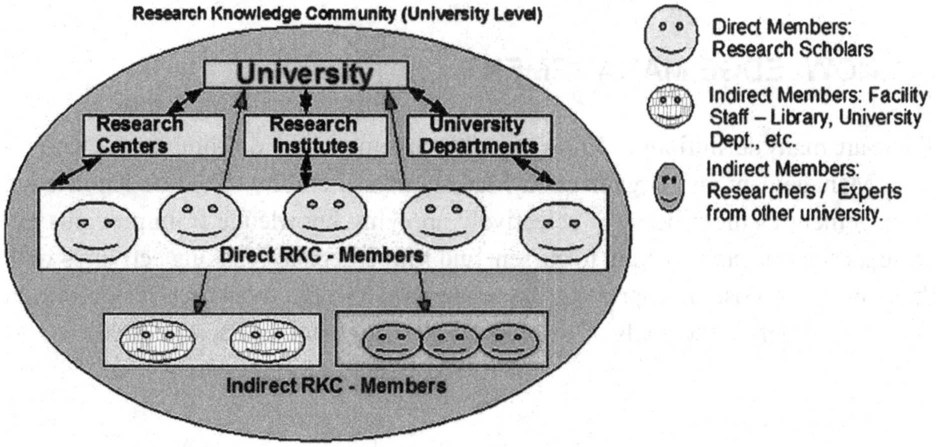

The RC is having a common interest, common goal of research. The research of university is important knowledge asset of the nation. The government is always motivating the scholars for the research activities through offering different research student's scholarships and research project grants.

The RC would be a special kind of community which always needs interaction, communication, and sharing of knowledge from various streams and disciplines for innovative research work. These community members are trying to regularly contact and interact with each other for sharing knowledge and information of research, through different conferences, seminars, workshops and development programs, etc.

The RC is most important community and its individual member is a knowledge asset of the university. Since, till date there is no any such kind of community formed, or properly organized in the universities. Formation of RKC can make healthy environment for research in the university, by providing technology, tools, and various platforms for RC, to inculcate the importance of research knowledge in students. This would be helpful for the high quality research with more positive and proper output to the nation building.

The idea about research Information and Knowledge and their resources is given here further. The discussion about the steps of Research process and how it can be specifically synchronized for the knowledge Management of the research community is also given in this chapter. This is a big challenge to manage existing Research Knowledge and upcoming new Research Knowledge for the design of the open source solution. The Open Source Solutions for Research Community should be managed or governed by an authorized organization to ensure security and integrity of this open source - research Knowledge Management System.

The Research Community, in true sense needs an open source solution as a knowledge management system, which could be used and managed by university level as an online web application. Hope it will be a fruit full work in the one step of the required open source solution for research community.

4. KNOWLEDGE MANAGEMENT

There are many definitions of Knowledge Management here we combine the Knowledge Management and Organization Management literature to define Knowledge Management as the process of selectively applying knowledge from previous experiences of decision-making to current and future decision making activities with the express purpose of improving the organization's effectiveness. This definition allows us to define the goals of Knowledge Management as: (Servin 2005)

- Identify Critical Knowledge,
- Acquire Critical Knowledge in a Knowledge Base or Organizational Memory,
- Share the stored Knowledge,
- Apply the Knowledge to appropriate situations,
- Determine the effectiveness of using the applied knowledge,
- Adjust Knowledge use to improve effectiveness.

4.1 What Is Knowledge?

Academics have debated the meaning of "knowledge" since the word was invented, but let's not get into that here. A dictionary definition is "the facts, feelings or experiences known by a person or group of people" (Collins English Dictionary). Knowledge is derived from information but it is richer and more meaningful than information. It includes familiarity, awareness and understanding gained through experience or study, and results from making comparisons, identifying consequences, and making connections. Some experts include wisdom and insight in their definitions of knowledge. In organizational terms, knowledge is generally thought of as being "know how", or "applied action". The last point is an important one. Today's organizations contain a vast amount of knowledge and the NHS is certainly no exception. However, in applying knowledge management principles and practices in organization, knowledge is not end, but the means for further action. What we are trying to do is to use knowledge to get better at doing what we do. (Servin 2005)

4.2 Why Research Communities Need Knowledge Management

Knowledge management is based on the idea that an organization's most valuable resource is the knowledge of its people. This is not a new idea – organizations have been managing "human resources" for years. What is new is the focus on knowledge. This focus is being driven by the accelerated rate of change in today's organizations, communities and in society as a whole. Here authors are focusing on Knowledge Management of RC (Servin 2005). Knowledge management recognizes that today nearly all jobs in research and administration of University involve "knowledge work" and so every RC member is a "knowledge worker" to some degree or another – meaning that their job depends more on their knowledge than their manual skills. This means that creating, sharing and using knowledge are among the most important activities of nearly every person in RC. Do we know everything we need to know or are there gaps in our knowledge? Of course there are. Government policies are constantly evolving as a management practices. The current modernization programme requires us to let go of what we knew and to learn and apply new knowledge. To get idea about the need of KM for RC, we should ask few questions to RC members:

- Do we share what we know?
- Is the knowledge of individuals available to RC?
- Is the knowledge of RC and University available to all?
- Not at present. How many times have we lost valuable knowledge and expertise when a staff member moves on?
- How many times have we "reinvented the wheel" when we could have learned from someone else's experience?
- Do we use what we know to best effect? Not always.

Clearly our knowledge has not always been applied to best effect, and we have fallen behind the times. How many times have we had an idea about how a process or an activity could be improved, but felt we lacked the time or resources to do anything about it? How many times have we had an idea that might help our colleagues, but we keep quiet because our colleagues might not appreciate us "telling them how to do their job"? How many times have we implemented a new initiative, only to find we reverted back to the "old way" a few months later? In terms of how that is done, the processes of knowledge management are many and varied. As knowledge management is a relatively new concept, organizations are still finding their way and so there is no single agreed way forward or best practice. This is a time of much trial and error. Similarly, to simply copy the practices of another organization would probably not work because each organization faces a different set of knowledge management problems and challenges. Knowledge management is essentially about people – how they create, share and use knowledge, and so no knowledge management tool will work if it is not applied in a manner that is sensitive to the ways people think and behave. (Deshpande et al.,2015)

4.4 Definitions of Knowledge Management

- *The creation and subsequent management of an environment, which encourages knowledge to be created, shared, learn't, enhanced, organized and utilized for the benefit of the organization and its customers.* – Abell & Oxbrow, tfpl Ltd, 2001
- *The capabilities by which communities within an organization capture the knowledge that is critical to them, constantly improve it, and make it available in the most effective manner to those people who need it, so that they can exploit it creatively to add value as a normal part of their work.* – BSI's A Guide to Good Practice in KM

- *Knowledge is power, which is why people who had it in the past often tried to make a secret of it. In post-capitalism, power comes from transmitting information to make it productive, not from hiding it!* – Peter Drucker
- *Knowledge management is not about data, but about getting the right information to the right people at the right time for them to impact the bottom line.* – IBM
- *The capability of an organization to create new knowledge, disseminate it throughout the organization and embody it in products, services and systems.* – Nonaka & Takeuchi, 1995

4.5 Types of Knowledge: Explicit and Tacit

Knowledge is often classified into two types: explicit knowledge and tacit knowledge. *Explicit knowledge* is knowledge that can be captured and written down in documents or databases. Examples of explicit knowledge include instruction manuals, written procedures, best practices, lessons learned and research findings. Explicit knowledge can be categorized as either structured or unstructured. Documents, databases, and spreadsheets are examples of structured knowledge, because the data or information in them is organized in a particular way for future retrieval. In contrast, e-mails, images, training courses, and audio and video selections are examples of unstructured knowledge because the information they contain is not referenced for retrieval (Servin 2005).

Tacit knowledge is the knowledge that people carry in their heads. It is much less concrete than explicit knowledge. It is more of an "unspoken understanding" about something, knowledge that is more difficult to write down in a document or a database. An example might be, knowing how to ride a bicycle – you know how to do it, you can do it again and again, but could you write down instructions for someone to learn to ride a bicycle? Tacit knowledge can be difficult to access, as it is often not known to others. In fact, most people are not aware of the knowledge they themselves possess or of its value to others. Tacit knowledge is considered more valuable because it provides context for people, places, ideas and experiences. It generally requires extensive personal contact and trust to share effectively (*Géraud Servin, July 2005*).

4.6 Research Knowledge and Its Resources

We have seen, what is knowledge? And what are the different types of knowledge? Now, we need to think here about what is research knowledge? Research Knowledge is information collected, created, generated through analysis and stored in minds of researchers in form of experiences, stories, conclusions and suggestions. Research

Knowledge is conclusive information that forms the basis for thoughts, actions, and beliefs related to research." It includes the theories and experiments of scientists, who collaborate to establish our knowledge of the external world. Research knowledge is a scientific knowledge which is generated by proper scientific Research methods. Research Knowledge is having its own value in the research field and interdisciplinary research too. (Deshpande, Kulkarni 2014),

Research Knowledge is majority concerned with researchers, is the information created and stored in their minds like their experiences, actions, thoughts, observations and beliefs during the time of research work. We can store and manage the explicit knowledge. The data can be managed in the different forms like text, images, charts, audios, videos, etc. but really managing the tacit knowledge is very different, we have to convert this tacit knowledge in readable and transferable format can try to represent this type of knowledge using the few formats like we can store videos, audios, images and stories about the exact experiences during their research experiences. These data would be managed in data server, which can make available to the researchers to share the knowledge or tacit knowledge. This would help the researchers to prepare future plan in their research.

Around the world in each and every field research projects are executing. Every research project is having its own social, scientific, financial, informative and correlative value for the nation. These projects are generating new knowledge, which would be useful information for the human being; it might be useful or applicable in any research field. Hence Research Knowledge would be available for the researchers. A Knowledge Management System Model can play important role in such type of research knowledge Management.

Figure 2 gives idea about, what is research knowledge? And how it can be produced and procured? Research Knowledge sources in academic research are different like Research Papers, Research Conferences/Seminars, Research Journals, Research Articles and Research Thesis/dissertations. Now, this information is available on line in form of textual data in research repository, research database and few on line tools like Google Scholar, Research Gate and Mendeley. But this information is not searchable form and easily accessible form. Knowledge Management techniques and tools can be used to properly arrange this research knowledge and can be more effectively used for further actions and research. Explicit and Tacit research knowledge can also be produced in different formats to avail it on online formats as shown in figure. Tacit research knowledge can be Researcher's ideas, real or live experiences, observations; which can be produced in form of Interview Videos and Audio clips, Simulations and Animation clips. While explicit research knowledge can make available in the general way of textual, image, graphs, tables, and chart form of database. This information can be available easily for researchers.

Figure 2. Research knowledge resources

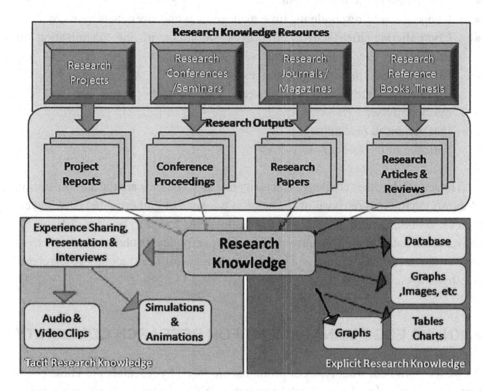

5. CHALLENGES/PROBLEMS FACED BY RESEARCH STUDENTS

Research students and Researchers are facing lot of challenges in their research project. Few researchers have published their research papers on topic, "Problems faced by researchers during their Research". The Researchers are mostly facing problems, which related to research knowledge or research information, are given in these research papers which are mentioned here as it is, given below (Anna 2013):

- Identification of researchable issue and construction of research title.
- **Research Methodology Concepts:** Constructions of interpretation, analysis, findings, conclusions and recommendation.
- **Statistical Analysis Tools:** Problem on the statistical treatment of data or what statistical tool to use.
- **Secondary Data Collection:** The collection and choice of related studies/ theories as bases to support.
- **Questionnaire Design:** Researcher made questionnaire formulation.

- Formatting of the text content.
- Cooperation of respondents, time management and stress management.
- Contradicting ideas/narrow mindedness/conflict in the organization of thoughts between research partners.
- Limited period in conducting the research.
- Conflicting interpretations between the student- researcher and the teacher-adviser.
- Inexperienced researcher.
- Patience of the teacher-adviser.

The few of the other challenges faced by research students are the administration of questionnaire and retrieval of the same is a means of gathering the data; nevertheless, visibility and availability of the respondents found to be very difficult for the student-researchers. To approach unfamiliar respondents and convince them to answer the survey questionnaire could be very hard for the student – researchers. (Deshpande et.al., 2014)

6. KNOWLEDGE MANAGEMENT FOR RESEARCH COMMUNITY

As we have studied, what types of problems are faced by researchers? These problems are mostly related to research knowledge. We have also study about academic research knowledge and its different resources. The Problems can have solutions by use of knowledge management tools in the academic researcher groups. The research knowledge can be managed using knowledge management tools in following six steps as shown in Figure 3 (Deshpande et al. 2014):

1. Generating research knowledge,
2. Eliciting, extracting research knowledge,
3. Consolidating and organizing research knowledge,
4. Synthesizing, analyzing research knowledge,
5. Packaging and repacking research knowledge package,
6. Sharing, disseminating and communicating research knowledge.

Using above six steps of Knowledge Management, we can manage the research knowledge, which would be efficiently managed and make available for reuse or reference by the new researchers. (Servin 2005)

Figure 3. Steps in research knowledge management

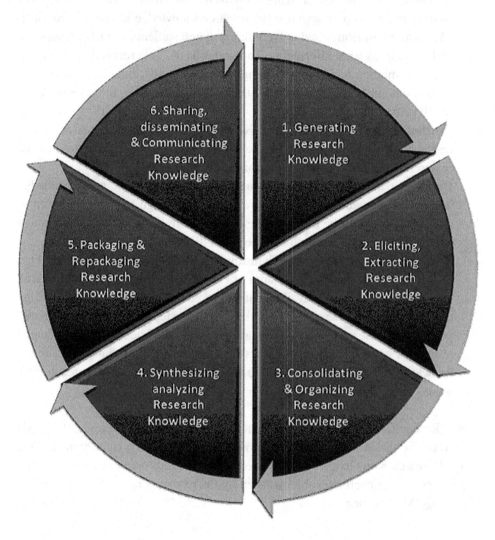

1. **Generating Research Knowledge:** The available Knowledge Management tools and ICT tools, RKC can generate the research knowledge through the RKC members. They will update their research work related video/audios clips, photos, reports, charts, tables, reviews and experiences on regular basis. This will generate the scattered knowledge in research knowledge repository of open source system.
2. **Extracting Research Knowledge:** The generated and newly updated research knowledge can be extracted or obtained as per requirement of the researchers and used for their further research. This might be easily available on one search related to their research topic.

3. **Consolidating and Organizing Research Knowledge:** This OSS - KMS System would help to organize the research knowledge in centralized form. The different institutes and universities research students and researchers can update their research information on regular basis. This research information can be combined together and strengthened. This distributed and physically located data in library can be organized in proper manner, to make available for all researchers.

4. **Synthesizing, Analyzing Research Knowledge:** The centralized and organized research information and knowledge can be synthesized and analyzed as per requirements, would be produced for the researchers.

5. **Packaging and Repacking Research Knowledge Package:** Knowledge Management system can put this research knowledge together, and due to packaging it would be available easily in required format. Researchers can again rearrange this research knowledge in different forms and repack it.

6. **Sharing, Disseminating and Communicating Research Knowledge:** Due to Knowledge Management System of Research knowledge, the all research knowledge can be made available at single point. This Research knowledge can be shared by researchers; the research knowledge can be disseminated properly by Research Knowledge Management tools. The researchers, located at various states or locations can easily communicate and share their subject knowledge, research related knowledge, which can help them to reach their goals.

The Research Knowledge Management System can manage the research knowledge to utilize the available research knowledge in right way, right manner. Due to this Research Knowledge can be shared, disseminated, organized and communicated easily. The current problems faced by the researchers would be solved by Knowledge Management.

7. OPEN SOURCE SOLUTION

7.1 What Is Open Source?

A definition Founded in 1998, the open source initiative (OSI) is a non-profit industry-recognized approval authority that acts as a steward for the open source definition (OSD), a set of rules that determine if a software product meets strict guidelines for open source compliance. The OSI is comprised of a board of directors from the IT industry who support the ideals of the open source community and include key representatives from firms such as Google, Apple Computer, MySQL

AB, FSF Latin America, and Thyrsus Enterprises. As listed on the OSI's web site (www.opensource.org/docs/osd), official open source products must meet the following criteria:

1. **Free Distribution:** The license shall not restrict any party from selling or giving away the software as a component of an aggregate software distribution containing programs from several different sources. The license shall not require a royalty or other fee for such sale.
2. **Source Code:** The program must include source code, and must allow distribution in source code as well as compiled form. Where some form of a product is not distributed with source code, there must be a well-publicized means of obtaining the source code for no more than a reasonable reproduction cost preferably, downloading via the Internet without charge. The source code must be the preferred form in which a programmer would modify the program. Deliberately obfuscated source code is not allowed. Intermediate forms such as the output of a preprocessor or translator are not allowed.
3. **Derived Works:** The license must allow modifications and derived works, and must allow them to be distributed under the same terms as the license of the original software.
4. **Integrity of the Author's Source Code:** The license may restrict source-code from being distributed in modified form only if the license allows the distribution of "patch files" with the source code for the purpose of modifying the program at build time. The license must explicitly permit distribution of software built from modified source code. The license may require derived works to carry a different name or version number from the original software.
5. **No Discrimination against Persons or Groups**: The license must not discriminate against any person or group of persons.
6. **No Discrimination against Fields of Endeavor:** The license must not restrict anyone from making use of the program in a specific field of endeavor. For example, it may not restrict the program from being used in a business, or from being used for genetic research.
7. **Distribution of License:** The rights attached to the program must apply to all to whom the program is redistributed without the need for execution of an additional license by those parties. Gaining competitive advantage
8. **License Must Not Be Specific to a Product:** The rights attached to the program must not depend on the program's being part of a particular software distribution. If the program is extracted from that distribution and used or distributed within the terms of the program's license, all parties to whom the program is redistributed should have the same rights as those that are granted in conjunction with the original software distribution.

9. **License Must Not Restrict Other Software:** The license must not place re-strictions on other software that is distributed along with the licensed software. For example, the license must not insist that all other programs distributed on the same medium must be open-source software.

10. **License Must Be Technology-Neutral:** No provision of the license may be predicated on any individual technology or style of interface.

7.2. Why Open Source?

Information and communication technologies (ICTs) are widely recognized as tools contributing to the realization of the Millennium Development Goals. However, in terms of being well equipped to make informed decisions on ICT architecture and choice of platform, countries from the South are lagging behind, and are therefore still unable to harness the full potential of these tools in the eradication of poverty. This knowledge arrear contributes to incompatible information systems, expensive and ineffective maintenance of ICT infrastructures and resource-draining software licenses. By addressing this issue, communities can be better equipped to develop local expertise and markets, based on ICT knowledge, and can develop a stronger domestic ICT-industry, such as we have seen developing in Asia over the past decade (Hedgebeth 2007; Neus & Scherf 2005).

Open source technologies developed by librarians, archivists, technologists and researchers who share the goal of creating and preserving long-term access to the world's digital heritage. For these stewards of knowledge, open source software has several important advantages over proprietary software. Open source is developed through free sharing and the transparent exchange of ideas and resources among peers. This makes it possible for us to leverage the enormous talent of self-motivated participants contributing expert skills and knowledge from all over the world.

Governments, business firms, military organizations, and educational entities have incorporated open source software into their enterprise functions to counter tightened budgets and rising operational expenses. In addition to cost savings, the open source model provides customers with the ability to modify applications specific to particular user needs, and fosters collaboration among global user communities for activities such as product enhancements and bug fixes.

Europe has long been an active player in the open source movement. The libre software community has contributed heavily to the worldwide open source move-ment we know today. Pioneers of open source include Linus Torvalds of Finland (Linux kernel), Michael Widenius of Sweden (MySQL), Guido van Rossum of The Netherlands (Python), Matthias Ettrich of Germany (KDE), and The MandrakeSoft Company of France. (Mandrake Linux and the ability to download entire open source distributions on the Internet) and Symbian of the UK (Symbian OS – operating system for mobile devices). China benefits from strong government support for open source software, and has a stated national goal to "boost the domestic software industry to realize the transition of China from IT consumer to IT provider" by "playing a leading role in the Linux/Open Source Software community, in the hope of being recognized as one of the global standard makers and enablers" (Yeo et al., 2006).

India has introduced the Open Source Simputer project, e-governance, and CoIL-NET & TDIL localization projects to adopt open source methodologies. Additionally, software sponsored by the Indian Government has been used to establish an open source software-based center of excellence in the country's Hubli Software Technology Park (Sharma & Adkins, 2006).

NASA Open Source Software, NASA conducts research and development in software and software technology as an essential response to the needs of NASA missions. Under the NASA Software Release policy, NASA has several options for the release of NASA developed software technologies. These options now include Open Source software release. This option is under the NASA Open Source Agreement "NOSA". The motivations for NASA to distribute software codes Open Source are: To increase NASA software quality via community peer review

8. PROPOSED OPEN SOURCE - KNOWLEDGE MANAGEMENT SYSTEM (OS - KMS) FOR RESEARCH COMMUNITY

The different KMS tools are configured or structured to support KM activities. This research provides an overview of KMS tools that required implementing the proposed KMS architecture. As shown in the Figure 4, the first layer is a presentation layer. It allows the KMS and the end users to interact with each other through via User Interface (UI). The users submit a knowledge request using formulated keywords to the presentation layer. The presentation layer services communicates with different knowledge processing tools to retrieve useful content knowledge that can satisfy user requests. The personalized search may also display contact address of potential experts in RC or external knowledge sources if the actual content is not found in the existing knowledge Base. Linking users with potential knowledge sources is one of the goals of OS-KMS. The presentation service should also support visual navigation by organizing concepts by their relationships, User Interface Controls and other required external components. It also facilitates knowledge externalization to update existing knowledge resources in the database (Jennex, 2008).

The second layer is an application layer. It contains different applications and services such as Chatting, Sharing, Profile Management, Audio/Video streaming,

Figure 4. Proposed N-Tier OS-KMS model for RC

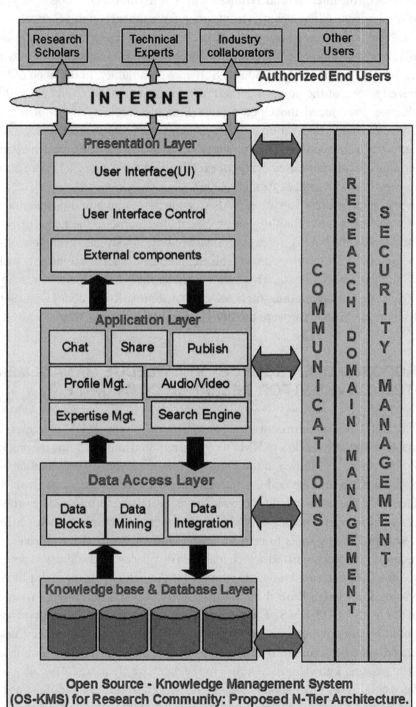

search engines and various applications. The layer provides knowledge management tools for the authorized end users for communication in RC. The knowledge processing tools receive requests from the presentation layer and respond results to presentation layer that meet the specific user's needs. The knowledge processing tools response can be the actual content of the knowledge or a reference to the knowledge sources such as contact address of the experts. Retrieving the location of knowledge is one piece of knowledge required by knowledge seekers to fill their knowledge gap. Hence application layer would be helpful for end users to easily search, retrieve, update, create required knowledge through this OS-KMS.

The third layer is a Data Access Layer. It contains different databases related tools like data block for regularly accessed data, Data Mining for searching the knowledge base and data requirements of the users. Data Integration tools to maintain the integrity of the Research Domain wise Data and knowledge base records. The Data Access Layer mainly support the system to maintain the data access more secure and reliable.

As shown in the Figure 4, next layer in this model is shown as Knowledge Base & Database Layer stores research knowledge contents and research related database and file formats, to be manipulated by the OS-KMS tools in the Application and Data Access Layer. Knowledge stored in the knowledge base and database should accessible by the knowledge seekers, which is useful to be used in task related activities. It will reduce unnecessary efforts to filter useful knowledge. This layer contains content database, expert database, reference database and ontology database.

This design model needs to evaluate from Research Scholars. As per their expectations, a design model must solve current problems when it is implemented. With regard to Institute or University capability, it refers to organization readiness to implement the proposed design. With respect to user requirements, the proposed OS-KMS Model may have high acceptance because of its capability to reduce social and distance barriers to access existing knowledge resources. It also serves as additional communication channels to create flexibility in the use of communication channels for knowledge sharing. Knowledge owners will not be interrupted by simple questions that can be solved by referring existing knowledge base. It also serves as a data store for knowledge shared through personal interactions that has the potential for later reuse. The main challenge is the lack of skill to develop an integrated KMS that can support its strategic objectives. The proposed architecture is assumed to solve currently observed KM problems in the RC.

9. CONCLUSION, RECOMMENDATIONS AND FUTURE WORK

9.1 Summary of Findings

This theoretical study pertained to the academic research, research knowledge, difficulties encountered by student-researchers, knowledge management as a tool for the solution to manage the Research knowledge. Findings show that the item which contributed a very great extent to the difficulty of the students in conducting their research study is to get a research methodology knowledge, Research topic formation issues, and similar knowledge sharing related issue (Tian, J., Nakamori, Y., & Wierzbicki, A. P. (2009). The study shows that research related research information resources; research knowledge resources are available in proper extent. Research Information and Knowledge resources are produced by different research projects conducted by research students and researchers. The overview study of knowledge management, and given six steps of knowledge management shows the way, how to manage the available research knowledge. Hence if we apply the Knowledge Management in academic research field, which is successfully used in different business organizations and multinational companies, would definitely benefit the Researchers'.

9.2 Conclusion

The light of this study the researcher concludes that the researchers having lot of challenges in their research work. The lack of availability of information, knowledge resources, distance barriers are major problems for them. Elucidation for the researcher's problems with the research information resources and research knowledge resources the related study of knowledge management is more effective. Implications of Knowledge Management in academic research can provide good solution for the problems of the researchers.

The Open Source is best solution for the developing countries to implement the high tech solutions for the different sectors. In Institute and University level research community need the Knowledge Management System as a solution for their Research related issues. OS-KMS would be developed and implemented for the research knowledge Management at university level.

9.3 Recommendations

The following recommendations are advanced:

1. The proper study of academic research in different subjects and different fields should be studied for the common goal implementation of Knowledge Management.
2. The research should be conducted on the research problems and knowledge management as solutions for it; view of researchers.
3. The Special initiative should be taken for development of OS-KMS as pilot project for Research Knowledge Management at Institute or University level.

9.4 Future Work

This is a conceptual study to propose OS-KMS for RC, hence it is at very initial level, lot of things should be performed in the process of implementation of OS-KMS. The main aim of proposing OS-KMS model for RC is to provide a idea for the Open Source Community to develop such a nice KMS for the Research Community. For this lot of things should be done which we can remind here as, putting proposal towards OS community for developing this project. The proper analysis and design of the OS-KMS data base, Developing Architecture Model for Network, Database, tools selection for development of OS-KMS, implementation, training, evaluation of OS-KMS. Then convert this project from a conceptual model to a working open source system for the benefit of the research scholars.

REFERENCES

Armbrecht, Jr., Chapas, Chappelow, & Farris. (2001). Knowledge management in research and development. *Research Technology Management, 44*(4), 28.

Baskerville & Dulipovici. (2006). The Theoretical foundation of Knowledge Management. KMR&P.

Bocar. (2013). Difficulties encountered by the student researchers and the effects on their research output. *Proceeding of the Global Summit on Education 2013.*

Chappelow. (2004). The Future of Knowledge Management: An international Delphi Study. *Journal of Knowledge Management.*

Deshpande, D. S., & Kulkarni, P. R. (2014). Use of Knowledge Management in Academic Research: A Study Report. *International Research Journal, 4*(2), 1-5.

Deshpande D. S, Kulkarni P. R., Metkewar P. S. (2015). A Knowledge Management approach for Developing Research Community. *International Journal of Engineering, Business and Enterprise Applications, 11*(1), 73-77.

García, V. H. M., & Torres, D. A. S. (2012). Knowledge Management Model for Research Projects Masters Program. In Proceedings of World Academy of Science, Engineering and Technology (No. 70). World Academy of Science, Engineering and Technology.

Hedgebeth, D. (2007). Gaining competitive advantage in a knowledge-based economy through the utilization of open source software. Vine, 37(3), 284–294. doi:10.1108/03055720710825618 doi:10.1108/03055720710825618

Jasemi & Piri. (2012). Knowledge Management Practices in a Successful Research and Development Organization. *Open Journal of Knowledge Management*, (5).

July, G. S. (2005). ABC of Knowledge Management. Published by Community of Knowledge.

Keskin, S. (2013). Communication and Management of Knowledge in Research and Development (R&D) Networks. *Journal of US-China Public Administration*.

Kidwell, J. J., Vander Linde, K., & Johnson, S. L. (2000). Applying Corporate Knowledge Management Practices in Higher Education. EDUCAUSE Quarterly, 23(4), 28–33.

Kidwell, J. J., Vander Linde, K. M., & Johnson, S. L. (2000). Applying Corporate Knowledge Management Practices in Higer Education. EDUCAUSE Quarterly, 4.

Magnier-Watanable, Berrton, & Daisenoo. (2011). *A study of Knowledge Management enablers across countries.* KMR&P.

Neus, A., & Scherf, P. (2005). Opening minds: Cultural change with the introduction of open-source collaboration methods. IBM Systems Journal, 44(2), 215–225. doi:10.1147/sj.442.0215 doi:10.1147/sj.442.0215

Oakley, A. (2003). Research evidence, knowledge management and educational practice: Early lessons from a systematic approach. London Review of Education, 1(1), 21–33. doi:10.1080/14748460306693 doi:10.1080/14748460306693

Ondari-Okemwa. (2006). Knowledge Management in a Research Organisation: International Livestock Research Institute. *Libri, 56*, 63–72.

Razak, N. A. (2009, August). E-Rakan Universiti: A Portal for bridging knowledge and digital divide among the varsity and the community. In *Computer Science and Information Technology, 2009. ICCSIT 2009. 2nd IEEE International Conference on* (pp. 429-432). IEEE. doi:10.1109/ICCSIT.2009.5234676 doi:10.1109/ICC-SIT.2009.5234676

Rodriquez, Anuro, & Stanishy. (2004). Knowledge Management Analysis of the Research and Development & Transference Process at HERO's. *Journal of Universal Computer Science.*

Scacchi, W. (2010, November). The future of research in free/open source software development. In *Proceedings of the FSE/SDP workshop on Future of software engineering research* (pp. 315-320). ACM. doi:10.1145/1882362.1882427 doi:10.1145/1882362.1882427

Sharma, A., & Adkins, R. (2006). OSS in India. In C. DiBona, D. Cooper, & M. Stone (Eds.), Open Sources 2.0 (pp. 189–196). Sebastopol, CA: O'Reilly Media, Inc.

Smokotin, V. M., Petrova, G. I., & Gural, S. K. (2014). Theoretical Principles for Knowledge Management in the Research University. Procedia: Social and Behavioral Sciences, 154, 229–232. doi:10.1016/j.sbspro.2014.10.141 doi:10.1016/j.sbspro.2014.10.141

Tian, J., Nakamori, Y., & Wierzbicki, A. P. (2009). Knowledge management and knowledge creation in academia: A study based on surveys in a Japanese research university. Journal of Knowledge Management, 13(2), 76–92. doi:10.1108/13673270910942718 doi:10.1108/13673270910942718

Toral, S. L., Bessis, N., Martinez-Torres, M. R., Franc, F., Barrero, F., & Xhafa, F. (2011, November). An exploratory social network analysis of academic research networks. In *Intelligent Networking and Collaborative Systems (INCoS), 2011 Third International Conference on* (pp. 21-26). IEEE. doi:10.1109/INCoS.2011.49 doi:10.1109/INCoS.2011.49

Wenger, E. (1998). Communities of Practice. Learning as a social system. *The Systems Thinker, 9*(5), 2–3.

Wenger, E. (2007). *Learning in communities of practice: a journey of the self.* Academic Press.

Witt, N., McDermott, A., Peters, M., & Stone, M. (2007). A knowledge management approach to developing communities of practice amongst university and college staff. In ICT: Providing choices for learners and learning. Proceedings ASCILITE. Academic Press.

Yeo, B., Liu, L., & Saxena, S. (2006). When China dances with OSS. In C. DiBona, D. Cooper, & M. Stone (Eds.), Open Sources 2.0 (pp. 197–210). Sebastopol, CA: O'Reilly Media, Inc.

Chapter 7
Software Engineering for Technological Ecosystems

Rajeshwar Vayyavur
California Intercontinental University, USA

ABSTRACT

Software engineering for technological ecosystems also referred as Software Ecosystems (SECOs) focuses on the concept of software engineering field. The study of SECOs started in early 90s under business schools, mainly focused on software engineering based on the software product lines approach that aimed to allow external designers and developers to contribute to hitherto closed platforms. The chapter gives background, various dimensions, framework, architectural challenges of SECOs, and explains various limitations and different recommendations and solutions to provide a better and conclusive platform for the technology ecosystems.

DOI: 10.4018/978-1-5225-0905-9.ch007

INTRODUCTION

Software engineering for technological ecosystems referred as software ecosystems (SECOs) focuses on the concept of software engineering field. The study of software engineering for technology ecosystems started in early 90s under business schools. These studies mainly focused on software engineering based on the software product lines approach that aimed to allow external designers and developers to contribute to hitherto closed platforms. Various research directions developed by industrial and literature cases provides a lot of relevant perspectives to be examined such as architecture, business considerations, modeling, social networks, organizational based management, and mobile platforms (Urban, Bakshi, Grubb, Baral, & Mitsch, 2010). Besides that, software ecosystems require a multidisciplinary treatment that includes law, business, economy, communication, as well as sociology. The studies are motivated through the software vendor's routine for there is no longer function that is independent and has the potential to deliver separate products.

These products have become dependent on other software vendors for relevant software infrastructures and components, for instance, platforms, component stores, libraries, operating systems, and other important and needed software elements. Over the past years, most institutions and firms have established Free Software and open source developments that cover technological needs, for the internal processes management and the public facing visibility. Universities, large firms, and SMSs generates a large amount of data when carrying out their operations. In order to support their emerging needs and improve the type of information systems they are using, companies search technological solutions. There are several of open source solutions that cover the basic ICT needs of business platforms, from decision-making tools to content management systems or project management software. Most of these solutions are referred to as technological ecosystems and allows focusing on information as well as knowledge to put aside the underlying technology concepts (Adomavicius, Bockstedt, Gupta, & Kauffman, 2012).

BACKGROUND

Software ecosystems give a phenomenon in the field of software engineering based on the rapid and ever evolution in the present times. The software product lines approach motivated the study of SECOs in the software engineering community. Focus was aiming on the acceptance of external developers so as to contribute to hitherto enclosed platforms. Various research activities contributed by industrial cases and literature reinforce a lot of relevant perspectives that need to be explored, like mobile platforms, modeling, social networks, and business considerations. On top of these, software ecosystems require a multidisciplinary treatment that comprises law, business, economy, communication, and sociology. Most of the above studies are motivated by the existing software vendors' routine, for they no longer operate in independent manner that has the potential to deliver different products. Study show that they have become more dependent on other software vendors for key software components plus infrastructures. For instance, they include platforms, libraries, operating systems, and component stores (Dos Santos & Werner, 2011).

In other words, software vendors do resort to virtual integration that comes through alliances to establish and keep networks of interoperability and influence factors responsible in generating SECOs. There certain challenges that emerges from the direction taken making it technical for the realization of ideal results. One thing is that software vendors in the software engineering field should be have skills and knowledge on the materials that they are using. With that, they will be in a better position to develop and create a better platform that focuses on all the needs and strategies to carry out all related concepts. Most develops have always focused and need to use the same notion, something that ensures right measures are used at all times. In the software engineering field, it is essential to operate with well-defined standards that will help get desirable results. To get these true, software vendors need to know all concepts that relates to the SECOs (Still, Huhtamäki, Russell, & Rubens, 2014).

Operating on the SECO scope is not easy and calls for ideal activities something approved by various studies. Vendors should have an overview of possible ways towards opening up the firm's platform without the exposure of intellectual property at all cases. Most cases of SECO have failed simply because it has become difficult for vendors to ensure that the concept of intellectual property has been maintained and protected in the required manner. In that way, challenges that prevents proper and ideal way of completing set projects becomes manageable at all costs. More than that, vendors wants also to be aware of the key strategies on survival that are in the SECO's stakeholders' platform. Survival strategies in all areas of technology development help designers to engage in suitable operations. Within software engineering for technology ecosystems, software vendors need to have clear survival strategies on what they are required to carry on when they conduct their projects (Bosch, 2009).

SOFTWARE ENGINEERING FOR TECHNOLOGICAL ECOSYSTEMS

To understand the field of SECOs requires one to have a focus on the scope of system engineering within various fields of operations. Various levels used comprise of different research challenges that begin from the effect of system architectural changes towards development of general metrics and the measures of software engineering for technology ecosystems health. Challenges in this case might be articulated by defining general properties of target objects like the outputs, interaction, competition, performance, value sharing, and inputs among others. Beyond the scope of the system, various dimensions that develop from software engineering for technology ecosystems levels need to be considered so as to represent the pillars that are derived from the literature researchers. In other concept, most firms engage in different past and current system engineering process models in the market where they are mixed with the business models. These involvements with the developers who are the third part as well as open product platform and architecture give a clear system explanation (Zacharias & Gianni, 2008).

From challenges highlighted, they help in defining and the monitoring of the ideal system for a given situation. The goal is to have a clear understanding of generated aspects from different SSNs during their lifetime. It's a process that must consider three levels of scope and allow identification of new software engineering for technology ecosystems. Established proposal has a structure that is set in a way that steps are related and classified based on the SECO tridimensional view that was initially developed by Campbell and Ahmed.

- **Architectural Dimension:** It focused on the system platform such as technology and market based on the platform domain engineering process, variability management and commonalties, and developed architecture designed and defined by the system.
- **Business Dimension:** The aspect of business dimension examines on the flow knowledge; artifacts, information, and resources, based on a business innovation and strategic planning. It helps medium and small companies to allow proper in products and processes through the involvement of industry, institutions, and government through their process of maintaining and developing a suitable system for operation (Urban, Bakshi, Grubb, Baral, & Mitsch, 2010).
- **Social Dimension:** Its focus in the software engineering for technological ecosystems is based on stakeholders in realization and balancing the proposition for understanding the reason stakeholders integrates and modify knowledge. Promotions on the way parties engage and participate are implicit and explicitly recognized. Another aspect determined in the process is the knowledge that aims at the focus of what open source development, collaboration plus other social network opportunities do contribute to the system stakeholders (Zacharias & Gianni, 2008).

Architectural Issues and Problems

The section will present the architecture issues and challenges that are within the current SECOs platform in the technology. So as to simply the problems and issues within SECOs platform, they are divided into independent application development as well as independent platform development. It's an element that presents the challenge in different from the two distinct perspectives. On top, it is aggregated independent platform development with interface stability, although the two challenges are strongly related. Research shows that most of the issues and controversies within the SECOs platform are much related; hence they cannot be treated whatsoever separately (Still, Huhtamäki, Russell, & Rubens, 2014).

The models below offers various challenges for the topic developed in this paper. It is a collection that comprises the issues that have becomes as critical towards the respective issues and the collaboration models in the SECO setting. A good number of the results in this chapter tend to be generalized to similar further ecosystems (see Figure 1).

Platform Openness Dilemma

Platform openness dilemma focuses on the selection of an appropriate point in time where the existing platform requires to be opened to end users. There exist some

Figure 1. Architecture challenges for SECOs

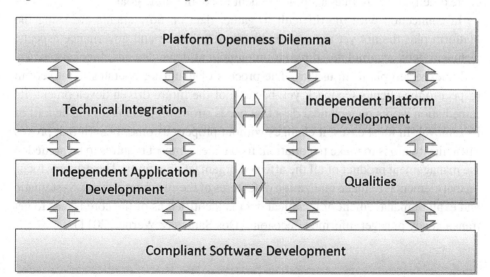

contrary forces that do justify either an early platform that opens the ideal of SECO for the system within the organization setting. Apart from that, study indicates that concepts in engineering performed in the company units require the best knowledge in the domain used for the firm system operations. In such a case, early involvement of the clients becomes essential so as to understand the development use cases for the company. Offering a platform to clients who develop, maturing, and changing almost inevitably results in certain technical debt that calls to be costly re-factored as part of the elements of maturing process. The great concern in such a concept is the level on which maturity is needed before operating any platform. Also, it examines the level at which the client's business pressure and the needs are missed given a situation where a platform is operated in future. As for SECOs, the plan pressure for its products releases on various client's needs on the key stone to be used as the platform in early development phases (Barbosa & Alves, 2011).

Product line engineering (PLE) attracts a lot of challenges during the system operation. PLE for SECOs in the platform opening approach requires the core clients' needs that differ based on the business objectives. They are involved in architecture decision making in that the coming to mutual agreements ends in the ideal manner plus takes significant amount of time. On top, users develop required use case to help the operation. The cases are not completely fixed right from the start, something that gives it a great challenge. Its mission to meet the different as well as partially unknown needs led to SECO to an optimistic opening element that helps in support of various concepts. There are large numbers of interfaces that are publicly accessible plus they are implemented extensibility. Such development context delivers more than a single element to get the same goal.

In connection with the difficult to gather data on how clients are using the platform plus the not yet matured architecture guidance and governance aspects, technical debt accumulates through unintentional dependencies, inconsistencies, and unexpected platform usages. The process of maturing operates iteratively in respect to the client's feedback yet, because of the future driven development. Its remediation works on technical debt that needs strong arguments for the benefit of its removal. In most cases, it changes without proper customer benefit that proves difficult situations to make negotiation. Its business impact requires to be argued to the management product of all the affected organizational units. The primary focus on that element is to make realization of features of the customer request. Systematic and explicit management of technical debt is identified as of the core issues to get transparency plus get informed decisions (Dos Santos & Werner, 2011).

Technical Integration

The challenge with technical integration is all about architecture measures and process that requires to be used to help customers to use their applications into the platform. Basing on the product line engineering at this case, the keystone plus clients core develops a common set of products that are distributed jointly. In that way, synergies among client applications do generate added aspects for clients. Customers in most cases require expanding the platform with different specs functionality that is not provided as commonality. Study shows that all the applications used for such elements require to be integrated deeply into all layers of the architecture whenever the organization uses or applies its operations. There are certain cases where it required managing the integration among customer or client applications. They do increase complexity in different levels. It is clear that the deep integration used implies dependencies that do restrict independent development. Another thing is that the coupled product release schedules strong interconnected architecture requiring short integration cycles plus comprehensive understating of the contributions (Lungu, 2009).

Most researchers in the field of software engineering have various responsibilities and duties to integrate the applications. They have the capacity to select the best integration frequency independently. In most practice aspects, the need for added features, feedback, and improved call for achieving short integration cycles. It has been discovered that they shorten of the comparatively long loops that develops critical factors for decision so as to become a core customer. Despite that the platform is not explicitly aligned with the measured customer elements, requirements inevitably results in much more integration efforts. Awareness on such plus ideal measures are essential for customer success at all levels. For example, in a situation with proactive investigations about a quarter of work towards contributing to platform development plays a significant role. There are those client-consumer related applications that are not only developed upon the platform, but they are also on top of various core applications that get to be reused. It is believed that they are the applications that were initially not meant or designed as platform; hence they have no stability guarantees and they also lack supporting architecture (Zacharias & Gianni, 2008).

SECO comprises various extended core consumers with autonomous software engineering life cycles that decoupled release schedules. It's something that reuses selected core assets of the platform within the organization setting. In that way, it is true that there is the need for integration processes plus architecture measures that helps them to independently use their applications towards the provided sets of the core assets. On top, these applications also require to integrate existing components that are required for the reuse. Research shows that there still exists the challenge to cope with interoperability, as some of the existing components are designed and developed for various runtime software engineering infrastructures (Jansen, Cusumano, & Brinkkemper, 2013).

Independent Platform Development

Study shows that independent platform development aims the capacity of platform to develop independently. It's a platform that in most cases requires incorporating new features to satisfy the requirements of its clients. On the same, the outdated features require to be removed so as to keep the technicality of the platform within the system manageable. The most challenging situation in this case is that the accumulated technical debt requires being re-factored (Urban, Bakshi, Grubb, Baral, & Mitsch, 2010). Experts claim that the architecture problem is twofold hence it needs proper strategies in order to come up with a clear and sound strategy. In the first place, the keystone needs to be considered dependences to customer applications, something that restrict the keystone's possibilities of system action. The second thing is that breaking changes at all levels must be managed plus communicated because they require to be developed out incrementally. It's something that goes over a long period to provide clients enough time to use their applications in the best and appropriate manner (Adamides & Mouzakitis, 2009).

Dependency management is a great challenge in SECOs as mentioned above. The optimistic opening approach shows a vast level of interfaces accessible at any start of the system software engineering. Based on the initially lacking elements, the technology ecosystem of architecture eroded as customers applied non-matured or in case improper interfaces, in various parts explicitly accepted by the keystone because of the lack of the alternatives. It's something that led to undesired dependencies that decreases the overall evolution capability of the system platform. As one of the main element in the maturing process, the concept had become more clear something that interfaces need to be exposed to concerned parties. In the current times, there is the need not to widen the platform relatively, in respect to client's feedback. On top, the reactive closure necessitates refactoring activities that generally do require interfaces plus if the situations have commodities needed by the system. Within the software engineering for technology ecosystems, keystones in the first place need to provide the best alternatives (Dos Santos & Werner, 2011).

So as to handle and deal with the challenge in the required manner, study shows that there is great need to manage all the dependencies explicitly. In other words, the existing dependencies require to be removed incrementally at the time when alternatives are available. Something else on top of this is that new undesired dependencies require to be tracked and they are only allowed temporality based on explicit consultation. In that case, consensus between all parties affected is needed as the existing keystone relies on the client's cooperation as adherence to architecture guidelines that may not be strictly enforced. Another challenge is the issue of breaking changes something that its interfaces may not be kept static and requires evolving over given time. In that way, the keystone must ensure that breaking changes for the elements linked to interfaces that are explicitly intended for client use. Study has it that breaking changes not only concerns the syntax for there are times when non-functional aspects, such as assumptions and behavior do turn out to become the key challenge (Barbosa & Alves, 2011).

As consensus is by all means desired, the core clients become veto in the system adaptation where they manage to provide conclusive arguments and used at the right point. It also have the need to establish change process that do allow various negotiation and communicate changes that are ahead of time of adjustments to offer clients the opportunity to assess the impact, hence align and vote their application when a mutual agreement is established.

As for platform reuse for SECO, the platform evolves at time when needed by the firm of the core clients. At the case when the adaptation breaks applications of consumer clients, the same elements become operational for the designed system. However, the key keystone used in the ecosystem tries to establish their needs plus platform adaptations. They are not appropriate at times when they endanger the firm success of the clients and other parties. The main difficult and issue is rooted in the various business cases, where the low influence in platform decisions and scope, for SECO which is the large organization distance. Study indicates that keystone does not allow on the interface dependencies of parties to the platform. So as to consider them, there is the need to offer the exact information to the parties along with the estimates of the impact of a potential adaptation of the system used by the organization (Lungu, 2009).

The element of breaking changes linked to core clients develops semantic changes turned out to be the key problem. Just as mentioned earlier, clients and customers are parties of low priority. In such a manner, they do have the possibility to veto changes as much more restrained. In ensuring that the entire thing functions in the required angle, parties restrict the independence of system keystone only to a limited extent and operation for the system.

Independent Application Development

At the time of developing software engineering for technological ecosystems, it is clear that a good number of clients are self-contained in respect to profit centers. The focus is to preserve the independence for being in a position to optimally get their objectives. In that way, there are those clients who chose to explicitly decouple on their development form the keystone. It helps fulfill on their varying business cases so as to reduce the impact of platform adaptations. More of that, not all changes and features needed may be processed through the help of the keystone in an instant manner. For innovations even if there is reuse potential among parties, sometimes they do side with customers and clients. So as to help reuse afterwards, the innovations either requires to be given over to concerned parties plus need to be shared directly with other clients (Popp & Meyer, 2010).

One main issue on this concept is the decoupling of the software engineering for technological ecosystems. The core clients and keystone in this case develop products that are common and they are jointly distributed. In that way, synergies do get and generate added value for the clients. The decoupling of customer applications is at all times partially desired. Customers at times require decoupling so as to optimally achieve their objectives plus reduce the impact of platform changes. Change requests and feature plays a significant role. There exist limited crucial challenges for both ISECOs for the keystone development capacities. Working as a bottleneck the keystone might slow down the innovation potential of the entire ecosystem. Various customers call for plenty of platform adaptation as well as features (Urban, Bakshi, Grubb, Baral, & Mitsch, 2010).

The reusable and generic implementation within the platform of the ecosystem is always time consuming. Commonalities do not get realized most of times on customer side. In fact, keystone aspect may frequently not satisfy the great demand at all time, something that results to in long waiting times. Consequently, at some instances, customers of both ISECOs tend to develop the needed innovations with platform impact by themselves based on the ecosystem requirements. Clients at times want to reuse those developments afterwards. It helps reuse the exchange mechanisms that get needed so that the either keystone may incorporate the innovations into the platform. At that level, clients do share the innovations directly among each other. The situation is a challenge that mostly affects the ideal platform for the ecosystem activities plus related development plans by the clients (Barbosa & Alves, 2011).

The architecture challenges at times turn twofold. In the first place, the transfer does implicate loss of control plus the effort for the ecosystem at large. The second thing is the keystone required to incorporate the element into the platform without the aspect of breaking applications developed upon. The aspect has challenged various experts for there has not been immediate benefit for other customers who still operate with the old variant of components. Due to such aspect, the keystone requires have a better platform that allows maintenance of both variants of the ecosystem. So as to reduce the maintenance effort, the old components requires discontinuation in its future operations. Customers do either require adapting their code or do take over the maintenance for the old components (Bosch, 2009).

As mentioned earlier, platform adaptations generally get performed what they get needed by the core business platform. The change process is with no means aligned with the needs of customer. Instead, it has to take the initiative so as to get informed about changes plus estimate the exerted impact. The resultant high effort from the changes more so for those that were not announced in due time, is a challenge that all clients get concerned when they are in need of the ecosystem activities. Study shows that, the situation is the most crucial element for clients to turn into core customers. As a result, clients must decouple all the applications they have to a large extent so as to reduce the impact of changes, even if it's at the expense of other qualities such as lower performance. It's believed that the changing interface of the entire evolving platform resulted in adaptation effort plus the final decision that calls refactor of the application that is less dependent on the platform (Jansen, Cusumano, & Brinkkemper, 2013).

When clients decouple their applications right from the start, there are some who initially builds their application directly upon the platform. The changing interfaces of the evolving platform results in the adaptation effort plus the final decision towards refactor application of the dependent platform. Because of the low funding of the deliveries, large firms distance additional features plus the changes that requires to get requested officially. In some instances with the top management support of the company, there are things that become technical to operate in a suitable manner. These are of lower priority plus processed dependent on the current work load that is for the core business as well as the urgency of the request. It often results in long waiting times and requests that may lack processed at all, hence requires workarounds by the consumer of the system (Lungu, Lanza, Gîrba, & Robbes, 2010).

All the extended core customers have a different business case plus partially needs to design decisions different that is from the keystone's recommendations. Clients may want to execute core assets to the dedicated processes, without the use of the container which offers keystone elements. The focus in such a setting is on the degree of independence to the extended core clients required for fulfilling business cases as well as the level of error sources get provoked through the additional flexibility. It is a controversial issue that most parties of the collaboration model discuss. Independence is a relevant characteristic that the keystone needs to enable for more architecture so as to hinder architecture erosion that the additional ecosystem flexibility enables (Popp & Meyer, 2010). Based on the study developed by experts, the limited development capacities on the keystone are crucial problems for the collaboration model. On top, the keystone's core competence does not exist in the application domain of extended core customers. Given that several customers requires or wants the same feature, the work of keystone might not be able to offer it in a better manner. In summary, same to PLE for ISECO, there is the need to establish the features on the client side, suitable at collaborative aspects across client organizational units (Adamides & Mouzakitis, 2009).

Qualities

Another problem within the technological ecosystem aspect in software engineering is the quality aspect. Products developed within the ecosystem consist of developments of various firm units. The compliance with quality requirements entirely requires to get managed across all parties involved. Most of the prominent qualities are the system developers' habitability as well as maintainability with regard to the internal software reliability and quality. Memory utilization and time behavior utilization with respect to the external software quality also forms part of the basics. Internal software quality focuses on the varying needs of the various clients that requires for generic highly extendable and configurable platform. Such a move happens by means of metadata as well as internal domain specific languages under which it exists limited tool support for the ecosystem. For the two ISECOs, it leads to an uncomfortable and error-prone development context for metadata plus DSLs. The error sources are not obvious and they do only identified by means of time consuming debugging (Urban, Bakshi, Grubb, Baral, & Mitsch, 2010).

On top, the resulting complexity extends the settling in periods for new developers during system development. Most of the interviewees claim that there exist the needs to focus on a more habitable development environment that do support developers. Such a move allows understanding the intentions and construction of the system in such a mover. Customers feel the need for the support of efficiency by providing more developer governance and guidance with an early feedback. The respective issues are specific to the development context plus the creation of system plus maintenance of counteractive measures, like the tool support which might cost the company more than expected (Bosch, 2009).

Interviewed architects platform considers it important to strive for consistent internal quality as well as balance it with feature development of the software engineering for technological ecosystem. The external quality issues that exist with direct customer as well as product management visibility tend to have more attraction. For the purpose of achieving transparency, there exists the need for getting quality model that does correlate respective measures that is relevant for the product objectives of the firm. Core customers develop applications on a common platform aspect and do shares available resources for technology ecosystem (Lungu, 2009). So as to preserve the reliability of the software engineering ecosystem, there is the need to ensure that applications at all levels not impair each other. For the elements of the system, the above situation leads to challenges that relates to time behavior plus memory utilization. It requires the keystones for the management of resource consumption, such as restrict memory use of the system developed. Memory utilization, time behavior and reliability are the required qualities the interviewees get concerned at all times (Barbosa & Alves, 2011).

In frequent ways, the quality issues do not arise or come up with some development angles until several levels of applications gets extensions. In such a manner, they require to get handled jointly by the multiple clients and keystone. As for the both ISECOs, there is the need to establish guide developers with quality patterns. On further explanation, there exist the need for measures that do allow visualizing and effecting and causes of quality challenges across firms unit. It is something that requires explanations and should not be done close. All measures within ecosystem ensure that proper explanations get those who are for self-interest. It also carries out the aspect of analyzing effects and causes of various and quality challenges across organization units. It is something done close to point in time where code gets created so as to offer assistance to all the developers with unique and early feedback for the technological ecosystems (Urban, Bakshi, Grubb, Baral, & Mitsch, 2010).

Based on the conducts of developers' habitability, it's something similar as for core clients. The challenge develops in that measures and platform do not explicitly gear to the needs of consumer clients. For example, at times where some interfaces reveal too much aspect or do not play any role, it means that some needed functionality is missing from the ecosystem software engineering system. It is something that may result in the orientation points for the system developers. The low priority for the system support, complicate the identification of suitable contact persons, the access to architecture, and the larger organizational distance counts for a suitable setting and platform. Based on the issue of habitability with software engineering for technological ecosystems, the end client user's architecture operates in charge so as to get the alignment for the government with the trusted developers and the needs at hard (Adamides & Mouzakitis, 2009).

Compliant Software Development

Compliant software development is an aspect that generally looks or relates to the challenges and problems discussed in the previous sections. The aspect targets regulations that require proper focus on the ecosystem. It also examines the execution and establishment of architecture so as to help and check for compliance. Study shows that it is something that requires deciding on topics that are relevant for the ecosystem, for deciding on processes as similar to execute the system and defines responsibilities and roles the system definitions. That moves helps understand the ecosystem and supports the operation of various components. One of the issue in this case is the aspect of topic decide. Major topics get covered by all challenges established so far and target intended platform reuse. The issue that requires to get regulated across the company platform requires suitable measures; for example coding styles, interface changes, and architecture dependencies (Popp & Meyer, 2010). An important element towards the development of compliance is through having the firm enabled for the compliance exercising. In that way, benefits and costs need transparent to all firm units upfront and areas agreed. Something that counts is to establish a consistent understanding and consensus on the topics plus the respective regulations. Various expectations may lead to effort on all sides of the development. For example, in software engineering for technological ecosystems, there are no consistent understandings on the parts of the platform those servers as sample application alone. They are not intended for the direct reuse at whatever cost. It leads to the undesired dependences, in which in the current times increases maintenance effort.

One step important towards establishment of compliance is on ways to have the organization enabled that looks at exercise compliance of the technological eco-system software. Based on that, benefits and costs requires transparent to all firm units upfront as well as agreed. The most common thing that matters is to develop a consistent consensus and understanding on respective regulations and topics as per client request. Different system expectations lead to effort on all sides (Hossain, Bujang, Zakaria, & Hashim, 2015). As for the PLE for ISECO, decide on measures and processes forms another major area of focus. So as to enable and facilitate compliant software development, there exists the need for communication within architectural intentions plus the imposed regulations. Study show that the standard that is applied based on the management of technical knowledge is expectably high compared to the decentralized context or nature of the component. It's claimed that relevant information requires to be tailored plus communicated coherently based on the varying development use cases of all firm units.

It is important to come up with a process that does support architecture G&G activities. The activities execution calls for an effective collaboration across organizational units. More on that, there is the need to offer tools that helps govern developers for compliance, then foster their mindset through an early feedback plus motivate them through defined goals as well as continuous improvement activities. There exists the need to offer tools to support architectures to systematically and continuously put some level of monitoring. For the purpose of reducing the effort, compliance process must have some level of automation where possible at all times. Manual checks like reviews are then unavoidable since the expert knowledge is often needed. As the establishment of processes and tools is based on time consuming, the active contribution by the clients is required.

Since such a move is consensus in respect to the environment, some strict measures must apply to help people adhere to the standards and guidelines. Such a move helps in the operational field because it's not all guidelines may be forced across the ecosystem platform. Study shows that it is the sole responsibility of those firm units to maintain compliance at whatever cost. Apart from that, it is necessary to form an organizational mindset towards compliance. Schedule and feature pressure within the two ISECOs regularly results to the violations by several organizational units. This requires countermeasures so as to avoid architecture erosion. More on that, regulations, measures, and processes are not fully defined at the start of the project establishment. They are evolved progressively as the project develops over the time. More on that aspect, there is the need to accept for pragmatism if need arise. Although violations must get managed explicitly so as to keep the issue in mind plus remedy them incrementally later on the project completion.

Dimension Architecture

The first dimension in the software engineering for technological ecosystems is based on the firm, and the scope levels of SSNs as compared to the level of SECO for it focuses on the platform element. The dimension used in this case focuses at understanding the way SE is used to develop platform conception, maintenance, and development based on the following steps.

Step 1: Contextual Platform Development and Project: The first step comprises a number of activities that helps in the development of the proposed system. It corresponds to the concept of system analysis phase that is conducted through three main activities. Select platform is the first activity that represents a suitable decision point in selecting a platform for the purpose of the study and depends on the SECO boundary. The second activity is the process of identifying roles something that aims at defining the actors of the system. It also considers the different elements that were previously pointed by the business ecosystem literature at the specialization of a business ecosystem. Analysis of health is the final activity in the first stem and helps quantify a number of elements within system indicator (Adomavicius, Bockstedt, Gupta, & Kauffman, 2012).

Step 2: Plan the system Process: It is a step that corresponds to the system platform and usually helps during the design phase after the above activities are complete. The step also has three activities namely specification of levels, delineate factors, and the last activity is the define licenses. The step is more of a design phase for the software engineering for technological ecosystems. These activities help restrict the participation of the actors that exist in the platform through the obligations and rights that allow governance of the system process towards opening the ideal architecture (Zacharias & Gianni, 2008).

Step 3: Balances Architecture Transparency and Modularity: Within the software engineering implementation phase, various activities are completed. The step comprises of various activities that offer direction on how to perform and undertake all the ideal aspects. It consists of defining all the platform accessibility mechanism and extension that develops conditions that govern the entire system (Adamides & Mouzakitis, 2009).

SOLUTIONS AND RECOMMENDATIONS

There are various limitations that have developed in this study and different recommendations and solutions have been developed to provide a better and conclusive platform for the technology ecosystems. Limitations and generality elements covered in this study offer a suitable explanation on the software engineering towards the operations of technological ecosystems within organization. One of the main solutions to the above challenges is by handling and focusing on the threats towards construct validity. It's something that concerns the relation that exists between observation and theory of software engineering. Interviews are developed that relates to the statements made by participants and that have the capacity to develop elements of subjectivity (Bosch, 2009). So as to limit the effects, findings are based exclusively on statements that are confirmed by multiple interviews. Moreover, questions of interview might be handled in various ways by interviewees and researchers. A better way to handle such a move is through reflecting on the notion of decentralized software engineering. The move aims at the established projects as well as collaboration focused at the start of project operation. On matters of completeness, we tend to close each session with open forum to check whether there are problems that the project needs to handle and discuss on time (Behrens & Dicerbo, 2014).

Focusing on threats to internal validity is another recommendation based on the limitations and generality of SECOs. The element concerns the co-elements that might influence the results of the software engineering platform. In this case, participants may provide information on their responses that slightly fail to reflect on the reality as they were recorded. For the purpose of addressing this situation, experts conducts and ensures anonymity and assures that they do seek for ideal and relevant feedback on conclusions to avoid misunderstandings. The results in this case might be biased since researchers tend to focus on interviewed architects and there are no other roles. Because of the high level of firm units, the concept was necessary to establish the effort manageable in software engineering. It is clear that all architects involved must be experienced, in central positions of system operations, and they must work closely together with organization product developers and managers. Research indicates that they must consider each and every level that is used in the software engineering for technological ecosystems (Dos Santos & Werner, 2011).

Threats to conclusion validity have been a major concern towards challenges affecting software engineering. The element concerns the relationship between results and treatment. Since the concept developed is a qualitative aspect, data analysis used depends on the approach used for interpretations. Main work during project operation helps to develop better and conclusive results that offer ideal results. Recommended methods help to improve quality, like the triangulation, spending sufficient time with the cases, member checking, and study protocols (Popp & Meyer, 2010).

Various recommendations in relations to studies show that a lot needs to be established in the software engineering for technological ecosystems. Another concept is the threats to external validity something that concerns the generalization of the results from the system operations. In most cases, various elements are investigated so as to provide a suitable and conclusive result to the project developed. With no doubts, it has been discovered that there are chances that there are some results that are specific compared to others. Findings from this study stem from features of the respective collaboration models plus it doesn't depend on technologies, tools, and programming language used during software development. Most of the findings are confirmed by data of various independent firm units, where the interviewees' level of professional experience becomes the central point of focus. In this case, it's believed that different findings do also hold for other SECOs that use similar collaboration models (Lungu, Lanza, Gîrba, & Robbes, 2010).

FUTURE RESEARCH DIRECTIONS

Discussed proposal above gives a framework that allows and guides to deeper researches that relate to the support of software engineering for technology ecosystems. Results offered in the analysis give points out the various concepts offered; hence it can be realized that understanding software engineering for technology ecosystems calls joining a lot of unstable IT elements in an entity concept. It adds software engineering elements that later affects concepts during the ecosystems maintenance, development, and creation. Future work in this field consists of expanding the applied proposal with other research concepts plus integrates it to the other two aspects in a unified engineering platform. Above that, future work should support component-based architecture software engineering for technology ecosystems and its development for the tool has more mechanism with the potential to help social and business dimensions (Lungu, Lanza, Gîrba, & Robbes, 2010).

CONCLUSION

Due to the lack of applied research and theoretical concept in SECOs management based on software engineering point of view, various things have changed in this field to make it better established in academic research. The above discussion offers a better proposal for software engineering for technological systems to offer set of steps that contains three different dimensions of SECOs plus joins various existing perspectives in the field and research literature through an ideal survey. Preliminary contribution of this concept was establish understanding on how software engineering for technology ecosystems is treated plus integrates the works offered at the two first IWSECO platforms. The key focus in the first instance is architecture while the others are studied as well as linked to the architecture since it might in some ways become impossible to treat pure engineering concept (Adomavicius, Bockstedt, Gupta, & Kauffman, 2012).

Intra firm has a decentralized software projects that do involve various self-contained organizational units that requires suitable architectural measures instead of detailed managerial orders that ensures proper coordination is achieved during project operations. Having conducted and developed a high in-depth case on the software engineering for technological ecosystems that indicates architecture challenges, results have it decentralized software projects calls for proper operations must be put in place. Three collaboration models were established that ranged from low to high coupling (Jansen, Cusumano, & Brinkkemper, 2013). In each of the models, there were identified a range of recurring condensed and issues that accounted for the future progress. The approach enabled practitioners who finds themselves in one of the system models, hence carefully reason towards suitable architecture measures that are developed. More on that, practitioners outline a high broad field of real world on system challenges that requires to be investigated through future and further research in the field of software engineering for technological ecosystems (Popp & Meyer, 2010).

REFERENCES

Adamides, E. D., & Mouzakitis, Y. (2009). Industrial ecosystems as technological niches. *Journal of Cleaner Production*, *17*(2), 172–180. doi:10.1016/j.jclepro.2008.04.003

Adomavicius, G., Bockstedt, J., Gupta, A., & Kauffman, R. J. (2012). Understanding Evolution in Technology Ecosystems. *Communications of the ACM*, *51*(10), 117–122. doi:10.1145/1400181.1400207

Barbosa, O., & Alves, C. (2011). A Systematic Mapping Study on Software Ecosystems.*Proceedings of the Workshop on Software Ecosystems*.

Behrens, J. T., & Dicerbo, K. E. (2014). Technological Implications for Assessment Ecosystems: Opportunities for Digital Technology to Advance Assessment. *Teachers College Record*, *116*(11), 1–22. PMID:26120219

Bosch, J. (2009). From Software Product Lines to Software Ecosystems. *Proceedings of the13th International Software Product Line Conference*. Carnegie Mellon University.

Dos Santos, R. P., & Werner, C. M. L. (2011). A Proposal for Software Ecosystems Engineering. In *Proceedings of the Workshop on Software Ecosystems*.

Hossain, M. S., Bujang, J. S., Zakaria, M. H., & Hashim, M. (2015). The application of remote sensing to seagrass ecosystems: An overview and future research prospects. *International Journal of Remote Sensing*, *36*(1), 61–114. doi:10.1080/01431161.2014.990649

Jansen, S., Cusumano, M. A., & Brinkkemper, S. (2013). *Software Ecosystems: Analyzing and Managing Business Networks in the Software Industry*. Edward Elgar Publishing. doi:10.4337/9781781955635

Lungu, M., Lanza, M., Gîrba, T., & Robbes, R. (2010). The small project observatory: Visualizing software ecosystems. *Science of Computer Programming*, *75*(4), 264–275. doi:10.1016/j.scico.2009.09.004

Lungu, M. F. (2009). *Reverse Engineering Software Ecosystems*. (Doctoral dissertation). University of Lugano.

Popp, K., & Meyer, R. (2010). *Profit from Software Ecosystems: Business Models*. Norderstedt, Germany: Ecosystems and Partnerships in the Software Industry.

Still, K., Huhtamäki, J., Russell, M. G., & Rubens, N. (2014). Insights for orchestrating innovation ecosystems: The case of EIT ICT Labs and data-driven network visualisations. *International Journal of Technology Management*, *66*(2-3), 243–265. doi:10.1504/IJTM.2014.064606

Urban, R. A., Bakshi, B. R., Grubb, G. F., Baral, A., & Mitsch, W. J. (2010). Towards sustainability of engineered processes: Designing self-reliant networks of technological–ecological systems. *Computers & Chemical Engineering*, *34*(9), 1413–1420. doi:10.1016/j.compchemeng.2010.02.026

Chapter 8
Knowledge Structuring for Sustainable Development and the Hozo Tool

Jenny S. Huang
iFOSSF, USA

Kouji Kozaki
Osaka University, Japan

Terukazu Kumazawa
Research Institute for Humanity and Nature, Japan

ABSTRACT

The search for more actionable knowledge lies at the core of Sustainability Science and its implicit desire to improve the lives of various stakeholders without disrupting the balance of Nature and efficient use of all available resources. In this chapter, the authors have examined current shortfalls in knowledge-centric research and proposed the creation of an Ontology-based open-source tool to create a more practical approach for researchers to facilitate both thought and decision-making process in order to solve pressing issues with place-based actions. The effectiveness of the Hozo Tool is then examined and validated using four case studies in an attempt to both refine the current models and propose the necessary steps to create a more holistic knowledge ecosystem – one that might ultimately facilitate broader collaboration worldwide.

DOI: 10.4018/978-1-5225-0905-9.ch008

INTRODUCTION

While every scientific discipline aims to either create or discover new knowledge, there are specific attributes associated with Sustainability Science. This paper discusses knowledge management in the context of collaborative Sustainable Development projects.

Why is this topic important? According to Kates (2010), "Sustainability science is science, technology, and innovation in support of sustainable development—meeting human needs, reducing hunger and poverty, while maintaining the life support systems of the planet." Like agricultural and health sciences, Sustainable Science is use-driven, which means its methods are both integrative and translational in that they seek to link knowledge with action.

Instead of merely limiting itself to knowledge creation, Sustainability Science places greater emphasis on translating that knowledge into appropriate actions. According to Kates, it is a "field that is defined by the problems it addresses rather than by the disciplines it employs". In other words, it is use-inspired research as opposed to curiosity-driven research; where the solutions to a problem will often require multi-interdisciplinary stakeholders working together to achieve an more holistic understanding of the problem space to discover potential solutions.

Sustainable development projects are also place-based, meaning that the exact needs and solutions to any given problem will vary from place to place. Most of its case studies are snapshots of place and time. Knowledge retention is therefore crucial to successful outcomes. Just as best practices harvested from previous projects should be used as a foundation for new project development, prior local customization and refinements should also be applied to future projects to achieve resource efficiency. In addition, the knowledge management of Sustainability Science should always consider both local and global factors.

In summary, Sustainability Science and Sustainable Development projects consist of use-inspired research that focuses on finding solutions to targeted world problems. They are place-based and there is no one-size-fits-all solution. They aim to provide integrative understanding among multi-disciplinary stakeholders and to transform knowledge into action.

Based on the aforementioned attributes of sustainable development projects, this paper will seek to explore the benefits of a knowledge ecosystem that would help facilitate both the thought and decision-making process for appropriate place-based actions, with the ultimate goal of creating more shareable knowledge globally. An Ontology-based Open Source tool will be introduced, along with four case studies, to validate this hypothesis. Finally, several recommendations are provided on future research for the aforementioned creation of this knowledge ecosystem.

BACKGROUND

Sustainability Science is still a relatively new field, there is currently no well-established curriculum or infrastructure to facilitate multi-stakeholder knowledge creation and action. As a result, many of the Sustainable Development projects are still taking a silo approach – one in which researchers and scholars attempt to gain knowledge first and then figure out how that knowledge can be transformed into community action. In other words, many development projects take a top-down approach, one where end-user needs are not fully explored until much later in the process. The SEED Framework (Huang, Hsueh, & Reynolds, 2013) argues for a different approach: that is, creating a framework to foster an environment that channels the creativity of the community towards discovering opportunities for development. It assumes a knowledge-based approach that leverages global intelligence and then refines it for place-based applications and new-knowledge development. Its global and local multi/interdisciplinary development model can be implemented using the following six iterative steps for a knowledge driven innovation lifecycle.

Figure 1. Community focused innovation and knowledge ecosystem
Huang, Hsueh, & Reynolds, 2013.

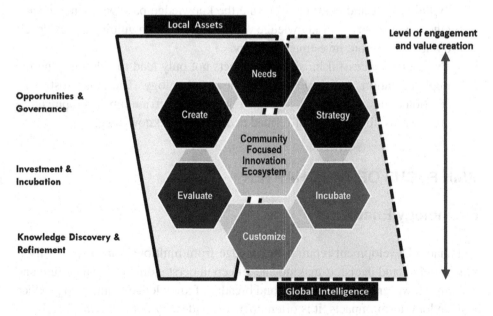

1. **Needs/Opportunities:** Start by identifying and taking inventory of local community needs and opportunities. Needs are captured in a semantically rich knowledge base to assist ongoing evaluation and to identify opportunities for development. Common needs from different communities are indicators of implementation priorities, as well as ways to reduce redundant investments.
2. **Strategy:** Global and local stakeholders can then jointly perform business analysis and modeling for value-based partnership ecosystems to find partners and build multidisciplinary teams. Governments, NGOs, businesses, trustees and research organizations can build on the knowledge base to both identify and organize target business cases.
3. **Incubation:** In this phase, stakeholders can leverage and identify existing research, appropriate technologies and best practices from the knowledge base in any given problem area. Partners and key stakeholders can then begin to define the project scope, investment, and execution strategy based on evidence from current data, policies and stakeholder inputs on both a local and global level.
4. **Customization/Localization:** Customize leveraged research, technology and best practices to suit local conditions and competences. In this phase, it will be important to continue to document the findings of local implementation in order to share new knowledge with similar communities in the future, thus reducing redundant investment.
5. **Evaluation:** Use benchmarks and metrics to determine the impact created by the project and continue to refine the knowledge base with findings and outcomes. This type of knowledge will be invaluable in guiding policy development and future investment strategy.
6. **Creation:** Successful incubation projects not only lead to solutions and the implementation and deployment of new technology. They also foster the creation of new businesses, jobs and educational curriculum development. In other words, the creation of refined and actionable knowledge.

MAIN FOCUS OF THE CHAPTER

Technology Enablers

Sustainable Development requires knowledge from multiple domains, interdisciplinary policy and decision-making and a deep understanding of local culture and customs. However, due to the depth and breadth of knowledge required to produce positive long-term impacts, it is often difficult to identify not only which problem to solve, but how best to solve it (Kumazawa, Saito, Kozaki, Matsui, & Mizoguchi, 2009).

A shift to promoting the local assets of the community has the potential to form a system that will facilitate inter-disciplinary problem solving and creative solution development. This knowledge base would be created by incorporating user-inspired research and proposing solutions that would be produced, implemented and tailored to local needs to create a field that is ultimately defined by the problem it addresses. This, however, presupposes the need for a new scientific discipline and ontology framework; one that takes into account all elements of local culture and includes social, environmental, and economic considerations.

Since the problems addressed in Sustainability Science relate to stakeholders and players from many different fields, the problem-solving process would naturally require the collaboration and partnership of all these players. Structuring this knowledge would in itself be an important task for Sustainability Science, as only a comprehensive strategy could address such complex and evolving problems. Understanding would also require consistent exploratory inquiry into a multitude of relevant domains, as well as networking those concepts in order to adapt to dynamic changes both within and between domains. In other words, researchers cannot meet the challenges of 'what to solve' and 'how to solve it' only by structuring knowledge. Knowledge structuring would need to support thinking processes as well (Kumazawa et al., 2014a).

Ontology Exploration for Collective Thinking Process

The models for knowledge management has been a long studied subject and real world practice for the academia and business alike, to best harness the collective intelligence to enhance organization performance ("Knowledge Management and Business Model Innovation," 2000). With the increasing proliferation and maturity of the Information and Communication Technologies (ICT) and the use of open source, the studies have turned into the emergence of applying processes, technologies combined with crowdsourcing to effectively create a knowledge ecosystem that span across personal and organizational boundaries. (Rubio, 2004), (Garcia-Holgado, 2014)

The knowledge management for sustainable development has its own challenges for the characteristics that described earlier. Developed at MIT, the Global System for Sustainable Development (GSSD) is one current example of a Sustainable Development knowledge base. It is a system that determines 'what to solve' by focusing on the content architecture levels, linkages and complexities that characterize the domain of 'sustainability'.

However, the challenge of Sustainability Science lies in identifying 'how to solve' the problems derived from the first challenge. Since these problems relate to various stakeholders from many different fields, the problem-solving process naturally requires the collaboration and partnership of these same players. Thus, while structuring knowledge is important in Sustainability Science, that alone cannot provide a comprehensive understanding when addressing complex and evolving problems. Instead, understanding requires consistent exploratory inquiry into a multitude of relevant domains in order to flexibly adapt to dynamic changes both within and between domains. In this paper, we introduced an ontology-based approach to address these challenges.

The reference model depicted in Figure 2 (Kumazawa et al., 2009) uses an ontology-based approach, which was proposed in the paper entitled "Toward knowledge structuring of sustainability science based on ontology engineering."

Layer 0: Refers to the Data layer. It stores raw data corresponding to the real world.
Layer 1: Refers to the Ontology layer. It stores the ontology for explaining and understanding the raw data in Layer 0. The ontology in this layer describes the concepts and relationships related to Sustainability Science that exist in the

Figure 2. A reference model for knowledge structuring in Sustainability Science using ontology
Kumazawa et al., 2009.

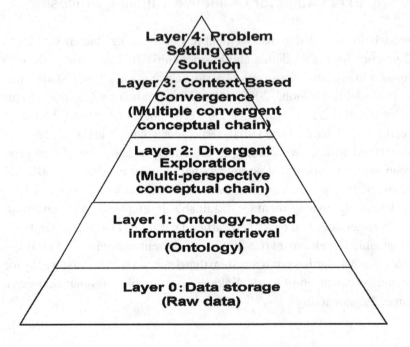

real world. However, some kind of guidance is needed to both support problem identification and to generate the ideas needed to solve Sustainability Science problems (Guilford 1950, 1967). However, the most innovative approach of this knowledge structure framework lies in Layer 2 & 3.

Layer 2: Refers to the Divergent Thinking layer 2. Layer 2 handles the dynamic information that reflects individual perspectives. The main task supported by this layer is the divergent exploration of the conceptual world realized in Layer 1. In Layer 2, the users explore the ontology from a variety of perspectives according to their own intentions. Because the ontology consists of both concepts and relationships, this exploration is achieved by choosing concepts and relationships that are of interest to them. As a result, they obtain a set of concepts with relationships among them. This is what is referred to as multi-perspective conceptual chains. Please note that these conceptual chains reflect their way of thinking.

Layer 3: Refers to the Convergent Thinking layer. Having reached this layer, the explorer can set the specific context to a problem that he or she actually treats and obtain 'multiple convergent conceptual chains' in accordance to the given context (Klein 2004). How to decide the contexts for convergent thinking in this layer is very important. It depends on the purpose of the convergence. For instance, in order to support consensus building among stakeholders, comparison among conceptual chains generated by them can be effective. In other cases, focusing on some combination of different paths may be useful to find an important chain.

Layer 4: Refers to the Problem Setting and Solution layer. Using all of the information and knowledge obtained from each sub layer, the explorer will pursue essential problem-solving tasks. This includes setting the conditions for solving a problem, searching for a new problem or fostering information integration, innovation and the abduction of new hypotheses. In this final layer, it is important to consider comprehensive usage of results obtained in all other layers.

SOLUTIONS AND RECOMMENDATIONS

Open Source Hozo Tool

Developed with the Sustainability Science Knowledge-base Reference Model in mind, the Hozo tool (http://www.hozo.jp) is a free software tool[1] based on the fundamental theories of ontology engineering used to capture the essential conceptual structure of the target world. Ontology engineering aims to assimilate common concepts into a well-organized knowledge base. Ontology exploration tools like Hozo can facilitate holistic framing and collaboration among various stakeholders on a particular issue. By using this system, users (stakeholders) can explore various conceptual linkages regarding their specific interests and create conceptual maps that display relevant concepts with semantic links (nodes) around the focal concept.

For example, individual or community concept maps can be built either through surveys/interviews or by using more sophisticated tools, such as Hozo. Those concept maps can then be assimilated at the global/local level to explore different stakeholder viewpoints and perspectives. The goal is to build consensus among stakeholders through discussion, by using the same maps that they generated. This is quite different from most of the semantic web applications that use ontologies as vocabularies to describe metadata and which are aimed at semantic processing. The Hozo efforts regard ontology as the target for divergent exploration of the ontology itself. The divergent exploration of ontologies enables users to freely explore a wide array of concepts in the ontology from a variety of perspectives and according to their own motivations. This exploration stimulates unique thought processes and

Figure 3. Collaboration between stakeholder analysis and ontology
Kozaki et al., 2012.

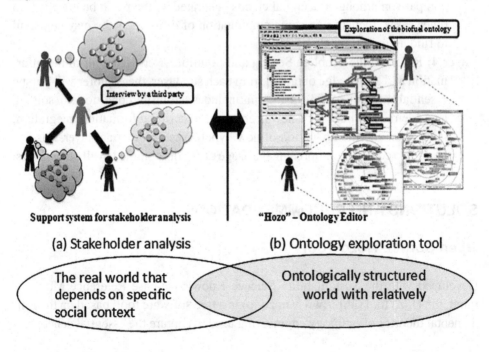

Support system for stakeholder analysis | "Hozo" – Ontology Editor

(a) Stakeholder analysis | (b) Ontology exploration tool

The real world that depends on specific social context | Ontologically structured world with relatively

ultimately contributes to a deeper understanding of the ontology and, hence, its target world.

Technical Details of Ontology Exploration Using Hozo

The divergent exploration of an Ontology can be performed by choosing arbitrary concepts from which, according to the explorer's intention, they can trace multi-perspective conceptual chains.

Figure 4 outlines the framework for ontology exploration. This chapter defines exploring the ontology and obtaining the multi-perspective conceptual chains as the interplay of the focal point and aspect. The focal point indicates the concept to which the user pays attention to as the starting point of the exploration. The aspect is the manner in which the user explores the ontology. Because ontology consists of concepts and the relationships among them, the aspect can be represented by a set of methods for extracting concepts according to its relationships. The aspect can then be represented by both a set of methods for extracting concepts according to its links and a direction to follow, either upward or downward. The multi-perspective conceptual chains are visualized in a user-friendly form – in other words, in a conceptual map.

Figure 4. Divergent exploration of ontology
Kozaki et al., 2011.

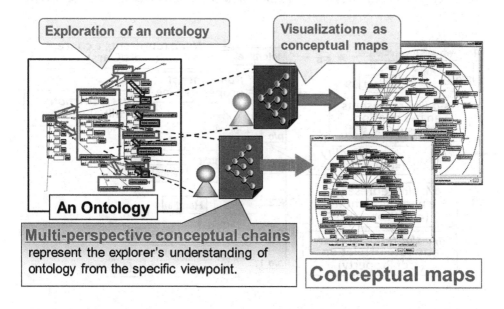

203

Here, the authors have implemented the divergent exploration of an ontology in two ways. The first is through the implementation of an additional function of Hozo, a client software using Java (Kozaki et al., 2011). The second is implementation through a Web based open-source software using a linked data technique such as RDF database and SPARQL (Kozaki et al., 2014). This section will explain the technical details common to both implementations.

Figure 5 shows an example of ontology representation in Hozo. Each concept is defined using two kinds of slots: part-of (denoted by p/o) and attribute-of (denoted by a/o). A slot consists of a role name, class constraint and cardinality - each corresponding roughly to restrictions on properties in a Resource Description Framework Schema (RDFS) and Web Ontology Language (OWL). In Figure 5, for instance, bicycle (class) has the restrictions owl:allValuesFrom Wheel and owl:cardinality 1 on the front-wheel property.

The left side of Figure 6 shows an example of a conceptual chain obtained by exploring Sustainability Science ontology, using the *destruction of regional environment* as the focal point. It shows the path *destruction of regional environment → a*ir pollution *→ sooty smoke*. In this example, the former path *destruction of regional environment → a*ir pollution is obtained by following its *is-a* link (relationship) upward, and the latter path *air pollution → sooty smoke.* is obtained by following its *external cause* link (relationship) upward. Similarly, other conceptual

Figure 5. A sample ontology representation in Hozo and its correspondence with OWL
Kozaki et al., 2011.

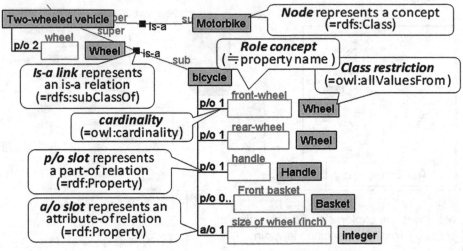

chains are also obtained through other links according to other aspects. A multi perspective conceptual chain is then obtained by combining all of them and displaying them in a user-friendly form, also known as a conceptual map (see right side of Figure 6).

The system provides the following functions for ontology explorations:

- **Manual Exploration:** The user chooses viewpoints for exploring each step by manual operation.
- **Search Path (Machine Exploration):** The system explores all combinations of conceptual chains (paths) from the selected start and end points.

Please note that the system also allows users access to post-hoc editing for extracting only interesting portions of the map. That is, the user explores ontologies using these functions in arbitrary order. In addition to these functions for explorations, the system also supports convergent thinking through the following functions:

- **Change View:** The system highlights specified paths of conceptual chains on the generated map, according to given viewpoints.
- **Comparison of Maps:** The system can compare generated maps and show the common conceptual chains on both of them.

Figure 6. An example of divergent exploration of an ontology
Kozaki et al., 2011.

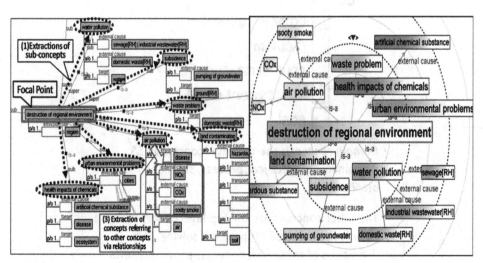

CASE STUDIES

This section discusses four case studies that demonstrate how to apply ontology exploration for the collective thinking process. Three of these studies occur in the Sustainability Science domain, while the last is a trial study to create idea support in Biomimetics. These case studies cover all the five layers discussed in the reference model of knowledge structuring in Sustainability Science using ontology (Kumazawa et al., 2009).

Case Studies 1-3: Usages of Sustainability Science Ontology

Sustainability Science ontology (SS ontology) seeks to clarify the inherent complexities and provide comprehensive approaches to solving sustainability issues (Kates et al. 2001; Kates 2011; Komiyama and Takeuchi 2006). The main characteristics of an SS ontology can be seen in its attempt to simultaneously conceptualize both its static domain and the dynamic process of problem solving as targets. Hence, two kinds of top-level concepts shall be set in the SS ontology: One is *domain concept* as a top-level concept of the SS domain and the other is *goal*, *problem*, *countermeasure*, and *assessment* as top-level concepts of problem solving (see Figure 7):

Figure 7. Top-level concepts of the SS ontology
Kumazawa et al., 2014b.

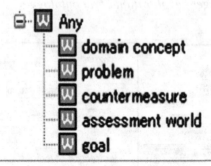

- *Domain concept* is the top-level concept of SS domain including *object, process, state* and *attribute.*

- The other concepts are the top-level concepts of the knowledge required for problem solving. The definitions of these four concepts provide criteria for classification into the sub-concepts of these.

- **Problem:** Covers problems related to sustainability.
- **Countermeasure:** Covers countermeasures implemented for problem solving.
- **Assessment:** Covers concepts to understand the present situation and state of the achievement.
- **Goal:** Covers concepts as controls for comparing with present states/ situations.

The authors then constructed an SS ontology using the Hozo ontology development tool discussed in the previous section. Hozo's greatest characteristic is its ability to deal with a role concept, which enables researchers to create a model to explicate what roles are played. For example, human, fruits or heating oil can play the role of teacher, food and fuel respectively. Making full use of this characteristic, the authors attempted to define, as strictly as possible, the concepts in the SS ontology. In the present implementation, the SS ontology had more than 4,500 classes and 13 hierarchical levels. These concepts were introduced based on a literature survey and experts' workshops. They were then systematized based on 36 discussions among experts in SS and knowledge science, which were held during monthly workshops (Kumazawa et al., 2008, 2009b). The authors constructed the *domain concept* to conform to YAMATO (Mizoguchi, 2010, 2012), which is a top-level ontology being developed by R. Mizoguchi et al. The *domain concept* class was divided into the *attribute*, *quantity*, *abstract object*, *concrete object*, *substrate*, and *spatial region* classes. *Concrete object* was further classified into *object* and *occurrent* classes. *Occurrent* was divided into the *process* and *event* classes. *Event* was divided into the *change* and *ordinary event* categories. V*alue* was a subclass of *quantity* (Figure 8).

Case Study 1: Understanding a Target Domain through Ontology Explorations

The first case study focuses on the first two layers of the knowledge structure model. In Layer 1, an ontology captures common understandings of the target domain. In Layer 2, the users explore the ontology according to their interests. This allows them to understand the target domain from various viewpoints through divergent expirations. In order to evaluate both the SS ontology and the ontology exploration for Layer 1 and 2, the following two experiments were conducted:

Figure 8. Sub-concepts of domain concept in the SS ontology
Kumazawa et al., 2014a.

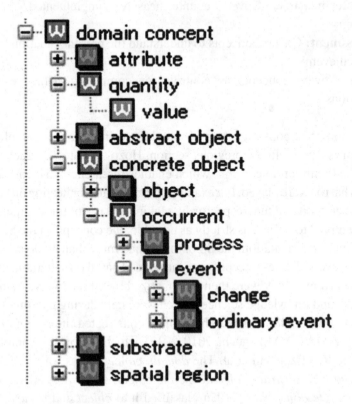

Evaluation of the SS Ontology from the Aspect of Relevance and Coverage

Twenty-eight Sustainability Science experts in Japan were invited to evaluate the SS ontology. As part of this evaluation, a questionnaire was developed to identify the problem, countermeasure and difficulty inherent in collaborations for SS research. The questionnaire items are listed below. A number of respondents also participated in a direct, in-depth interview. The authors then examined whether the SS ontology could represent/trace the results of the questionnaire survey by generating a map outlining the path from problem to countermeasure. Conceptual chains generated by experts (CGE) and chains generated from the SS ontology (CGO) were used to compare the survey results with the generated map.

For the purpose of this comparison, samples for map generation were prepared. In particular, the authors specified the problem classes from which the causal chain of the map corresponding to the result of the questionnaire survey began. Causal chains were extracted based on the survey answers in which both the problems and its countermeasures were involved in the SS ontology. The authors explored the likely classes in the SS ontology and specified a few such classes. As a result of exploring the classes in the hierarchy of *Countermeasure* as a goal of the causal chain, the research found 73 maps as potential candidates for the evaluation targets. The authors then selected the one map that was assumed to be most likely to contain the causal chain as a target for evaluation in the survey. This causal chain was selected by limiting the multiple aspects of similarity; either in countermeasure, in likeness with the actual causal chain of experts and of the concreteness of the comprised concepts. No less than 37 maps were obtained as a result of the evaluation targets.

The evaluation criteria used were:

1. The extents of abstractness-concreteness as the property involved in a point element, and
2. The extents of similarity in fields passing across the route composed of a line element.

As a result, 28 cases were found to be successful, 2 were close to failure and 7 were complete failure. The details are discussed below.

The three maps of 28 successful cases were judged to be likely chains (Table 1). All these cases had two characteristics:

- First, the respondents showed a comparatively short chain, and
- Second, the causal chains did not reach specific technologies or methods, although they reached the classes for differentiating general categories.

The SS ontology is supposed to fit the domain framework with larger grain. In 24 of the 28 successful cases, (more than two-thirds of all cases), the CGO was routed through rather abstract classes as compared to those terms in the CGE, although these classes cover the same research field. As a result of this experiment, it turned out that 24 out of the 37 cases appeared to be very successful. If one were to also consider another four cases that partially routed classes in different fields, the total number of successful cases rises to 28.

The SS ontology performed well when it came to the selection of countermeasures. Looking at three of the most successful cases, policy option (PV^2), supporting method (scenario) and governance system (democratic decision making) each had different targets, but all were countermeasures that would have been normally selected among multiple options. By its very nature, the ontology likely incorporates concepts concerning the selection of countermeasures. Another two cases were

Table 1. Cases in which CGE and CGO are judged to be sufficiently similar

ID	CGE	CGO
2	Sustainability of energy resources. • Expanding introduction of renewable energy and nuclear power generation • Photovoltaics	Exhaustion of fossil fuels(target). →*Resource(input)* →*Energy[RH]* ←*(objective)*「*photovoltaics_2*」
6	Defining socio-economic and actual lifestyle scenarios.	Shortage problem(target). →*Concrete object* ←*(target)Deterioration/loss of human security(impact)* →*Social system* ←*(target)Technology for scenario building*
21	[Comment about the countermeasures in the interview]. • Ensuring democratic decision-making or some sort of framework for participation and decision-making is essential for protection of rights. • Reflecting assertion by the weak to governance to overcome social inequality. • The weak are involved in social decision-making. • Sustainability is realized by striking a balance among assertions.	Balance problem in rights(disturbed goal). →*Sustenance of societies(is-a)* →*Sustenance of politics(is-a)* →*Appropriate distribution of power(is-a)* →*Participation in politics by minority*

Kumazawa et al., 2014a.

close to failure because they partially routed the classes in different fields and their end paths were too abstract.

However, in four of the seven failure cases that routed completely different field classes, the performance of the SS ontology was unsatisfactory, especially when CGE traced invisible terms such as rule, authority, mechanism and regulation and CGO traced visible concepts such as Communicating, Urban infrastructure and Cost. Since most of these invisible concepts were actual components of the system, the authors determined that the SS ontology requires the addition of sub-concepts of System and the enrichment of the slots for establishing strict definitions in the subclasses of System. It can therefore be concluded that the SS ontology and the exploration tool can be effective to a certain extent, although some extension of the ontology is required to reach a richer understanding.

An Evaluation Experiment for Divergent Exploration

In Layer 2, it is important to ensure that the user can obtain various conceptual maps and understand the target domain from various viewpoints through them. In order to evaluate the effectiveness of the ontology exploration tool, the authors asked four domain experts of Sustainable Science to use the tool in order to evaluate its practical performance. In this experiment, a previous version of SS ontology was employed (Kumazawa et al. 2009).

After receiving basic instruction regarding its use, the authors created 13 conceptual maps (three or four maps per expert) within an hour, in accordance with their specific interests. They then chose 61 conceptual paths (linkages between concepts in a map) from those 13 maps and evaluated those paths. As a result, 85% of the selected paths were evaluated as important or interesting for the domain experts; that is, the authors could ensure that domain experts could collect meaningful knowledge of conceptual chains through the divergent exploration of ontology using the tool. Furthermore, 75% of the conceptual chain paths generated in the experiment were not present when the ontology was constructed. It can therefore be concluded that the tool stimulated their thought process and contributed to obtaining unexpected conceptual chains that they had never thought of before (Kozaki et al., 2011).

Case Study 2: A Consensus-Building Support Based on Ontology Exploration

In Layer 3, the results of divergent exploration converge according to some contexts. In this case study, the authors presume that several stakeholders have their own contexts and try to reach a consensus about some problem through context-based convergence.

For an evaluation of consensus-building support, the authors designed an experiment through role-play discussion (Kozaki et al. 2012). In the experiment, researchers assigned several of the subjects the role of stakeholders on the topic of biofuel production and the policy making necessary for its successful implementation. The subjects were then asked to discuss the related topics by role-playing with ontology exploration tools in the following two steps:

Step 1: In the first step, each subject was asked to build a map after a brief instruction on how to use the system. The focal point was set to "production of biofuels" and each subject built a map by selecting three to five keywords from about 120 keywords prepared in advance. To make the maps compact and easy to interpret, subjects were asked to delete the paths they found uninteresting and to extend those paths that they wanted to explore further. By doing this, they generated maps that included only interesting and meaningful paths, from the stakeholder role they were asked to play (Figure 9).

Step 2: In the second step, these maps were integrated using the tool's *compare map* function. The subjects then engaged in discussion using the integrated map presented on the touch table (Figure 10). On the integrated map, each node is colored according to the subjects (stakeholders) who created its original map. Table 2 shows the number of nodes included in each map and built by each subject, as well as the overlapping nodes between them. The number of overlapping nodes indicates the extent to which the stakeholders shared common interests. The authors believe any function that produces quantitative information between stakeholders to be one of the merits of the system.

Figure 9. An example of a conceptual map generated from the point of view of an Environmental NGO
Kozaki et al., 2012.

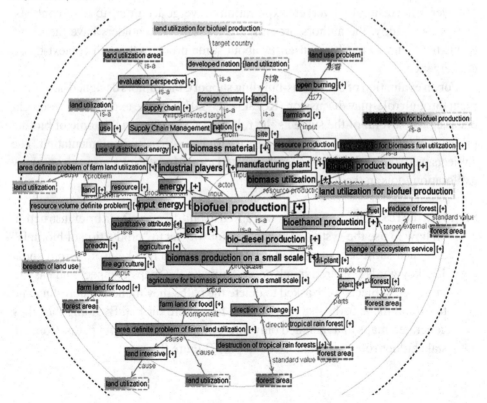

Figure 10. A snapshot of the discussion around the touch table
Kozaki et al., 2012.

Table 2. Number of nodes and overlapping nodes

	Number of Nodes in the Map	Number of Overlapping Nodes			
		a: Industry	b: Government	c: EMployees	d: Environmental NGO
a: Industry	110		16	21	10
b: Government	88	-		12	5
c: EMployees	187	-	-		49
d: Environmental NGO	115	-	-	-	

Kozaki et al., 2012.

Although there is still plenty of room for system improvement, the following positive feedback was obtained from the subjects:

- Visualization of conceptual maps is helpful to understand in what respects we are different by identifying what concepts we share and don't from the map.
- It sometimes helps us to better realize the issues by explicating unexpected relations or dependencies between concepts.

Case Study 3: Issue Explorations in Community Workshops toward Regional Sustainability

This case study aims to practice problem setting and solving in local society using Layer 4. To achieve this, the authors introduced an issue using the knowledge-structuring framework in workshop cases in Takashima City, Shiga Prefecture in Japan. This case allowed the opportunity to apply the knowledge structure based on the SS-SESs ontology[3] to issue exploration on the workshops and to design the business scheme contributing to regional sustainability. These workshops, which set the goal of proposing small business needs focused on nature, tourism and elderly people, were held on five separate occasions between July 2014 and January 2015.

The authors conducted these workshops through the following five steps.

Step 1: First, they extracted the terms and the rough relationships between these terms from the work products those participants produced in groups (Figure 11).
Step 2: They then formulated sentences using these terms and consisting of subject, predicate and object, like RDF triples (Figure 12).
Step 3: In the third step, they added new classes and instances into the SS-SESs ontology by using these terms categorized into subject, predicate and object.
Step 4: They then determined and set the central concepts of exploration by means of the ontology exploration tool.
Step 5: Finally, they designed the customized structural maps to facilitate people's understanding (Figure 13).

In several cases, it was discovered that some researchers and citizens who were not accustomed to this method of ontology engineering found it difficult to understand the conceptual map generated by the ontology exploration tool without any explanation. This would suggest that there is ample room to improve the current tool for supporting knowledge-sharing and issue exploration. This is why original maps generated by the tool were not used. Instead, customized maps were used to facilitate participant understanding.

Case Study 4: Keyword Exploration for Idea Creation in Biomimetics

This case study shows the process of idea creation support based on ontology exploration in Biomimetics. It is an advanced usage of knowledge structuring model based on Layer 4.

Biomimetics is innovative engineering created through the imitation of the models, systems and elements of nature (Shimomura, 2012). Based on the notion that

Figure 11. One of the work products in the second workshop

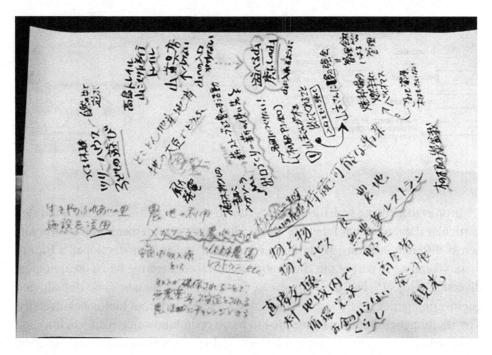

Figure 12. Sentence design by means of the terms in the work product

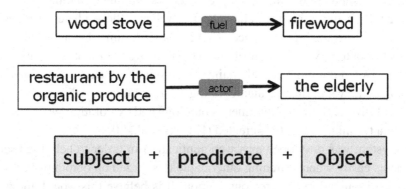

studying nature aids in the development of technology, Biomimetics has caught the attention of many people. Well-known examples include paint and cleaning technologies that imitate the water repellency of the lotus; adhesive tapes that mimic the adhesiveness of gecko feet; and high-speed swimsuits that imitate the low resistance of a shark's skin. These results integrate studies on the biological mechanisms of organisms with engineering technology to develop new materials.

Figure 13. An example of a customized map used in the workshop

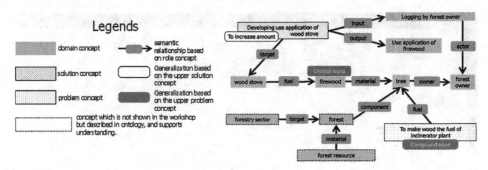

In order to facilitate such Biomimetics-based innovations, it is necessary to develop particular databases that integrate knowledge, data, requirements and viewpoints across different domains. With this need in mind, the authors developed a Biomimetics database as part of the "Innovative material engineering based on biological diversity" project[4]. The project aims to create both a new academic domain and engineering paradigm by systemizing knowledge gained from biological diversity. The Biomimetics database is intended to be an open innovation platform bridging various domains: including natural history, biology, agriculture, materials science, mechanical engineering, information science, environment and policy science and sociology. It is expected to assist engineers in creating innovative ideas for new technological development through an improved understanding of biological diversity.

The authors believes this motivation matches well with those inherent in knowledge structuring in Sustainability Science. That is, they presume that a development of Biomimetics ontology would contribute to the improvement of knowledge interoperability between the biology and engineering domains. Furthermore, linked data technologies are very effective in integrating existing biological diversity databases (Heath and Bizer, 2011). A Biomimetics ontology and exploration system based on linked data techniques was thus created (Kozaki et al., 2015).

The system was developed as a web application in order to help the user employ results easily when searching other databases, based on ontology exploration techniques discussed in the previous section. It is believe this would allow users to find important keywords for retrieving meaningful knowledge from a variety of perspectives, based on their own motives. This exploration would stimulate new thought processes and ultimately contribute to a deeper understanding of the ontology and its target domain, that being Biomimetics. As a result, users could discover what interests them. What's more, they might find unexpected conceptual chains from the ontology exploration that they would have otherwise never thought of.

On the more technical level, the authors implemented the ontology exploration tool using HTML5 and Java Script to enable it to work on web browsers on various platforms, including PCs, tablets and smartphones. The Biomimetics ontology was then converted to RDF format and stored in a RDF database so that the exploration methods could be implemented based on Simple Protocol and RDF Query Language (SPARQL) queries.

Figure 14 shows the result of one such exploration of the Biomimetics ontology using the system. In this example, the user selected *Antifouling* as the focal point (starting point) and obtained conceptual chains to some *Organism* as the end point. The system searched all combinations of aspects (relationships) to generate conceptual chains from the starting point specified by the user. As a result, the system displayed all conceptual chains between the selected concepts as a conceptual map. By clicking the nodes on the map, the user could see detailed information about each path. Furthermore, the user could then use the selected information to search

Figure 14. A snapshot of the Ontology Explorer for Biomimetics
Kozaki et al., 2015.

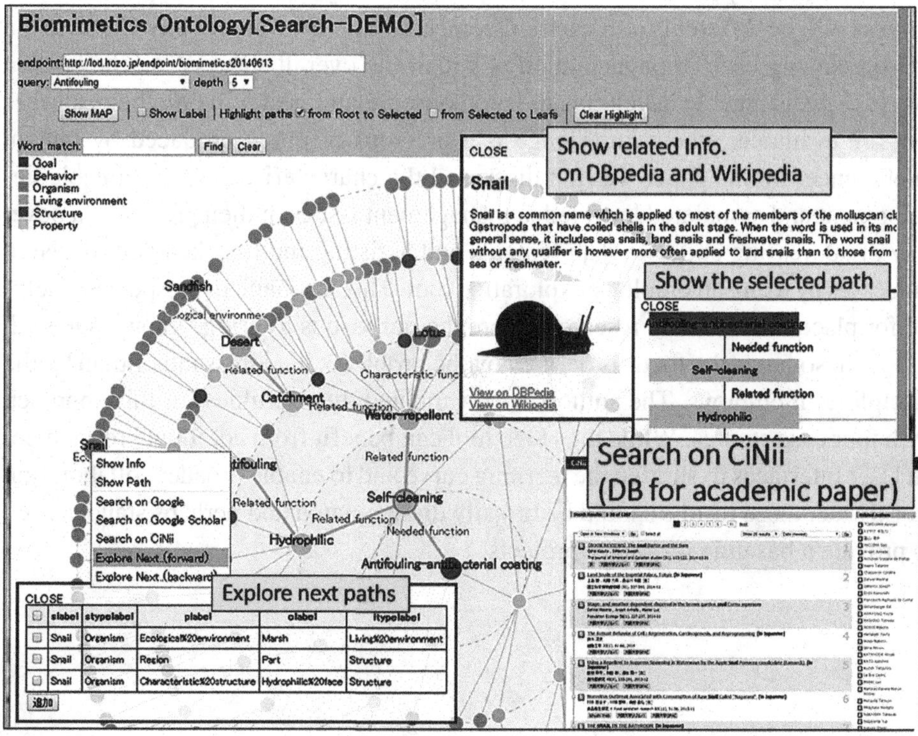

other Linked Data, such as DBpedia and databases. Though the current version supported only a few LODs and databases, it could have been easily extended to others.

Although the current ontology is a small prototype, some interesting conceptual chains (paths) can be obtained from it, such as those shown in Figure 14. One interesting example is the path Antifouling-antibacterial Coating → Antifouling → Water-repellent → Catchment → Desert → Sandfish. Sandfish (known as Scincus scincus) is a species of skink that lives in the desert. It was a reasonable yet unexpected candidate for antifouling function, even though it is well known to have a low-friction-surface skin designed to move in sand. This is an example of the kind of results the system could yield; ones based on rough inference for abstract concepts that bridge missing links among domains.

The Biomimetics ontology with keyword exploration system is available at the URL: http://biomimetics.hozo.jp/ontology_db.html.

CONCLUSION

Sustainable development is an urgent topic that is aimed at addressing many critical issues faced by all countries globally. The priority and solution to the issues it address will be different from each implementation, however, effective knowledge sharing among each implementation is key to the overall success. As the bottom line is that sustainable development is to conserve and best utilizing the resources that are available; where knowledge is a precious resource produced by human intelligence. In this paper we first discussed the characteristics of sustainable development and associated knowledge management issues, it then presented a novel way of addressing end user requirements and assisting multi-stakeholder decision processes by using an ontology exploration tool. This mechanism is especially helpful for place-based action research where the purpose is to bridge knowledge with action, in so far as the focus is defined by the problems it address rather than by the disciplines it employs. The authors have validated the usefulness of this approach with four case studies. While the Hozo tool can benefit from additional refinement on User Interfaces to shorten the learning curve and to enable broader collaboration worldwide, these results should be broadly disseminated and perhaps standardized to provide a baseline for future projects.

REFERENCES

Garcia-Holgado, A., & Garcia-Penalvo, F. J. (2014). Architectural pattern for the definition of eLearning ecosystems based on Open Source developments. *2014 International Symposium on Computers in Education (SIIE)*. doi:10.1109/SIIE.2014.7017711

Heath, T., & Bizer, C. (2011). Linked Data: Evolving the Web into a Global Data Space. Synthesis Lectures on the Semantic Web: Theory and Technology, 1(1).

Huang, J. S., Hsueh, K. A., & Reynolds, A. (2013). *A Framework for Collaborative Social, Economic and Environmental Development*. Paper presented at the 2013 7th IEEE International Conference on Digital Ecosystems and Technologies (DEST), Menlo Park, CA. http://web2.research.att.com/techdocs/TD_101166.pdf

Kates, R. W. (2010). *Readings in Sustainability Science and Technology* (C. f. I. Development, Trans.). CID Working Paper. Cambridge, MA: Harvard University.

Kates, R. W. (2011). What kind of a science is sustainability science? *Proceedings of the National Academy of Sciences of the United States of America, 108*(49), 19449–19450. doi:10.1073/pnas.1116097108 PMID:22114189

Kates, R. W., Clark, W. C., Corell, R., Hall, J. M., Jaeger, C. C., & Lowe, I. et al. (2001). Environment and development:sustainability science. *Science, 292*(5517), 641–642. doi:10.1126/science.1059386 PMID:11330321

Knowledge Management and Business Model Innovation. (2000). doi:10.4018/978-1-878289-98-8

Komiyama, H., & Takeuchi, K. (2006). Sustainability science: Building a new discipline. *Sustainability Science, 1*(1), 1–6. doi:10.1007/s11625-006-0007-4

Kozaki, K., Hirota, T., & Mizoguchi, R. (2011). Understanding an Ontology through Divergent Exploration. *Proc. of 8th Extended Semantic Web Conference (ESWC2011)*:305-320.

Kozaki, K., & Mizoguchi, R. (2015). A Keyword Exploration for Retrieval from Biomimetics Databases. In *Proc. of 4th Joint International Conference* (JIST 2014) (LNCS), (vol. 8943, pp. 361-377). doi:10.1007/978-3-319-15615-6_27

Kozaki, K., Saito, O., & Mizoguchi, R. (2012). A Consensus-Building Support System based on Ontology Exploration. In *Proc. of International Workshop on Intelligent Exploration of Semantic Data (IESD 2012)*.

Kumazawa, T., Kozaki, K., Matsui, T., Saito, O., Ohta, M., Hara, K., et al. (2009). Development of ontology on sustainability science focusing on building a resource-circulating society in Asia. In *Proceedings of the 6th international symposium on environmentally conscious design and inverse manufacturing* (EcoDesign 2009).

Kumazawa, T., Kozaki, K., Matsui, T., Saito, O., Ohta, M., Hara, K., ... Mizoguchi, R. (2014). Initial Design Process of the Sustainability Science Ontology for Knowledge-sharing to Support Co-deliberation. *Sustainability Science, 9*(2), 173-192. doi: 10.1007/s11625-013-0202-zK

Kumazawa, T., & Matsui, T. (2014). *Description of social-ecological systems framework based on ontology engineering theory*. The 5th Workshop on the Ostrom Workshop (WOW5).

Kumazawa, T., Matsui, T., Hara, K., Uwasu, M., Yamaguchi, Y., & Yamamoto, Y. et al. (2008). Knowledge structuring process of sustainability science based on ontology engineering. In *Proceedings of the 8th international conference on eco balance*.

Kumazawa, T., Saito, O., Kozaki, K., Matsui, T., & Mizoguchi, R. (2009). Toward knowledge structuring of sustainability science based on ontology engineering. *Sustainability Science, 4*(2), 315. doi:10.1007/s11625-009-0076-2

Mizoguchi, R. (2005). *Ontology Kougaku*. Ohmsha. (in Japanese)

Mizoguchi, R. (2010). *YAMATO: yet another more advanced top-level ontology*. Available online at: http://www.ei.sanken.osaka-u.ac.jp/hozo/onto_library/upper-Onto.htm

Mizoguchi, R. (2012). *Ontology Kougaku no Riron to Jissen*. Ohmsha. (in Japanese)

Rubio, E., Ocón, A., Galán, M., Marrero, S., & Nelson, J. C. (2004). *A personal and corporative process-oriented knowledge manager*. Retrieved from http://www.cicei.com/index.php/publicaciones/congresos/111-congresos/425-a-personal-and-corporative-process-oriented-knowledge-manager-suricata

Saito, O., Kozaki, K., Hirota, T., & Mizoguchi, R. (2011). The application of ontology engineering to biofuel problems. In *Sustainability Science: A Multidisciplinary Approach (Sustainability Science 1)*. *United Nations University Press*.

Shimomura, M. (2012). Engineering Biomimetics: Integration of Biology and Nanotechnology. In Design for Innovative Value Towards a Sustainable Society, (pp. 905-907). Academic Press.

ENDNOTES

[1]   Hozo is not Open source but free software. The authors do plan to publish it as open source in the future. However, an implementation of ontology exploration tool is published as an open source web-based software.

[2]   Solar power generation (PV) is generally viewed as a "measure" related to "choice" in order to be discussed in the context of choosing solar power generation from among the many kinds of renewable energy sources.

[3]   It is an extend version of Sustainability Science(SS) ontology focusing on Social-Ecological Systems (SESs).

[4]   This project is supported by the KAKENHI program of the Japan Society for the Promotion of Science (JSPS) 24120002.

Chapter 9
Trying to Go Open:
Knowledge Management in an Academic Journal

Özgün Imre
Linköping University, Sweden

ABSTRACT

Theoretically, open source solutions are a good match with the resource scarce organization such as a young academic journal to make the publication process and the knowledge shared explicit to the participants in the system. This paper uses a case study approach to investigate how the decision to have such a system depends on a myriad of factors, and tracks how the editorial team decided to adopt an open source journal management system for their knowledge management issues. The study argues that these components should not be taken in isolation by showing how the previous decisions can become a hindrance as these components change over time. The results show that some factors, though initially thought to be unimportant, can become major forces as the journal matures, and a more holistic approach could help to side-step the problems faced.

DOI: 10.4018/978-1-5225-0905-9.ch009

INTRODUCTION

Recent years saw an increase in number of scientific journals (Larsen & von Ins, 2010). This has been to large extent facilitated by the increased use of information technology (IT), not only because IT enabled easy access to information and dissemination channels, but it also made possible to connect to people – reviewers, authors, editors more easily than before. IT has also enabled the creation of systems for knowledge management and handling of the information flows that previously necessitated expert knowledge and other resources not easily attained through these systems.

An academic journal, though how small and young it may be, consists of several parts that need to be managed with rather tight schedules, and often without visible gains for those involved with the work. Most of the work, if not all, is done voluntarily, with commitments of those people to other institutions taking precedence over the journals' needs. Though these invisible rewards may bear fruit in the long run, i.e. if the journal becomes and remains successful, usually the editors and the management of the journal are occupied with the short run survival of the journal. They need to attract papers, review them, send them for peer-review, assess these reviews, reject/accept the papers based on these reviews, ask for copyright and check if all the copyright laws are followed in the accepted paper and finalise the editing. All these tasks necessitate that the editors and managers have the required information to perform accordingly, and these tasks themselves generate knowledge to be used either directly later in the process, or to be used for future volumes. The papers generated are the products of the journal, to be used by the academia – their main customer – while at the same time, the papers also play the role of input for the authors for their future evaluations, and for other research that will use these papers in one form or another. Thus, the rather seemingly simple act of publishing a scientific journal (see Figure 1 for a basic workflow of a submission derived from the case organisation) actually is a complex combination of various actors and factors.

IT and information systems (IS) come at this stage to play several roles. Most of the mentioned tasks and the input and output of these tasks take place in a virtual setting, rendering the IT and IS that are used as a form of infrastructure. On the other hand, IT and IS also play the role of a platform where the knowledge necessary to run the journal is collected, created and shared, which serves as the focus of this chapter. The issues related to this role have become to the forefront of the case organisation's (to preserve anonymity, hereafter Business Journal) editors' and managers' minds as they have gone through a growth phase in the Business Journal. This growth phase highlighted the shortcomings of the existing ad-hoc ways of

Figure 1. Basic workflow of Business Journal

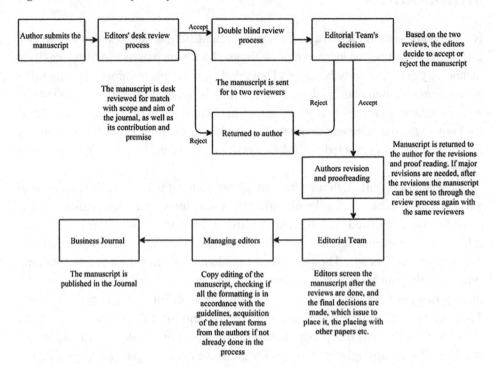

knowledge management they had initiated previously in the 5 years of the Journal's existence. This issue has been raised in a coffee room talk the author had with one of the editors, who hinted that such decisions to implement IT and IS have usually been taken without consideration of the other factors in the work systems (WS) they operate.

Thus the WS around the scholarly publishing becomes an interesting phenomenon to investigate to understand how decisions regarding IS and knowledge management are made, and how they affect the business as the journal matures.

This chapter broadly aims to investigate how and why does a scientific journal invest in an information system. To achieve this aim the chapter looks at how the previous decisions were reached, what their aims were and how they affect the knowledge management in the journal. To do this, the case is presented in 3 time intervals: when Business Journal was established and the route to that decision in 2011, when it began to grow and when finally it entered into a maturity stage in early 2015 and decided to adopt an open source (OS) journal management system (JMS). These three stages highlight how things have evolved with time, as well show how a WS approach could have solved some of the existing problems. Previously, adoption of OS JMSs have been discussed in the literature (see Hunter, 2010; Solomon,

2007) providing the respective authors' accounts for their journals. In this work, a similar adoption would be analysed by positioning the adoption in a WS framework and employing a case study design.

Following this brief introduction, the chapter continues with a brief section on WS, followed by the method used. The next section provides the case description, in which the case is presented in three temporal episodes. After the discussion of the case the chapter closes with a conclusion section.

ON WORK SYSTEMS

The term "work system", as Alter (2006) argues, has been used in the IS literature for some time. He however emphasizes that there was no attempt to define what a WS was in those early references, or use it as an analytical concept, and defines WS as "a system in which human participants and/or machines perform work (processes and activities) using information, technology, and other resources to produce specific products and/or services for specific internal or external customers." (Alter 2008, p. 451) His work coincides with the time when others were questioning the definition of what IT, IS and IT-artefact is (Benbasat & Zmud, 2003; Orlikowski & Iacono, 2001), and proposes that IS are a special form of a WS. Following several iterations of developing this concept – one step including the debate around the Jasperson, Carter, and Zmud (2005) paper on post-adoptive behaviour (see: Alter, (2006) and the letters to the editor in the same issue) – WS has been criticized as being too rigid and lacking a social theory of work (Korpela, Eerola, Häkkinen, & Toivanen, 2004). In line with this argument Petersson (2008) suggests that work practice theory can be an answer to this issue. WS approach is not alone in such criticisms, as the call for relevance and rigour is well established in the IS discipline. However as Alter (2003) argues, works systems approach can help bridge the "rigour vs. relevance dichotomy": the use of WS can help generalizability issues outlined in Lee and Baskerville (2003), highlight adoption as on-going use thus show how issues other than immaturity of the products can effect the adoption behaviour, and provide a better understanding between different disciplines as well as better communication with professionals. Additionally, WS framework have been used not only for IS but for a wide range of topics, from knowledge mobilization capabilities (BenMoussa, 2010), to investigating success factors in customer relations management (Kampath & Röglinger, 2010) and how to create high performing teams in IS environments (De Leoz & Petter, 2013), making it applicable for this study (see Alter (2013) for a brief review of research using WS), where the components aside from IS play a role in the system when coupled with the prescriptive elements of the framework (Alter 2004).

Alter's proposal of WS can be grouped under two frameworks, a static one that can be used to answer "what WS we are analysing", and a dynamic one – the WS life cycle model - to analyse how the WS change over time. There are nine components (see Table 1) that create the WS, four of them constituting the core of the system: processes and activities, information, participants and technology. These four components are taken as the core performing the actual work, and as such are directly related to the rationale of the system at hand. The other five components – customers, products and services, infrastructure, environment, strategies – complement the WS to create the WS framework.

Participants are people who perform non-automated tasks in the WS, using – and further creating – information. The participants are further helped in their tasks by the technologies, though the use of technology by the participants varies depending on the task performed and the roles that the participants play.

This system needs to be built on an infrastructure, a set of resources that are necessary for the system to function. As the infrastructure is not managed by the system, and as it might be shared with other WS, the infrastructure is not a part of the WS. Environment – organizational, regulatory cultural, technical – component

Table 1. Components of a work system

Participants	People who perform the non-automated work in the WS.
Information	Codified and non-codified information used and created as participants perform their work
Technologies	Tools that help people work more efficiently, tailored to specific business situations, involving a combination of general-purpose tools and specialized techniques.
Processes and activities	All of the activities within the WS, may combine information processing, communication, decision-making, coordination, sense making, thinking, and physical actions.
Customers	Direct beneficiaries/users/receivers of whatever a WS produces, plus other customers whose interest and involvement is less direct.
Products and Services	Combination of physical things, information, and services that the WS produces for its various customers
Environment	The organizational, cultural, competitive, technical, and regulatory environment within which the WS operates
Infrastructure	Resources that the WS relies on, managed outside of WS, and shared with others
Strategies	The guiding rationale and high-level choices within which a WS, organization, or firm is designed and operates

Compiled from Alter (2006, 2008).

is also not a direct component of the WS but is included as it influences the performance of the WS.

To operate, this system needs to be built on an infrastructure, a set of resources that are necessary for the system to function. As the infrastructure is not managed by the system, and as it might be shared with other WS, the infrastructure is not a part of the WS. Environment component is, like infrastructure, not a direct component of the WS as the system is not necessarily dependent on it for functioning, but a part of the framework as it influences the performance of the WS.

This WS results in products and services that are created for its internal and external customers – direct users/beneficiaries of these products and services, as well as those that are less directly involved with the products and services. The production strategy of the WS as well as its value proposition for its customers are composed in line with the overall strategies of the WS.

As can be seen, all the components of the WS framework are intrinsically connected with each other. A change – both planned and unplanned – in one of the components necessitate the involved parties to adapt accordingly. These changes, especially at operation and maintenance phases of the WS - are the drivers of new cycles of initiation, development and implementation, which are taken as iterative processes that provide a more dynamic view of the WS (Alter, 2006, p. 302).

Following this short description of WS, the WS under study – the scientific publishing conducted by a young international journal – can be briefly sketched to tie in with the case later on.

The primary participants in this WS are the editors, the reviewers, and the authors. They have different tasks related to the WS, with authors sending their submissions, the editors conducting an initial review of the submissions, with the reviewers reviewing the accepted submissions. These processes are mostly conducted with the help of computers and internet based technologies, both for the actual performing of the tasks, as well retrieving and storing information related to the submissions. The product of the system, the scientific paper serves both as an information product itself to the customers – the scientific community that the author is usually a part of, as well as information for future use within the WS. This core part of the WS is regulated within several overlapping environments i.e. the universities' regulations that the editors are working for, issues related to copyright and plagiarism that are institutionalized in scientific publishing industry etc. Various resources, such as access to Internet and having an established community constitute the infrastructure that the journal is built upon. The strategy, which has changed from the early days of the journal, establishes that the journal will provide scientific journals of a certain quality in applied business and economic research, and has shaped the choices that the editors have taken to operate the WS.

As can be seen, in this WS, some components overlap: the university/organizational environment plays a part of the technologies used –editors working by the computers provided to by their universities – as well as the infrastructure – internet access, access to scientific databases. Furthermore, university is also a customer – through their subscription to the scientific databases, as well as the organization that houses the individual scientists that are the customers of the Journal. To provide a more focused understanding of the WS at hand – and due to the space limitations – some of these issues would not be treated as deeply as others. The main impetus in deciding how to treat these components was how the respondents treated them during the case study: one clear elimination occurred as the editors heavily mentioned the university as the environment that they operate but have not brought it up as an organization that is a customer to their product.

As the underlying aim of this study was to analyse how and why a journal would invest in an IS regarding their knowledge management issues, a further choice to to treat IS as "technologies". This is not to say that IS are not WS, however, as the interviews have shown, the common understanding of the editors regarding their choices was more akin to a tool view, similar to the "technologies" that Alter (2015, p. 57) suggests that are "viewed as tools used by users or as automated agents that perform work autonomously once launched."

Choosing the technology as a focal point is similar to the arguments raised by Adomavicius et al. (2007) when analysing an ecosystem. WS framework with its focus on interdependencies among different constituents is similar to an ecosystem view that stresses resilience and adaptability of the ecosystem to survive, with multiple actors affecting each other both positively and negatively (Mars, Bronstein, & Lusch, 2012; Wareham, Fox, & Cano Giner, 2014). As will be seen in the case description, the different parts of the WS evolved throughout the Journal's lifetime and interacted in various ways, with the overall WS adapting.

THE STUDY DESIGN

In this research, a single case study design was employed, following the interpretative tradition (Walsham, 1995, 2006), and informed by the principles laid out by Klein and Myers, (1999). The main reason for choosing such a design was ease of access to the journal editors, as one of them, James, (all names are pseudonyms to ascertain anonymity and confidentiality to the case and the individual editors) works at the same institution as the author, and has provided further data gathering opportunities by contacting other editors as well as providing the opportunity to observe the WS in real life. Coincidently, as mentioned earlier, this research began as a friendly talk at the coffee room, thus informal observations where the topic came up naturally during such settings during the study provided a deeper access than other venues would have. This ease of access also made it possible observe how the journal had evolved during the last two years, thus introducing the longitudinal aspect of the study. In addition to ease of access to data and this longitudinal aspect, both termed as possible rationales for a single case study (Yin, 2009), the single case study designs relative strength to display dynamic processes (Siggelkow, 2007) was deemed a positive attribute to highlight evolution of the WS. Furthermore, as the journal is a relatively new journal with scarce resources, it also fits to some of the considerations of the open source software (OSS) literature: cost as a prime reason for choosing an OSS; that flexibility of OSS to offset the demands of agility to balance against changes of the environment; ability of OSS to side-step lock-in situations (Riehle, 2007; Serrano & Sarriei, 2006).

Familiarity with scholarly publishing process also influenced the analysis. This familiarity is akin Klein and Myers' (1999, p. 82) "principle of dialogical reasoning", the need to be open about the possible biases the researcher has. Knowing some of the general issues that might influence adoption behaviour of OSS, and that the scientific publication can be costly, one preconception that the researcher had was the issue of price forcing the choice of OSS. Also it was assumed the voluntary nature of work would influence how the editors and other participants worked. However, as the data collection and analysis progressed, a more system-oriented lens to account for the issues that did not have a direct effect on the choice of IT/IS solutions was needed, Rather, as the case showed that these factors worked together with others and to better understand this complex picture the WS framework was adapted.

After a pilot field observation regarding the daily work of an editor to narrow the issues of interest and to map how the editors engage with their activities, the data for the study was collected using semi-structured qualitative interviews with open-ended questions. To supplement the interview data two observations were done to see how the editors worked with the Journal. Though the author was previously involved with similar WS as an author and as a reviewer, such observations made it possible to see how the editors – the primary participants from the knowledge management role of the IS – work within the system, and how the components affect each other. Such observations of the editors' work for the Business Journal made it possible to analyse how the workflow for the Journal is usually interrupted as the editors are often playing several roles within the day, and contrast it with the interview data. During these observations the use of the existing IS solutions, and how the editors dealt with the situations and negotiated the next step were witnessed. Notes taken during the observations were summarised and rewritten to be used in the analysis. 3 of the 5 editors that sit at the editorial team were interviewed, with each interview consisting of approximately 1 hour. The editors were asked about their daily work with the journal, how they use the IT/IS with regards to their work, and how – and why – they moved from on IT/IS solution to another. These interviews were digitally recorded and summarized, and compared with each other. A follow up interview with each editor was placed after the initial analysis of the data was conducted to fill out any gaps that the author identified in the editors' accounts, as well as to provide the opportunity for the interviewees to review how their previous interviews were analysed by the author.

These follow up interviews, as well as having the summaries to discuss with the interviewees provided an opportunity similar to the hermeneutic circle of Klein and Myers (1999): as time passed and more iterations occurred between different parts of the data the Journal's WS emerged. Similarly this iteration between author and the editors enabled both parties to see the issue at hand from different perspectives. Similar to what they argue, the work-systems framework is used as a sensitizing device to analyse the data.

The summaries of the interviews, as well as the notes taken during the interview and the observations were analysed iteratively. The initial analysis was done with the main purpose of identifying the components of the WS framework within the journals own WS. After the new data was gathered by follow up interviews and observations, the summaries were updated accordingly, and the data was analysed contextually. The results of the analysis solidified the emerging understanding that there are distinct temporal zones within the Business Journal's WS - take-off, growth and maturity phases – that showed variety in how the knowledge management issues were tackled with, and how the investment in IS were done in light of these knowledge management issues.

The summaries and notes were analysed to identify the components of the Business Journal's WS, and to reveal the links among them to see how their interconnection resulted in unseen circumstances as the Journal progressed. Where necessary, the informal talks with one of the editors were used as a guide to delve into some parts of the collected data to provide a better understanding of the issue at hand.

A JOURNAL WORK SYSTEM

Business Journal was founded by a group of colleagues five years ago. This group of colleagues decided that their main scope would be studies of emerging markets, and situated the Journal in economics and business research, with emphasis on empirically grounded papers. In line with this scope and aim, they achieved to attract authors from various sectors and disciplines, with topics ranging from more macro level studies concerning oil prices and stock markets, to more micro level studies concerning value creation in a magazine, and as can be seen in Figure 2, Business Journal has been in the business for five years now. During these five years, the editorial team managed to assemble an international advisory board and published 18 issues by the time of writing this chapter, and was accepted into various academic indexes. While this chapter has been under review, the Journal was accepted to the Norwegian Register for Scientific Journals, Series and Publishers, and the editorial team is now thinking of applying to Scopus for indexing.

Figure 2. Business Journal's evolution

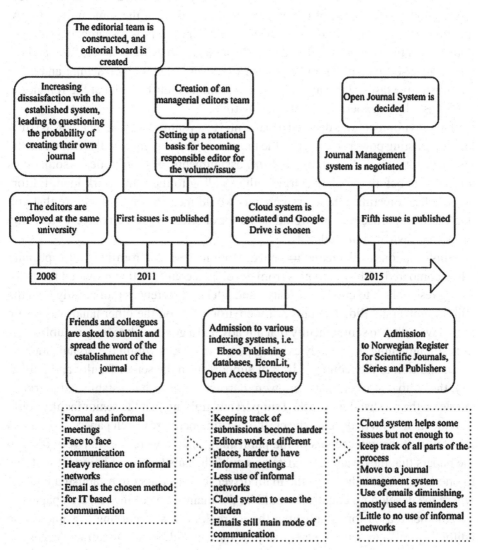

The role of IT/IS to address knowledge management issues has evolved since the founding of the journal. While the issue was not consciously termed as a knowledge management issue at the beginning, today the editors talk about IS as a solution to their knowledge management and communication problems. In the following parts, how this view of IT/IS has changed over the years, as well as how it sits within the WS of the Business Journal is detailed.

The Naïve Beginnings

Though the first issue of the Business Journal was published in 2011, the story starts around 2008, when some of the editors were employed at the same university. At the time, the would-be-editors were beginning their careers as researchers, and were going rather turbulent times. The demands put on them by the senior faculty and the university itself meant that most of their time was taken up by teaching and other administrative tasks, and thus, they had to conduct their research at the remaining time – usually in expense of their private time.

This environment was deemed detrimental to a young researchers career, as Chris put, the existing power structure of the university/department usually meant that the junior faculty would "need to take *extra* assignments on short notice – sometimes a few hours before the class started", thus adding to the usual work load. Editors argued that sometimes these assignments would mean teaching a lecture that you don't have expertise in, thus would add a lot of stress when compared to teaching from your own area of study.

This situation, as all three editors have mentioned, was far from the ideal, especially when compared with universities from developed countries that provided funds for young researchers to conduct research and attend conferences more easily than the editors' university did. The university environment, on the other hand was set up more favourably to senior faculty that already had a good track record of publishing, thus strengthening the already existing power distances within the organization.

In addition to the feeling of lack of support from the senior faculty and university, the editors also felt that there were barriers to publish in established journals. While on the one hand they lacked support and training that the senior faculty could provide them with to develop the craft of writing better research papers, the editors also felt that the gatekeepers of the publishing system were also not very open to the papers that they wanted to write and publish. This feeling of being left out due to one reason or another, was the main driver for the editors to establish a journal, where the developing countries would be the main scope of the research papers.

Another reason for establishing the journal, at least according to some of the editors was also to act as a career step. If they would be able to attract successful papers and authors to their journal, they would be able to present Business Journal as a success story in their work environment, and further use it as a networking tool for future purposes.

At this stage Business Journal did not have a clear-cut strategy to guide its editors. As hinted previously, most of their motivation was coupled with their dissatisfaction with their work environment, and their idea to have their own journal that would answer some of their frustrations was more of a reactionary act. However, as they have moved to consolidate their ideas, the strategy began to emerge as an on-going iterative understanding of what they need to guide their project.

To set off, they began to contact their colleagues and friends in business and economics fields, and present their idea of Business Journal as a publishing outlet, that would have legitimacy during the upcoming years. They have decided to use a similar tactic to use their existing network to find people who could be reviewers. However, at this stage, the editors themselves had to take the additional role of acting as a reviewer, as most of their contacts turned down their request. On this issue, the editors argue that even today, it still was a hard job to secure the reviewers, reflecting a general tendency in academia from their other experiences.

One conscious strategy of the editors was to set up Business Journal as an open access one, so that a wider audience could reach the published papers. This is also in line with the growth of scientific journals adopting an open access model, aiming to attract more readers (Laakso et al., 2011; Mann, von Walter, Hess, & Wigand, 2009). Similar to these other journals, the editors decided to forego a paper version of the journal, as they had neither the resources to publish a paper version, nor the established market that would demand such a product. As an online journal, a website for the journal was created, and the journal was registered in North America officially.

In this rather informal stage, the editors used only an email system, and have appointed one email address for all incoming mails. The appointed managing editor for that issue would then check the mail, distribute them accordingly to other editors, and contact the authors and reviewers by using this email account. However, as the submissions grew, the managing editors began to lose track of the processes. While the editors were colleagues and knew each other before hand, thus being able to communicate in other forms, the communication with the authors and the reviewers began to deteriorate. As sometimes they needed to send several emails to reviewer to get a final answer, some of these answers were misplaced or were not fully communicated to the other editors. This resulted in late answers to the authors as well as rather rushed reviews that were not on par with the expectations of the editorial team.

This *communication mess*, as one editor recalled during the interview, resulted in some friction among the editors. As the managing editor was tasked to keep track of what was happening for the overall journal for that issue, any shortcomings during that period were seen – to some extent – as a fault of the managing editor. On the other hand, the managing editor, who had overseen the whole process felt that the other editors were calling the shots even though they were unaware of how the paper was progressing. With all the editors keeping notes of what they have done, and what they think is the next appropriate stage for the submissions, most of them were not informed about the others' ideas. Their own expertise in their consecutive fields were not fully utilized. The documents that they sent each other regarding the submissions were usually not put in a uniform – coherent – format, and when asked to reflect upon these initial documents, were commented as not able to capture what editors really thought. The ad-hoc way of doing the business, and sending documents that were not able to codify the information resulted in use of more informal ways of doing the business, mostly face-to-face meetings, or through phone conversations.

At this rather naïve stage, the editors informally tried to find out if they would be able to secure some help from their university/department. These informal feelers however were turned down. This resulted in some unforeseen – or more likely predictable when taken in hindsight – consequences, as the editorial team had to pay to keep the website running for the Business Journal. In similar fashion, when one of the editors wanted to introduce an anti-plagiarism software to scan the submissions, they had to use their personal accounts to do so, as the university was not willing to set aside a budget for the Journal. This lack of resources, the infrastructure that Business Journal needed to be built upon, necessitated the editorial team to cover up those expenses from their own budgets, as well as taking up considerable amount of their time – when they had no access to anti-plagiarism tools.

After facing these various issues, the editorial team decided that they needed to make some changes if they wanted to succeed, and decided that the email system that they relied on was not adequate enough. Near the end of second volume, they decided to change how to tackle their increasingly obvious knowledge management problem.

Growth Pains

After the initiation phase, several things have changed in the WS. Even though one of the editors had been working partly in another institute, nearing the end of the second volume, she was offered a full time position at another university, in another country. One of the editors likewise began working at another university whereas another editor moved to work in another faculty. While these employment related issues were in their minds for some time, when it was finalized it was still considered as an external, unplanned change. And this change triggered a new way of thinking about how to continue with Business Journal. Amanda said,

All of us had problems about this or that [...] So changing places was always some-how there, you know. But you never know if you will get it. We didn't plan to move at the same time, it just happened. We were happy for each other [...].

This separation meant that the face-to-face meetings – or even telephone chats to some extent – were not feasible anymore. While they would still be able to use video conferencing when needed, this usually was seen as not as natural when compared with before: a direct threat to escalate their already existing knowledge management issues.

With the change of universities, the editorial team met different university environments – bound up with different regulations and norms. Though varying in intensity, all three new places put emphasis on publishing more, being more international and being visible more on the Internet. "Being international and visible on the internet," James commented during one informal session "was what we thought we would be getting by having Business Journal – turned out this is not how the university saw it."

Though changing universities meant different environments, the general attitude towards Business Journal from the higher ups seemed to be same. Especially with the emphasis of internationalization, the editorial team thought they would have a good chance of getting support, as their two-volume track was evidence that they didn't have when they started. "We really thought this would prove our point," Chris commented on the issue, "but it wasn't apparently what they wanted".

The support that the editorial team wanted was mainly on IT related issues, a hosting space, some help with setting up a server. This need for help came in two different strains: " [...] was more of the financial kind, yes we take our turn to pay for the hosting and server and it is not a full salary, but it adds up. And you have the talk about helping faculty to internationalize, to create awareness of the university and research, and... And on the other hand, if we had university backing it would have added to the legitimacy of Business Journal. Now we are a stand-alone new journal, we could have been more if we had Business Journal cooperation with *University X*. It would have helped to make the journal known better. And we would feel more secure that if something goes wrong it would be our people that we can ask for help." (James)

Others hinted at this security concern too, as they expressed they don't feel that they have the expertise to host the journal on their own, so they have to rely on some external party to do that for them. Though as of yet they haven't had a serious problem, the probability of something happening is still there, and thus they keep their own version of the papers in several copies "just in case". "Of course, then we would need to upload the whole thing to a new server/host and try to keep track of what went wrong at the first place, but better be safe than sorry" (James)

At this stage the editors also got the chance of further networking, and were able to achieve some success to encourage their new colleagues to support their Journal, by sending either their research papers, or asking them to review the submitted papers. Around this time Journal was included in some scientific indexes, like Ebsco and EconLit, providing a form of legitimacy and increasing submissions. However, as earlier, things were not as smooth as expected, as the publication system still did not favour new journals, but asked the researchers to publish in established journals with high rankings. Reviewer problems continued, prompting the editors to send several reminder emails before they received a definite answer, thus adding to the stress of the editors to provide a timely publication. On this issue, editors remarked that it felt nice to have enough papers in the pipeline for the next issues, but it is a stressful process to finalise the papers, and usually everything settles at the last minute.

Previously, the use of emails for communication and coordination had become rather problematic rather quickly for the editorial team. This was proven once again when the editorial team decided to ask for help in their editorial duties and used their network to recruit junior faculty to provide help as managerial editors. These new recruits were mostly PhD students that the editorial team had worked/had been working at the time, and just like the editorial team, were working on a voluntary basis. However, with all these people having access to submitted papers, the reviews, and other communications - on papers and the issue - the email system began to reproduce the same problems as before.

"We were producing a lot of emails," James commented, "and most of those emails turned into chains as everybody was added to the mail list, so that no body missed information. Soon our mail boxes were full of these emails". This issue became apparent during an observation session, where until the definitive answer of "I have it" was sent, the issue was taken up by others, trying to remember who was responsible, what the paper was about, and also talking about not Business Journal related issues.

This situation, and the changes in the availability of IT solutions resulted in adoption of a cloud service – Google Drive – to upload the related material to the publishing to the cloud, so that everyone would be able to see what they were looking for there. Furthermore now they would be able to have real time access to the information, rather than waiting for others to answer an email. They decided to upload these different pieces of information in different folders and give access to the editors to see and edit these documents. While it was easy to just put the copyright permission forms to a folder, it did not work as well for the information regarding the individual submissions and publications.

As mentioned at the previous section, the editors kept their own version of what they had done regarding the publications: their reasoning behind their decisions, and how the process went for those papers were left uncodified. This problem persisted: as the editorial team did not have a conscious strategy that went deep into the knowledge management issues, the metadata they put in to the cloud solution hindered its ability to perform the desired tasks. The metadata found in the spreadsheet document created for this purpose was limited to basic information about the paper, i.e. who reviewed it, if the copyright notice was received. While it provided an easier way to track if some of the steps in the publishing process were done, it didn't provide the editorial team with any extra decision making ability.

These not realized expectations became more apparent when the editors regarded updating the documents in the cloud service as an administrative job. Prompted by their earlier experience with email chains, this time some preferred to update the documents at the end of the process rather than in real time. While this solved the administrative workload, it worked against real time expectancy.

As can be seen, at this growth stage, the editors have taken more conscious steps in choosing their IT solutions. They have once again began their search for help from their respective universities, and when it didn't result in what the editors wanted, they chose a free cloud service that provided them with easy and real-time collaboration tools. However, though in theory the cloud service could solve some of their issues, problems occured due to low levels of participation. While now they had easier access to information they still needed somebody to put the relevant data in, relying on the editors keeping track of these different bits of information and uploading them in a timely manner, and the system didn't provide them with any input for future decision making.

Maturity and Wisdom

I guess we fall to the same mistakes that we warn our students about. We saw it [cloud service] as a solution, but we didn't think too much about it somehow. We knew it might not be enough but at the time it was what we did. Tight schedules, exams to correct, you know. You cannot not do them, so you give up from your own time to keep the Journal alive. – James

When James commented on this choice of the cloud service being possibly not the best but perhaps the only option at the time, the idea of looking at the decision as a part of the WS becomes even more relevant. While on hindsight all the editors agree that they could have done differently, they did not have so many alternatives to follow at that time. They were just starting the Journal and were resource constrained, and did not have the back up they imagined they would get from University. This resulted in reactionary decisions to the problems they faced, rather than taking a proactive stance. This changed in the maturity phase of the Business Journal.

It takes time to get a grip about what you need. You know it [publishing process], but you don't know it until you are in it. We had to learn the tricks to ease the process. – Amanda

It took some time for the editorial team to identify what was needed to be able to cope with the publishing process. While the process itself has not changed, the steps related to gathering data and disseminating information about the submissions, and more importantly the technology around, could have been worked around in different ways. This has shown itself at the maturity phase when the editorial team decided to tackle the problem directly by setting up a strategic way to decide what they should do. James commented,

On the one hand we were a classic example – we know what to do, what information we need, but we didn't do it, but you also know how it gets at some point that you don't have any time left for your own things. So at that summer we decided to decide on what we want from the future.

It was at that summer meeting when the editorial team argued that one part of the problem were actually the systems they had been using. While both emailing and the later cloud service served a purpose, they were not a holistic solution to the knowledge management issues they faced increasingly. As the Business Journal became more established, the editors acquired knowledge about how to treat the submission, who to send for reviews, how to respond to questions from the authors increased. However, none of the systems they had could provide a standardized way of putting this kind of information in a readily accessible way. They were able to upload the files such as copyright notice, but they had no way of linking all these different parts of information to a single framework. So, the first step taken was to identify what they want from their new system, and to see if it provided a solution to the issue at hand, or if there was an underlying problem that surpassed the technology related problems.

In the end they decided that though some of the issues were related to their own practices, a new system would be able to transform the situation for the better. They have created a list to determine what they thought would be needed in the new system and once again asked their already existing network to see if anybody had experience with such a system. This phase resembled the early beginnings of the Business Journal where the face-to-face meetings were used extensively for the operation of the journal. This time however, the meetings were with other people that they worked with in their work life, not just with the editors.

In the end we had several options, some matched us better than the others, but if you don't have the backing of the university, and if you don't expect the authors to pay for the cost of using such a system, you actually don't have that many options. – Amanda
We wanted to be able to have everything related to the paper under a single frame-work. When it was accepted, when it was sent to review, to whom, when we received the replies. And not just files and files in different folders, but to reach them with a click. Also we wanted to be able to see what is missing, and even get alerts from the system when a deadline is approaching. – James

In line with the more proactive thinking, one editor asked her division to see if they would be able to get some help to use such a system before they made a final decision, and if the university would this time provide some backing. However, the response from the university was that since this was not a university project they were not able to provide support for this undertaking. While the editorial team was expecting a similar answer, they were still disappointed as that meant they would have to deviate more resources to find such a system and set it up. "It would have helped to have somebody from the IT to help us. Not that they didn't but they have all the stuff that they have to do, and they only help between them" (James)

In the end an OS-JMS – Open Journal Systems (OJS), a widely used system (see Willinsky, 2005) – was chosen, and the implementation began. As none of the editors were tech-savvy, they decided not to change the system much let alone writing their own code, and went for a basic installation, using their requirements list with the help of the IT department. Similarly the financing issues also hindered the editors to employ a technician to customise the OJS, thus the choice of going for the basic installation. As of now, the editors are still using the cloud system, as well as the emails, however the intensity of the use of the system is increasing. As the new system asks the authors to register, it is much easier to track the submission process. As noted by editors, the process can be tedious and help in tracking "… was something we wanted to have before, but you need to shop around a bit until you find something like that" (Chris). This situation was coupled with the emergence of a new journal that had a very similar name, and catered to a very similar audience. The editorial team decided that the move to such a system would enable them to present a unified face, where the authors and reviewers would use a system rather than emailing the Journal. Though at the point the editors are not able to comment whether this issue of legitimacy will be reflected in future submissions, the feedback that they received from their colleagues that perform as reviewers so far seems to be positive.

As the editors argue, the ability to see who the reviewers are, and what they have reviewed is a great help. This provides them with an easy reminder of who to go for the new submissions, as well as the ability to search for additional reviewers using the provided tools within the system. Though the editors prefer to build up their own network of reviewers, the option to use such tools to search for some additional reviewers is considered as a potential benefit, just as the ability to see the previous authors that can be considered as potential reviewers.

Business Journal is open access from its initiation, thus the idea of subscription was not an issue that the editorial team has considered before. However, with the tools provided with the OJS they were able to manage their announcements easier, such as sending an announcement of when the new issue is coming, as well as send greeting or thank you notes at certain dates. As was discussed during an observation, the new system became another enabler of networking, as these mostly automatic announcements made it possible to have the journal maintain a certain level of visibility to its participants and users.

Around this time, the issue of continuity was put on the table. As James mentioned in informal talks, if one of the editors left the journal it would mean that a lot of intrinsic information would be lost, and the newcomers would have to establish a new set of contacts and try to make sense of the information in the cloud system. She argued that especially with the voluntary nature of the work, they were not able to have a concrete way of establishing a system that would enable them to "pass on the torch" to newcomers. As he was the one that provided a strong push to establish the journal, he felt that it was his duty to ascertain that if he leaves her position the journal would continue to operate as successfully as it is now. "So, we needed to have a system that I can rely on and understand as a newcomer that hasn't worked with this journal before" (James).

This issue was also reflected in choosing the OJS, as one of the criteria the editorial team used was to see if the system was widely used by others – to ascertain if the system will continue to exist – and see if they would be too tightly bound by the system to the point that they would be stuck with it. As from their research they have seen some organisations going through such lock-in situations, the OS solution was preferred as it provided some flexibility in case they decided to change their system later on.

DISCUSSION OF THE CASE

Following the case description, one can track the elements of the WS framework throughout the editorial teams' journey. At this section, some of the discussed issues would be presented in another format to highlight some aspects of this journey.

In words of James, this case can be seen as an example of "emergent strategy". From the beginning of the journey the editorial team had an overall strategy for the journal, both in terms of aims and scope of the Journal - be accessible to young researchers, focusing on developing economies – and more formal but mostly silent aim of being included in established academic ranking/indexing databases. However, the role of the IT did not receive attention during the set up of the journal. The infrastructure of access to internet and academic databases were taken for granted – as most often than not these were provided by becoming a member of faculty – however how the editors would use technologies in the publishing process were left untouched. The role of IT however evolved from using emails to using an OS-JMS. This process, as argued by Mintzberg (1978:946) is an organizational learning process, in which the "implementation feeds back to formulation and intentions get modified en route, resulting in an emergent strategy".

One reason why it took time for the editorial team to focus on the technologies to help them solve their knowledge management issues can be tied to the fact that these issues were not coined as knowledge management issues at the time, but rather as a situation that will resolve itself. On this issue all the interviewed editors commented that their first priority was to get through the take off phase. Most of their aspirations stemmed from their mostly negative experiences, and thus they were emotionally attached to the project to make it work even through turbulent times. As the take off of the Business Journal was achieved, the emotional attachment was followed by other forms of organizational commitment: as the editors were now a member of a highly involved group, they expressed that giving up would mean turning your back to your friends. To this end, in an informal discussion James expressed rather vividly that she – and other editors – felt duty bound to give work with the Journal, as it was their own project from the very beginning. Such organizational commitment is similar to the classification provided by Meyer and Allen (1991) – affective, continuance and normative – and while as they argue these might lead to positive results for the individual and the organization, in this case they might have resulted in a certain amount of blindness to other options. This issue has became apparent when the editorial team decided getting help from newcomers as managerial editors, as before the situation was resolved, all the editors' expressed that they were having extra stress but didn't want to leave the Journal behind. Furthermore, the editors also expressed that there was anxiousness until they were sure that these newcomers could handle the situation. The ability of the managerial editors to handle problematic instances on the other hand was constrained by the technologies that the Journal used to manage their knowledge management activities. By having this very close relation to the Journal the editorial team might have been hindered to act in a more strategic manner for several of their choices.

The choices regarding the technologies in Business Journal has usually followed an ad-hoc decision-making. It took several years until the editorial team was able to identify that they needed a more holistic technological solution to support their work processes. Up to that decision, their IT use has been most limited to emails when they first established the Journal, and adding a cloud service to store and work with the document related to submissions at the growth phase. While this intertwining of technologies (Robey, Schwaig, & Jin, 2003) helped them, the ad-hoc solutions were not able to provide long term solutions. Until they decided to use their OS-JMS they were not able to create a coherent way of information sharing and knowledge management, and though the intertwining was used consciously to help the OS system, it was more about saving the day at the growth phase, not taking the long term issues into consideration. This gradual adoption of a more systematic view resulting in OJS resembles the added pressure to become systemised in Solomon (2007).

This lack of long term planning, as the case hints can be explained – in part at least – as a result of the editorial team not having a conscious IT strategy and not seeing IT as a part of the whole. As a part of the WS framework, strategy affects the other components, as it directs the organization towards certain goals, however, as mentioned the strategy of the Journal did not take into account IT related issues. The nature of the IT strategy was more of an emergent one, and even though it seems to have resolved itself at this stage, it nevertheless is problematic that the editorial team did not think about the technologies that they would use in their work processes. Their belief that the chosen technologies would be enough can be considered as an example of the deterministic thinking of technology that might result in negative consequences that Leonardi and Barley (2010) warn about. Without thinking how the participants might actually use, and how they should use it to realize the potential benefits, the case of the technologies was left to resolve itself, creating further problems as the submissions and related tasks increased. Like other examples in the literature on OS publishing systems (see for example Hunter, 2010; Polydoratou & Moyle, 2008; Solomon, 2007) the objective of keeping costs down, streamlining the process, having easily accessible systems were present in this case too. However, until the editorial team has realised that technological solutions should be aligned with other parts of the WS and that such decisions should be made holistically, the piece-meal solutions only helped to save the day.

However, one should be cautious to say that the problems resulting from the technologies – or lack of a strategy for technologies and seeing how it will affect the other components – are only the result of how the participants used it. One of the chief hindrances the editorial team mentioned for the overall success of the Journal was that they had to take time out of their own personal life to work with the Journal. One of the editors argued that they hoped to get help from the university to have the faculty board consider working with the Journal as departmental duty, so that they would be able to compensate some of the time they worked for the Journal. However the university did not consider Business Journal as a university project, thus this option was not available. This is an example of how the short-term considerations can actually put the long-term survival of the Journal under question. While the editorial team today accepts that they wanted a better knowledge management system, to do so would mean they would need to divert considerable time to learning that system. This holistic understanding of technologies is definitely a desired view and would help the long-term survival of the Journal. Conversely, however, it would mean that the Journal would have either low quality due to lack of resources or the editorial team would live in a high-stress environment.

This lack of resources was also touched upon when the editors short-listed what they wanted from their new JMS. While some other system could have provided similar or perhaps better solutions to the knowledge management issues, the editorial team opted for an OS solution. While at the moment they are using the hosting services of the software, they have the option to use their own server without paying the license cost. As the editorial team pays for these fees from their own individual funds, this might mean that as they incorporate more tech-savvy people into their team or have the university support, they would be able to migrate the system to a server of their own and reduce the fees. Similar to the conscious thinking about the management system in general, the editorial team also have argued that if they need to change something in the future, the OS licensing would help them to do the changes. This shift from the near non-existent IT strategy to thinking about future use of OS code shows how the emergent strategy can become a part of psyche of the editorial team.

The decision to move to a more standardized system was also prompted by increased competition. As new journals emerged that had similar aims and scope, the editorial team argued that they needed to present a professional front, and one way to do so was to have a JMS. This legitimacy seeking behaviour is reminiscent of the isomorphic pressures of the neo-institutional theory (DiMaggio & Powell, 1983), and might be tightly linked to the strategy set up by considering the technologies as a tool to help the general strategy of the Journal. In line with this, another notice worthy situation is the ability of the system to actually influence the behaviour of the participants of the WS, in line with the technical isomorphism (Benders, Batenburg, & van der Blonk, 2006), in which the inscribed ways of communication in the system in turn effects the adopting organisation. As the JMS comes with scripted ways of doing the business, the effect of the implementation was more profound than expected. While the editors have discussed the need for sending reminders to reviewers and authors to complete their work, the system has also had the effect of having editors realize their own tasks in a standardized way. This, in turn, has resulted in the editors to identify instances where they skip in their information sharing practices and putting more effort to track their reasoning for their rejection/

acceptance decisions. Even though the editors still have a considerable amount of information uncodified, they also argue that with the new system they can see more of the decision process and the information regarding the submissions.

This change has been coupled with the more holistic view of the editorial team for the effect of the technologies they use as they continued their journey. Instead of the rather tool version of the technology, they have begun to see them as enablers of work. As the journal has matured, the editorial teams understanding of their environment and their strategy has become clearer, thus changing how they see the technologies they used, a shift from seeing IT as a tool – and as a constraint – to seeing IT as a part of their WS, and thinking about how they can use it. This, according to the observations of the author has on the one hand been partly a result of the built-in design of the OS system. Rather than the piece meal solutions that were used, with this system the editors were able to see the whole WS, and track the effects of actions. However, on the other hand this issue of built-in affordances (Norman, 1999) is not enough to explain how the participants of the WS changed their understanding of the technologies. When asked in an informal setting, James has argued that the value of the open source solution was realized because now they understand what needs to be done, and have a clear picture of the pieces. This is more in line with the more action oriented and relational aspects understanding of the affordances (Leonardi, 2011): as the participants interpret the technologies through their aims, the affordances provided by the JMS has been affected by the strategy of the Journal and experience of the editors. Moving from the ad-hoc decision making to seeing IT as a part of the WS and having a holistic view of the process was a lesson that the editorial team learned during the evolution of the Journal.

Similar to an ecosystem view, OJS can be conceptualized as a technological ecosystem, with similar technologies constituting a population (Saviotti, 1996). OJS, if taken as the focal technology in the analysis is connected with the computers used by the editors, various infrastructure components and standards – internet networks, routers, database languages – to the final product – a pdf file that is the accepted and edited manuscript. In such an ecosystem, multiple connections are possible, with the work flow chart provided before influencing how some of these connections are made in practice. With plug-ins the core OJS today can integrate for Google Scholar for indexing and provide RSS web syndication, showing how the ecosystem continues to extend. In this manner OJS takes the role of an ecosystem that provides services and tools that the actors use to achieve their goals (Iansiti & Levien, 2004; Iansiti & Richards, 2006).

As noted by Wallinsky (2005), OJS covers a wide range of activities, can be installed on various different operating systems and databases. However even if these affordances are found within the system it does not reflect actual usage. As already noted, while the editors seem to be happy about the ability to use the tool for finding additional reviewers, they have not done so. This shows that while OJS can be likened to a technological ecosystem, as of this moment, the potential has not been realised by the Business Journal. Most of the aspects that made the editors decide upon OJS – continuality, flexibility, ease of use can be traced back to this technological ecosystem that OJS can provide. With the OS community involvement, the evolution of the OJS is made possible, providing continuity. Similarly the high adoption rate of OJS can be taken as a signal for its resilience and adaptability, as well as survival. However, as can be seen, the other components of the WS have played an important role in using and adapting to this ecosystem, thus the adoption of a WS framework in this chapter.

CONCLUSION

This chapter began with the aim of examining how and why an academic journal invests in IS/IT. To achieve this aim a qualitative case study was conducted, using interviews and observations as main ways of gathering data. The case has shown that how the IS/IT was treated has shown differences in different temporal episodes.

When the journal was first set up, the use of technologies was not given much thought, and the editorial team did not consider it as a part of a bigger whole. They set up an email for Business Journal, and tried to use it as a way of communicating with the participants. However this resulted in an inefficient knowledge management tool, and was later on supplemented with a cloud system in which the editors uploaded the documents related to submissions.

This ad-hoc pattern of investing in IS/IT solutions contributed to the existing knowledge management problems, as the editors became more and more frustrated with the issue. As they later on realized, one reason for not having a sufficient system was that the tasks they performed were not reflected in their technologies, and to achieve their aims that needed to change. This in return meant that they had to set up a more strategic view of the technologies they used, taking into account that they face more competition from the environment and they have scarce resources.

This vision of taking the technologies as a part of a whole is what has actually been suggested in the WS framework (Alter, 2008), and the case showed that such an understanding could have helped the editors to iron out the problems they faced much earlier if they had followed such holistic view. However, the case also showed that, sometimes the long-term survival of the journal – and the technology investments for that – was curtailed by the short-term goals.

The case has also shown that by evolving with the Journal, the editors have also gained an understanding of the OSS and began to use a more WS approach for their technology choices. Even though they don't plan to modify the source code at this point, the ability to do so was one of the potential benefits they discussed during their summer meeting. The effects of the technology on the work processes and on realizing the strategy was highlighted, showing how they differed from their initial days when technology was seen only as a tool.

ACKNOWLEDGMENT

This paper acknowledges The Swedish Research School of Management and IT for funding this work.

REFERENCES

Adomavicius, G., Bockstedt, J. C., Gupta, A., & Kauffman, R. J. (2007). Technology roles and paths of influence in an ecosystem model of technology evolution. *Information Technology Management*, *8*(2), 185–202. doi:10.1007/s10799-007-0012-z

Alter, S. (2003). 18 Reasons Why IT-Reliant Work Systems Should Replace " The IT Artifact " as the Core Subject Matter of the IS Field. *Communications of the Association for Information Systems*, *12*, 23.

Alter, S. (2004). Making Work System Principles Visible and Usable in Systems Analysis and Design. In *AMCIS 2004, the Americas Conference on Information Systems* (pp. 1604–1611).

Alter, S. (2006). Work systems and IT artifacts - Does the definition matter? *Communications of the Association for Information Systems*, *17*, 14.

Alter, S. (2008). Defining information systems as work systems: Implications for the IS field. *European Journal of Information Systems*, *17*(5), 448–469. doi:10.1057/ejis.2008.37

Alter, S. (2013). Work System Theory: Overview of Core Concepts, Extensions, and Challenges for the Future Work System Theory: Overview of Core Concepts, Extensions, and Challenges for the Future. *Journal of the Association for Information Systems*, (February), 72.

Alter, S. (2015). The concept of "IT artifact" has outlived its usefulness and should be retired now. *Information Systems Journal, 25*(1), 47–60. doi:10.1111/isj.12048

Benbasat, I., & Zmud, R. W. (2003). The identity crisis within the IS discipline: Defining and communicating the discipline's core properties. *Management Information Systems Quarterly, 27*(2), 183–194.

Benders, J., Batenburg, R., & van der Blonk, H. (2006). Sticking to standards; technical and other isomorphic pressures in deploying ERP-systems. *Information & Management, 43*(2), 194–203. doi:10.1016/j.im.2005.06.002

BenMoussa, C. (2010). Exploiting Mobile Technologies to Build a Knowledge Mobilization Capability: A Work System-Based Method. In *2010 43rd Hawaii International Conference on System Sciences* (pp. 1–11). IEEE. doi:10.1109/HICSS.2010.197

De Leoz, G. M., & Petter, S. C. (2013). Infusing High Performance Teams in Information System Work Environments. In MWAIS 2013 (Paper 12).

DiMaggio, P., & Powell, W. W. (1983). The iron cage revisited: Institutional isomorphism and collective rationality in organizational fields. *American Sociological Review, 48*(2), 147–160. doi:10.2307/2095101

Hunter, B. (2010). Moving Open Access to Open Source: Transitioning an Open-Access Journal into the Open Journal Systems Journal Management System. *Technical Services Quarterly, 28*(1), 31–40. doi:10.1080/07317131.2010.500972

Iansiti, M., & Levien, R. (2004). Strategy as Ecology. *Harvard Business Review, 82*(3), 68–81. PMID:15029791

Iansiti, M., & Richards, G. L. (2006). Information technology ecosystem: Structure, health, and performance, The. *Antitrust Bull., 51*(1), 77–110.

Jasperson, J., Carter, P., & Zmud, R. (2005). A comprehensive conceptualization of post-adoptive behaviors associated with information technology enabled work systems. *Management Information Systems Quarterly, 29*(3), 525–557.

Kampath, N., & Röglinger, M. (2010). Operational and work system-related success factors for customer relationship management in "product sales" and "solution sales"–a descriptive case study. In *Proceedings of ECIS 2010, the 18th European Conference on Information Systems*.

Klein, H. K., & Myers, M. D. (1999). A Set of Principles for Conducting and Evaluating Interpretive Field Studies in Information Systems. *Management Information Systems Quarterly, 23*(1), 67–93. doi:10.2307/249410

Korpela, M. M., Eerola, A., Häkkinen, A., & Toivanen, H. (2004). IS research and development by activity analysis and development: Dead horse or the next wave? In Relevant Theory and Informed Practice: Looking Forward from a 20- Year Perspective on IS Research 15-17 July 2004, Manchester (pp. 453–471). Kluwer Academic Publishers.

Laakso, M., Welling, P., Bukvova, H., Nyman, L., Björk, B. C., & Hedlund, T. (2011). The development of open access journal publishing from 1993 to 2009. *PLoS ONE*, *6*(6), e20961. doi:10.1371/journal.pone.0020961 PMID:21695139

Larsen, P. O., & von Ins, M. (2010). The rate of growth in scientific publication and the decline in coverage provided by science citation index. *Scientometrics*, *84*(3), 575–603. doi:10.1007/s11192-010-0202-z PMID:20700371

Lee, A. S., & Baskerville, R. L. (2003). Gerneralizing Generalizability in Information Systems Research. *Information Systems Research*, *14*(3), 221–243. doi:10.1287/isre.14.3.221.16560

Leonardi, P. M. (2011). When flexible routines meet flexible technologies: Affordance, constraint, and the imbrication of human and material agencies. *Management Information Systems Quarterly*, *35*(1), 147–167.

Leonardi, P. M., & Barley, S. R. (2010). What's Under Construction Here? Social Action, Materiality, and Power in Constructivist Studies of Technology and Organizing. *The Academy of Management Annals*, *4*(1), 1–51. doi:10.1080/19416521003654160

Mann, F., von Walter, B., Hess, T., & Wigand, R. T. (2009). Open access publishing in science. *Communications of the ACM*, *52*(3), 135–139. doi:10.1145/1467247.1467279

Mars, M. M., Bronstein, J. L., & Lusch, R. F. (2012). The Value of a Metaphor: Organizations and Ecosystems. *Organizational Dynamics*, *41*(4), 271–280. doi:10.1016/j.orgdyn.2012.08.002

Meyer, J. P., & Allen, N. J. (1991). A three-component conceptualization of organizational commitment. *Human Resource Management Review*, *1*(1), 61–89. doi:10.1016/1053-4822(91)90011-Z

Mintzberg, H. (1978). Patterns in Strategy Formation. *Management Science*, *24*(9), 934–948. doi:10.1287/mnsc.24.9.934

Norman, D. (1999). Affordance, conventions, and design. *Interaction*, *6*(3), 38–43. doi:10.1145/301153.301168

Orlikowski, W. J., & Iacono, C. S. (2001). Research Commentary : Desperately Seeking the " IT " in IT Research — A Call to Theorizing the IT Artifact. *Information Systems Research*, *12*(2), 121–134. doi:10.1287/isre.12.2.121.9700

Petersson, J. (2008). Work system principles. In *Proceedings of the 3rd International Conference on the Pragmatic Web Innovating the Interactive Society - ICPW '08* (pp. 69–76). doi:10.1145/1479190.1479200

Polydoratou, P., & Moyle, M. (2008). Scientific journals, overlays and repositories: A case of costs and sustainability issues. Lecture Notes in Computer Science, 5362, 154–163.

Riehle, D. (2007). The Economic Motivation of Open Source Software: Stakeholder Perspectives. *IEEE Computer*, *40*(4), 25–32. doi:10.1109/MC.2007.147

Robey, D., Schwaig, K. S., & Jin, L. (2003). Intertwining material and virtual work. *Information and Organization*, *13*(2), 111–129. doi:10.1016/S1471-7727(02)00025-8

Saviotti, P. P. (1996). *Technology Evolution, Variety and the Economy*. Cheltenham, UK: Edward Elgar Publishing.

Serrano, N., & Sarriei, J. M. (2006). Open source software ERPs: A new alternative for an old need. *IEEE Software*, *23*(3), 94–97. doi:10.1109/MS.2006.78

Siggelkow, N. (2007). Persuasion With Case Studies. *Academy of Management Journal*, *50*(1), 20–24. doi:10.5465/AMJ.2007.24160882

Solomon, D. J. (2007). Handbook of research on open source software: Technological, economic, and social perspectives. IGI Global.

Walsham, G. (1995). Interpretive Case Studies in IS Research : Nature and Method. *European Journal of Information Systems*, *4*(2), 74–81. doi:10.1057/ejis.1995.9

Walsham, G. (2006). Doing Interpretive Research. *European Journal of Information Systems*, *15*(3), 320–330. doi:10.1057/palgrave.ejis.3000589

Wareham, J., Fox, P. B., & Cano Giner, J. L. (2014). Technology Ecosystem Governance. *Organization Science*, *25*(4), 1195–1215. doi:10.1287/orsc.2014.0895

Willinsky, J. (2005). Open Journal Systems. *Library Hi Tech*, *23*(4), 504–519. doi:10.1108/07378830510636300

Yin, R. K. (2009). *Case Study Research: Design and Methods* (4th ed.). Thousand Oaks, CA: Sage Publications.

KEY TERMS AND DEFINITIONS

Affordances: A concept from ecological theory of perception that argues objects (i.e. IT, knobs of an oven, a knife) have characteristics that provides a potential for action and realized by the interaction of the actor and the object.

Emergent Strategy: Result of organizational learning, in which participants as a reaction to changing needs incorporate new ideas to their work, which in time become part of the strategy.

Journal Management System: An information system used to manage and publish academic/non-academic journals, used by editors, authors and reviewers to produce digital/printed publications.

Open Source Journal Management System: Several journal management systems that are produced and distributed as open source software. Usually these systems provide hosting and support for additional fees.

Open Source Software: Software that is licensed under a licensing scheme satisfying the Open Source Initiatives' conditions (i.e. software can be freely given away/sold, source code given/obtainable etc.).

Work System: A system in which humans and/or machines perform work, using resources (i.e. technology, information) to provide products/services to the customers.

Work System Framework: A framework created by Steven Alter to conceptualise what a work system is, and how it is related to other components that are not part of the system but can not exist meaningfully studied without consideration (infrastructure, environment, strategy, customers, products/services).

Compilation of References

Adamides, E. D., & Mouzakitis, Y. (2009). Industrial ecosystems as technological niches. *Journal of Cleaner Production*, *17*(2), 172–180. doi:10.1016/j.jclepro.2008.04.003

Adams, E. (2010). *Fundamentals of Game Design* (2nd ed.). Berkeley, CA: New Riders.

Adell, J., & Castañeda, L. (2010). Los Entornos Personales de Aprendizaje (PLEs): una nueva manera de entender el aprendizaje. In R. Roig Vila & M. Fiorucci (Eds.), Claves para la investigación en innovación y calidad educativas. La integración de las Tecnologías de la Información y la Comunicación y la Interculturalidad en las aulas. Stumenti di ricerca per l'innovaziones e la qualità in ámbito educativo. La Tecnologie dell'informazione e della Comunicazione e l'interculturalità nella scuola. Alcoy, Spain: Marfil – Roma TRE Universita degli studi.

Adkins, B. A., Foth, M., Summerville, J. A., & Higgs, P. L. (2007). Ecologies of innovation: Symbolic aspects of cross-organizational linkages in the design sector in an Australian inner-city area. *The American Behavioral Scientist*, *50*(7), 922–934. doi:10.1177/0002764206298317

Adomavicius, G., Bockstedt, J. C., Gupta, A., & Kauffman, R. J. (2007). Technology roles and paths of influence in an ecosystem model of technology evolution. *Information Technology Management*, *8*(2), 185–202. doi:10.1007/s10799-007-0012-z

Adomavicius, G., Bockstedt, J., Gupta, A., & Kauffman, R. J. (2006). Understanding patterns of technology evolution: An Ecosystem perspective. In *Proceedings of the 39th Annual Hawaii International Conference System Science* (Vol. 8). IEEE.

Adomavicius, G., Bockstedt, J., Gupta, A., & Kauffman, R. J. (2012). Understanding Evolution in Technology Ecosystems. *Communications of the ACM*, *51*(10), 117–122. doi:10.1145/1400181.1400207

Agudo-Peregrina, Á. F., Iglesias-Pradas, S., Conde-González, M. Á., & Hernández-García, Á. (2014). Can we predict success from log data in VLEs? Classification of interactions for learning analytics and their relation with performance in VLE-supported F2F and online learning. *Computers in Human Behavior, 31*, 542–550. doi:10.1016/j.chb.2013.05.031

Alberer, G., Alberer, P., Enzi, T., Ernst, G., Mayrhofer, K., Neumann, G., et al. (2003). *The Learn@WU Learning Environment. In Proceedings of Wirtschaftsinformatik 2003*. 6th International Conference on Business Informatics, Dresden, Germany.

Alier Forment, M., Casañ Guerrero, M. J., Conde González, M. Á., García-Peñalvo, F. J., & Severance, C. (2010). Interoperability for LMS: The missing piece to become the common place for e-learning innovation.[IJKL]. *International Journal of Knowledge and Learning, 6*(2/3), 130–141. doi:10.1504/IJKL.2010.034749

Alier, M., Casany, M. J., Mayol, E., Piguillem, J., & Galanis, N. (2012). Docs-4Learning: Getting Google Docs to Work within the LMS with IMS BLTI. *Journal of Universal Computer Science, 18*(11), 1483–1500.

Alier, M., Mayol, E., Casañ, M. J., Piguillem, J., Merriman, J. W., & Conde González, M. Á. et al. (2012). Clustering Projects for eLearning Interoperability. *Journal of Universal Computer Science, 18*(1), 106–122.

Alter, S. (2004). Making Work System Principles Visible and Usable in Systems Analysis and Design. In *AMCIS 2004, the Americas Conference on Information Systems* (pp. 1604–1611).

Alter, S. (2003). 18 Reasons Why IT-Reliant Work Systems Should Replace " The IT Artifact " as the Core Subject Matter of the IS Field. *Communications of the Association for Information Systems, 12*, 23.

Alter, S. (2006). Work systems and IT artifacts - Does the definition matter? *Communications of the Association for Information Systems, 17*, 14.

Alter, S. (2008). Defining information systems as work systems: Implications for the IS field. *European Journal of Information Systems, 17*(5), 448–469. doi:10.1057/ejis.2008.37

Alter, S. (2013). Work System Theory: Overview of Core Concepts, Extensions, and Challenges for the Future Work System Theory: Overview of Core Concepts, Extensions, and Challenges for the Future. *Journal of the Association for Information Systems*, (February), 72.

Alter, S. (2015). The concept of "IT artifact" has outlived its usefulness and should be retired now. *Information Systems Journal, 25*(1), 47–60. doi:10.1111/isj.12048

Aram, M., & Neumann, G. (2015). Multilayered Analysis of Co-Development of Business Information Systems. *Journal of Internet Services and Applications, 6*(1).

Armbrecht, Jr., Chapas, Chappelow, & Farris. (2001). Knowledge management in research and development. *Research Technology Management, 44*(4), 28.

Arroway, P., Davenport, E., Guangning, X., & Updegrove, D. (2010). *Educause Core Data Service Fiscal Year 2009 summary report.* EDUCAUSE White Paper. EDUCAUSE.

Atkins, D., Ball, T., Graves, T., & Mockus, A. (1999). Using Version Control Data to Evaluate the Impact of Software Tools. In *Proc. 21st International Conference on Software Engineering.* doi:10.1145/302405.302649

Aubusson, P. (2002). An ecology of science education. *International Journal of Science Education, 24*(1), 27–46. doi:10.1080/09500690110066511

Avgeriou, P., Papasalouros, A., Retalis, S., & Skordalakis, M. (2003). Towards a Pattern Language for Learning Management Systems. *Journal of Educational Technology & Society, 6*(2), 11–24.

Barbosa, O., & Alves, C. (2011). A Systematic Mapping Study on Software Eco-systems.*Proceedings of the Workshop on Software Ecosystems.*

Barcellini, F., Detienne, F., & Burkhardt, J. M. (2008a). User and developer mediation in an Open Source Software community: Boundary spanning through cross participation in online discussions. *International Journal of Human-Computer Studies, 66*(7), 558–570. doi:10.1016/j.ijhcs.2007.10.008

Barcellini, F., Detienne, F., Burkhardt, J. M., & Sack, W. (2008b). A socio-cognitive analysis of online design discussions in an Open Source Software community. *Interacting with Computers, 20*(1), 141–165. doi:10.1016/j.intcom.2007.10.004

Barrios, O. (2000). *Estrategia del portafolio del alumnado. In Estrategias didácticas innovadoras* (pp. 294–301). Barcelona: Octaedro.

Bartle, R. (1996). *Hearts, Clubs, Diamonds, Spades: Players Who Suit MUDs.* Retrieved from http://www.mud.co.uk/richard/hcds.htm

Bartle, R. (2004). *Designing Virtual Worlds.* New Riders Publishing.

Baskerville & Dulipovici. (2006). The Theoretical foundation of Knowledge Management. KMR&P.

Baskerville, R. L. (1999). Investigating information systems with action research. *Communications of the AIS, 2*(3es), 4.

BBVA Innovation Centre. (2012). *The fun way to engage*. Retrieved from https://www.centrodeinnovacionbbva.com/en/innovation-edge/gamification/gamification-fun-way-engage

Behrens, J. T., & Dicerbo, K. E. (2014). Technological Implications for Assessment Ecosystems: Opportunities for Digital Technology to Advance Assessment. *Teachers College Record, 116*(11), 1–22. PMID:26120219

Benbasat, I., & Zmud, R. W. (2003). The identity crisis within the IS discipline: Defining and communicating the discipline's core properties. *Management Information Systems Quarterly, 27*(2), 183–194.

Benders, J., Batenburg, R., & van der Blonk, H. (2006). Sticking to standards; technical and other isomorphic pressures in deploying ERP-systems. *Information & Management, 43*(2), 194–203. doi:10.1016/j.im.2005.06.002

BenMoussa, C. (2010). Exploiting Mobile Technologies to Build a Knowledge Mobilization Capability: A Work System-Based Method. In *2010 43rd Hawaii International Conference on System Sciences* (pp. 1–11). IEEE. doi:10.1109/HICSS.2010.197

Bergeron, B. P. (2006). *Developing Serious Games*. Charles River Media.

Berger, P. L., & Luckmann, T. (1991). *The social construction of reality: A treatise in the sociology of knowledge*. Penguin.

Berlanga, A. J., Sloep, P. B., Brouns, F., Bitter-Rijpkema, M. E., & Koper, R. (2008). Towards a TENCompetence ePortfolio. *International Journal of Emerging Technologies in Learning, 3*, 24–28.

Berthelemy, M. (2013). *Definition of a learning ecosystem*. Retrieved from http://www.learningconversations.co.uk/main/index.php/2010/01/10/the-characteristics-of-a-learning-ecosystem?blog=5

Bienkowski, M., Feng, M., & Means, B. (2012). Enhancing teaching and learning through educational data mining and learning analytics: An issue brief. US Department of Education, Office of Educational Technology.

Bird, C., Pattison, D., D'Souza, R., Filkov, V., & Devanbu, P. (2008). Latent social structure in open source projects. In *Proceedings of the 16th ACM SIGSOFT International Symposium on Foundations of software engineering* (pp. 24-35). ACM. doi:10.1145/1453101.1453107

Birrer, A. J. F. (2006). Science-trained professionals for the innovation ecosystem: Looking back and looking ahead. *Industry and Higher Education, 20*(4), 273–277. doi:10.5367/000000006778175865

Bittner, E. A. C., & Leimeister, J. M. (2014). Creating Shared Understanding in Heterogeneous Work Groups: Why It Matters and How to Achieve It. *Journal of Management Information Systems, 31*(1), 111–144. doi:10.2753/MIS0742-1222310106

Blanch Gelabert, S., Bosco Paniagua, A., Gimeno Soria, X., González Monfort, N., Fuentes Agustí, M., Jariot Garcia, M., ... Forestello, A. M. (2011). *Carpetas de aprendizaje en la educación superior: una oportunidad para repensar la docencia.* Bellaterra: Servei de Publicacions Universitat Autònoma de Barcelona.

Blesius, C. R., Moreno-Ger, P., Neumann, G., Raffenne, E., Boticario, J. G., & Kloos, C. D. (2007). LRN: E-Learning Inside and Outside The Classroom. In B. Fernández-Manjón, J. M. Sánchez-Pérez, J. A. Gómez-Pulido, M. A. Vega-Rodríguez, & J. Bravo-Rodríguez (Eds.), *Computers and Education* (pp. 13–25). Springer. doi:10.1007/978-1-4020-4914-9_2

Blohm, I., & Leimeister, J. M. (2013). Gamification - Design of IT-Based Enhancing Services for Motivational Support and Behavioral Change. *Business & Information Systems Engineering, 5*(4), 275–278. doi:10.1007/s12599-013-0273-5

Bo, D., Qinghua, Z., Jie, Y., Haifei, L., & Mu, Q. (2009). *An e-learning ecosystem based on cloud computing infrastructure.* Paper presented at the Advanced Learning Technologies, 2009. ICALT 2009. Ninth IEEE International Conference on.

Bocar. (2013). Difficulties encountered by the student researchers and the effects on their research output. *Proceeding of the Global Summit on Education 2013.*

Bo, D., Qinghua, Z., Jie, Y., Haifei, L., & Mu, Q. (2009). An E-learning Ecosystem Based on Cloud Computing Infrastructure.*Ninth IEEE International Conference on Advanced Learning Technologies, 2009. ICALT 2009.* Riga, Latvia: IEEE.

Bollier, D. (2000). *Ecologies of innovation: The role of information and communication technologies.* Washington, DC: The Aspen Institute.

Bonjour, E., Belkadi, F., Troussier, N., & Dulmet, M. (2009). Modelling interactions to support and manage collaborative decision-making processes in design situations. *International Journal of Computer Applications in Technology, 36*(3/4), 259. doi:10.1504/IJCAT.2009.028048

Bosch, J. (2009). From Software Product Lines to Software Ecosystems. *Proceedings of the13th International Software Product Line Conference*. Carnegie Mellon University.

Bosch, J. (2010). Architecture challenges for software ecosystems. In *Proceedings of the Fourth European Conference on Software Architecture: Companion Volume* (pp. 93-95). New York, NY: ACM.

Bosch, J. (2010). *Architecture challenges for software ecosystems.* Paper presented at the Fourth European Conference on Software Architecture.

Browne, T., Hewitt, R., Jenkins, M., Voce, J., Walker, R., & Yip, H. (2010). *Survey of Technology Enhanced Learning for higher education in the UK*. Oxford, UK: UCISA - Universities and Colleges Information System Association.

Cater-Steel, A. (Ed.). (2009). *Information technology governance and service management: frameworks and adaptations*. Hershey, PA: Information Science Reference. doi:10.4018/978-1-60566-008-0

CeLTIc Project Wiki. (2014). *LTI/Best Practice/Introduction*. Retrieved February 13, 2015, from http://celtic.lti.tools/wiki/LTI/Best_Practice/Introduction

Chad, K. (2013, September). The library management system is dead – Long live the library ecosystem. *CILIP Update Magazine,* 18-20.

Chang, E., & West, M. (2006). *Digital ecosystems a next generation of the collaborative environment.* Paper presented at the Eight International Conference on Information Integration and Web-Based Application & Services, Yogyakarta, Indonesia.

Chang, E., & West, M. (2006). *Digital Ecosystems A Next Generation of the Collaborative Environment.* Presented at the 8th International Conference on Information Integration and Web-based Application & Services, Yogyakarta, Indonesia.

Chappelow. (2004). The Future of Knowledge Management: An international Delphi Study. *Journal of Knowledge Management.*

Chen, W., & Chang, E. (2007). *Exploring a digital ecosystem conceptual model and its simulation prototype.* Paper presented at the Industrial Electronics, 2007. ISIE 2007. IEEE International Symposium on.

Chen, W., & Chang, E. (2007). Exploring a Digital Ecosystem Conceptual Model and Its Simulation Prototype.*Proceedings of IEEE International Symposium on Industrial Electronics, 2007 (ISIE 2007)* (pp. 2933 - 2938). IEEE.

Clark, A. C. (1970). *Serious Games*. Viking Press.

Conde-González, M. Á., García-Peñalvo, F. J., Casany, M. J., & Alier, M. (2009). Adapting LMS architecture to the SOA: an Architectural Approach. In H. Sasaki, G. O. Bellot, M. Ehmann, & O. Dini (Eds.), *Proceedings of the Fourth International Conference on Internet and Web Applications and Services – ICIW 2009* (pp. 322-327). Los Alamitos, CA: IEEE Computer Society. doi:10.1109/ICIW.2009.54

Conde-González, M. Á., & Hernández-García, Á. (2013). A promised land for educational decision-making? Present and future of learning analytics.*Proceedings of the First International Conference on Technological Ecosystem for Enhancing Multiculturality* (pp. 239-243). ACM. doi:10.1145/2536536.2536573

Conde-González, M. Á., Hernández-García, Á., García-Peñalvo, F. J., & Sein-Echaluce Lacleta, M. L. (2015). Exploring student interactions: Learning analytics tools for student tracking.*Proceedings of the 17th International Conference, HCI International 2015*. Los Angeles, CA: Springer International Publishing.

Conde, M. Á., García-Peñalvo, F. J., Rodríguez-Conde, M. J., Alier, M., & García-Holgado, A. (2014). Perceived openness of learning management systems by students and teachers in education and technology courses. *Computers in Human Behavior*, *31*, 517–526. doi:10.1016/j.chb.2013.05.023

Cook, J. E., Votta, L. G., & Wolf, A. L. (1998). Cost-effective analysis of in-place software processes. *IEEE Transactions on Software Engineering*, *24*(8), 650–663. doi:10.1109/32.707700

COPLA. (2016). *Coneixement Obert i Programari Lliure a la Universitat d'Alacant*. Retrieved from http://blogs.ua.es/copla/

Crawford, C. (1982). *The art of computer game design*. Academic Press.

Crouzier, T. (2015). *Science ecosystem 2.0: How will change occur?* Luxembourg: Publications Office of the European Union.

Crowston, K., Howison, J., & Annabi, H. (2006). Information systems success in free and open source software development: Theory and measures. *Software Process Improvement and Practice*, *11*(2), 123–148. doi:10.1002/spip.259

CRUE TIC. (2014). *UNIVERSITIC 2014: Descripción, Gestión y Gobierno de las TI en el Sistema Universitario Español.* Madrid, España: Conferencia de Rectores de las Universidades Españolas (CRUE).

Csíkszentmihályi, M. (1996). *Creativity: Flow and the Psychology of Discovery and Invention.* New York: Harper Perennial.

Dalmau Espert, J. L. (2016). *Sistema multiagente para el diseño, ejecución y seguimiento del proceso de planificación estratégica ágil en las organizaciones inteligentes.* (Tesis Doctoral). Universidad de Alicante, Alicante. Retrieved from http://hdl.handle.net/10045/54217

David, P. A., & Shapiro, J. S. (2008). Community-based production of open-source software: What do we know about the developers who participate? *Information Economics and Policy, 20*(4), 364–398. doi:10.1016/j.infoecopol.2008.10.001

Davis, J., Miller, G. J., & Russell, A. (2006). *Information revolution: using the information evolution model to grow your business.* Hoboken, NJ: John Wiley.

De Leoz, G. M., & Petter, S. C. (2013). Infusing High Performance Teams in Information System Work Environments. In MWAIS 2013 (Paper 12).

Demetriou, N., Koch, S., & Neumann, G. (2006). The Development of the OpenACS Community. In M. Lytras & A. Naeve (Eds.), *Open Source for Knowledge and Learning Management: Strategies Beyond Tools.* Hershey, PA: Idea Group.

Dempsey, B. J., Weiss, D., Jones, P., & Greenberg, J. (2002). Who is an open source software developer? *Communications of the ACM, 45*(2), 67–72. doi:10.1145/503124.503125

Deshpande D. S, Kulkarni P. R., Metkewar P. S. (2015). A Knowledge Management approach for Developing Research Community. *International Journal of Engineering, Business and Enterprise Applications, 11*(1), 73-77.

Deshpande, D. S., & Kulkarni, P. R. (2014). Use of Knowledge Management in Academic Research: A Study Report. *International Research Journal, 4*(2), 1-5.

Deterding, S., Dixon, D., Khaled, R., & Nacke, L. (2011). From game design elements to gamefulness: defining "gamification". In *Proceedings of the 15th International Academic MindTrek Conference: Envisioning Future Media Environments (MindTrek '11).* ACM. doi:10.1145/2181037.2181040

Dhungana, D., Groher, I., Schludermann, E., & Biffl, S. (2010). *Software ecosystems vs. natural ecosystems: Learning from the ingenious mind of nature.* Paper presented at the Fourth European Conference on Software Architecture.

DiMaggio, P., & Powell, W. W. (1983). The iron cage revisited: Institutional isomorphism and collective rationality in organizational fields. *American Sociological Review, 48*(2), 147–160. doi:10.2307/2095101

Dinh-Trong, T. T., & Bieman, J. M. (2005). The FreeBSD Project: A Replication Case Study of Open Source Development. *IEEE Transactions on Software Engineering, 31*(6), 481–494. doi:10.1109/TSE.2005.73

Dini, P., Darking, M., Rathbone, N., Vidal, M., Hernández, P., Ferronato, P., . . . Hendryx, S. (2005). *The digital ecosystems research vision: 2010 and beyond.* Retrieved from http://www.digital-ecosystems.org/events/2005.05/de_position_paper_vf.pdf

Domingo, M. G., & Forner, J. A. M. (2010). Expanding the learning environment: Combining physicality and virtuality-the internet of things for elearning. In *Proceedings of 2010 IEEE 10th International Conference on Advanced Learning Technologies (ICALT),* (pp. 730-731). IEEE.

Domingo, M. G., & Forner, J. A. M. (2010). Expanding the Learning Environment: Combining Physicality and Virtuality-The Internet of Things for eLearning. *Proceedings of the IEEE 10th International Conference on Advanced Learning Technologies (ICALT 2010)* (pp. 730-731). IEEE. doi:10.1109/ICALT.2010.211

Dos Santos, R. P., & Werner, C. M. L. (2011). A Proposal for Software Ecosystems Engineering. In *Proceedings of the Workshop on Software Ecosystems.*

Duolingo. (n.d.). *Duolingo: Learn Spanish, French and other languages for free.* Retrieved 21 April 2016 from https://www.duolingo.com

Duval, E., & Verbert, K. (2012). Learning analytics. *E-Learning and Education, 1*(8).

Edery, D., & Mollick, E. (2009). *Changing the Game - How Video Games Are Transforming the Future of Business.* Upper Saddle River, NJ: FT Press.

Equipo BBVA España. (2012). *BBVA game: juega, gana y aprende.* Retrieved 21 April 2016 from https://www.blogbbva.es/bbva-game-juega-gana-y-aprende

European Commission. (2006). *Digital ecosystems: The new global commons for SMEs and local growth.* Academic Press.

European Commission. (2006). *Digital Ecosystems: The New Global Commons for SMEs and local growth*. Author.

European Commission. (2006). *Digital Ecosystems: The New Global Commons for SMEs and local growth*. European Commission.

Ferguson, R. (2012). Learning analytics: Drivers, developments and challenges. *International Journal of Technology Enhanced Learning*, 4(5/6), 304–317. doi:10.1504/IJTEL.2012.051816

Fernández Martínez, A., & Llorens Largo, F. (2009). *An IT Governance framework for universities in Spain*. Academic Press.

Fernández Martínez, A. (2009). *Análisis, planificación y gobierno de las tecnologías de la información en las universidades*. Universidad de Almería, Almería: Tesis Doctoral.

Fernández Martínez, A., & Llorens Largo, F. (2011). *Gobierno de las TI para universidades*. Madrid: CRUE TIC.

fragUA. (2016). *La fragUA*. Retrieved from http://biblioteca.ua.es/fragua

Friedkin, N. E., & Johnsen, E. C. (2011). *Social Influence Network Theory: A Sociological Examination of Small Group Dynamics*. Cambridge University Press. doi:10.1017/CBO9780511976735

Friedman, T. L. (2005). *The world is flat: a brief history of the twenty-first century* (1st ed.). New York: Farrar, Straus and Giroux.

Frow, P., McColl-Kennedy, J. R., Hilton, T., Davidson, A., Payne, A., & Brozovic, D. (2014). Value propositions: A service ecosystems perspective. *Marketing Theory*, 14(3), 327–351. doi:10.1177/1470593114534346

Fulantelli, G., Taibi, D., & Arrigo, M. (2015). A framework to support educational decision making in mobile learning. *Computers in Human Behavior*, 47, 50–59. doi:10.1016/j.chb.2014.05.045

Galanis, N., Alier, M., Casany, M. J., Mayol, E., & Severance, C. (2014, October). TSUGI: a framework for building PHP-based learning tools. In *Proceedings of the Second International Conference on Technological Ecosystems for Enhancing Multiculturality* (pp. 409-413). ACM. doi:10.1145/2669711.2669932

Garaizar, P., & Guenaga, M. (2014). A multimodal learning analytics view of HTML5 APIs: technical benefits and privacy risks. In F. J. García-Peñalvo (Ed.), *Proceedings of the Second International Conference on Technological Ecosystem for Enhancing Multiculturality (TEEM'14)* (pp. 275-281). New York, NY: ACM. doi:10.1145/2669711.2669911

García, V. H. M., & Torres, D. A. S. (2012). Knowledge Management Model for Research Projects Masters Program. In Proceedings of World Academy of Science, Engineering and Technology (No. 70). World Academy of Science, Engineering and Technology.

García-Holgado, A., & García-Peñalvo, F. J. (2014). Architectural pattern for the definition of eLearning ecosystems based on Open Source developments. In J. L. Sierra-Rodríguez, J. M. Dodero-Beardo, & D. Burgos (Eds.), *Proceedings of 2014 International Symposium on Computers in Education (SIIE)* (pp. 93-98). Institute of Electrical and Electronics Engineers. doi:10.1109/SIIE.2014.7017711

García-Holgado, A., & García-Peñalvo, F. J. (2013). The evolution of the technological ecosystems: An architectural proposal to enhancing learning processes. In F. J. García-Peñalvo (Ed.), *Proceedings of the First International Conference on Technological Ecosystems for Enhancing Multiculturality (TEEM'13)*. New York, NY: ACM. doi:10.1145/2536536.2536623

García-Holgado, A., & García-Peñalvo, F. J. (2013). The evolution of the technological ecosystems: an architectural proposal to enhancing learning processes. In *Proceedings of the First International Conference on Technological Ecosystem for Enhancing Multiculturality (TEEM'13)* (pp. 565-571). New York, NY: ACM.

García-Holgado, A., & García-Peñalvo, F. J. (2014). Knowledge management ecosystem based on drupal platform for promoting the collaboration between public administrations. In F. J. García-Peñalvo (Ed.), *Proceedings of the Second International Conference on Technological Ecosystems for Enhancing Multiculturality (TEEM'14)* (pp. 619-624). New York, NY: ACM.

García-Holgado, A., & García-Peñalvo, F. J. (2016). Architectural pattern to improve the definition and implementation of eLearning ecosystems. *Science of Computer Programming*. doi:10.1016/j.scico.2016.03.010

García-Holgado, A., García-Peñalvo, F. J., Hernández-García, Á., & Llorens-Largo, F. (2015). Analysis and Improvement of Knowledge Management Processes in Organizations Using the Business Process Model Notation. In D. Palacios-Marqués, D. Ribeiro Soriano, & K. H. Huarng (Eds.), *New Information and Communication Technologies for Knowledge Management in Organizations* (pp. 93–101). Springer International Publishing. doi:10.1007/978-3-319-22204-2_9

García-Peñalvo, F. J., Hernández-García, Á., Conde, M. Á., Fidalgo-Blanco, Á., Sein-Echaluce, M. L., Alier, M., . . . Iglesias-Pradas, S. (2015a). *Learning services-based technological ecosystems.* Paper presented at the 3rd International Conference on Technological Ecosystems for Enhancing Multiculturality.

García-Peñalvo, F. J., Hernández-García, Á., Conde-González, M. Á., Fidalgo-Blanco, Á., Sein-Echaluce Lacleta, M. L., Alier-Forment, M., . . . Iglesias-Pradas, S. (2015b). Mirando hacia el futuro: Ecosistemas tecnológicos de aprendizaje basados en servicios. In Á. Fidalgo Blanco, M. L. Sein-Echaluce Lacleta, & F. J. García-Peñalvo (Eds.), *La Sociedad del Aprendizaje. Actas del III Congreso Internacional sobre Aprendizaje, Innovación y Competitividad. CINAIC 2015* (pp. 553-558). Madrid, Spain: Fundación General de la Universidad Politécnica de Madrid.

García-Peñalvo, F. J., Hernández-García, Á., Conde-González, M. Á., Fidalgo-Blanco, Á., Sein-Echaluce Lacleta, M. L., Alier-Forment, M., et al. (2015b). Mirando hacia el futuro: Ecosistemas tecnológicos de aprendizaje basados en servicios. *Actas del III Congreso Internacional sobre Aprendizaje, Innovación y Competitividad (CINAIC 2015).* Madrid, Spain: Fundación General de la UPM.

García-Peñalvo, F. J. (2008). *Advances in E-Learning: Experiences and Methodologies.* Hershey, PA: Information Science Reference. doi:10.4018/978-1-59904-756-0

García-Peñalvo, F. J., Colomo-Palacios, R., & Lytras, M. D. (2012). Informal learning in work environments: Training with the Social Web in the workplace. *Behaviour & Information Technology, 31*(8), 753–755. doi:10.1080/0144929X.2012.661548

García-Peñalvo, F. J., Conde-González, M. A., Alier, M., & Casany, M. J. (2011). Opening Learning Management Systems to Personal Learning Environments. *Journal of Universal Computer Science, 17*(9), 1222–1240.

García-Peñalvo, F. J., Conde-González, M. Á., Zangrando, V., García-Holgado, A., Seoane, A. M., Forment, M. A., & Minović, M. (2013). TRAILER project (Tagging, recognition, acknowledgment of informal learning experiences). A Methodology to make visible learners' informal learning activities to the institutions. *Journal of Universal Computer Science, 19*(11), 1661.

García-Peñalvo, F. J., & Conde, M. Á. (2014). Using informal learning for business decision making and knowledge management. *Journal of Business Research, 67*(5), 686–691. doi:10.1016/j.jbusres.2013.11.028

García-Peñalvo, F. J., Conde, M. Á., Alier, M., & Casany, M. J. (2011). Opening learning management systems to personal learning environments. *Journal of Universal Computer Science, 17*(9), 1222–1240. doi:10.3217/jucs-017-09-1222

García-Peñalvo, F. J., García de Figuerola, C., & Merlo, J. A. (2010). Open knowledge: Challenges and facts. *Online Information Review, 34*(4), 520–539. doi:10.1108/14684521011072963

García-Peñalvo, F. J., Hernández-García, Á., Conde-González, M. Á., Fidalgo-Blanco, Á., Sein-Echaluce Lacleta, M. L., & Alier-Forment, M. et al. (2015a). Learning services-based technological ecosystems.*Proceedings of the Third International Conference on Technological Ecosystems for Enhancing Multiculturality (TEEM'15)*. New York: ACM. doi:10.1145/2808580.2808650

García-Peñalvo, F. J., Johnson, M., Alves, G. R., Minović, M., & Conde-González, M. Á. (2014). Informal learning recognition through a cloud ecosystem. *Future Generation Computer Systems, 32*, 282–294. doi:10.1016/j.future.2013.08.004

García-Peñalvo, F. J., & Seoane-Pardo, A. M. (2015). Una revisión actualizada del concepto de eLearning. Décimo Aniversario. *Education in the Knowledge Society, 16*(1), 119–144. doi:10.14201/eks2015161119144

Gardner, H. (1999). *Intelligence Reframed: Multiple Intelligences for the 21st Century*. Basic Books.

Gardner, H. (2011). *Multiple intelligences: Reflections after thirty years*. Washington, DC: National Association of Gifted Children Parent and Community Network Newsletter.

Gartner. (2015). *Gartner Hype Cycle*. Retrieved 11/07/2015, from http://www.gartner.com/technology/research/methodologies/hype-cycle.jsp

Ghapanchi, A. H. (2015). Investigating the Inter-relationships among Success Measures of OSS Projects. *Journal of Organizational Computing and Electronic Commerce, 25*(1), 28–46. doi:10.1080/10919392.2015.990775

Ghosh, R. A. (2003). Clustering and dependencies in free/open source software development: Methodology and tools. *First Monday, 8*(4). doi:10.5210/fm.v8i4.1041

Ghosh, R. A. (2005). Understanding Free Software Developers: Findings from the FLOSS Study. In J. Feller, B. Fitzgerald, S. A. Hissam, & K. R. Lakhani (Eds.), *Perspectives on Free and Open Source Software* (pp. 23–46). Cambridge, MA: MIT Press.

Ghosh, R., & Prakash, V. V. (2000). The Orbiten Free Software Survey. *First Monday, 5*(7). doi:10.5210/fm.v5i7.769

Gonzalez-Barahona, J. M., Robles, G., Andradas-Izquierdo, R., & Ghosh, R. A. (2008). Geographic origin of libre software developers. *Information Economics and Policy, 20*(4), 356–363. doi:10.1016/j.infoecopol.2008.07.001

Greenspun, P. (1999a). *Introduction to AOLserver*. LinuxWorld. Retrieved from http://philip.greenspun.com/wtr/aolserver/introduction-1.html

Greenspun, P. (1999b). *Philip and Alex's guide to Web publishing*. San Francisco, CA: Morgan Kaufmann Publishers Inc.

Grewal, R., Lilien, G. L., & Mallapragada, G. (2006). Location, location, location: How network embeddedness affects project success in open source systems. *Management Science, 52*(7), 1043–1056. doi:10.1287/mnsc.1060.0550

Gustavsson, R., & Fredriksson, M. (2003). Sustainable Information Ecosystems. In A. Garcia, C. Lucena, F. Zambonelli, A. Omicini, & J. Castro (Eds.), Software Engineering for large-scale multi-agent systems (Vol. 2603, pp. 123-138). Springer Berlin Heidelberg.

Gustavsson, R., & Fredriksson, M. (2003). Sustainable Information Ecosystems. In A. Garcia, C. Lucena, F. Zambonelli, A. Omicini, & J. Castro (Eds.), Software Engineering for Large-Scale Multi-Agent Systems (Vol. 2603, pp. 123-138). Springer Berlin Heidelberg.

Hars, A., & Ou, S. (2001). Working for free? - Motivations for participating in Open Source projects. In *Proceedings of the 34th Hawaii International Conference on System Sciences*. Retrieved from http://dlib.computer.org/conferen/hicss/0981/pdf/09817014.pdf

Heath, T., & Bizer, C. (2011). Linked Data: Evolving the Web into a Global Data Space. Synthesis Lectures on the Semantic Web: Theory and Technology, 1(1).

Hedgebeth, D. (2007). Gaining competitive advantage in a knowledge-based economy through the utilization of open source software. Vine, 37(3), 284–294. doi:10.1108/03055720710825618 doi:10.1108/03055720710825618

Henkel, J. (2006). Selective Revealing in Open Innovation Processes: The Case of Embedded Linux. *Research Policy, 35*(7), 953–969. doi:10.1016/j.respol.2006.04.010

Hernández, R., & Grumet, A. (2005). OpenACS: robust web development framework. In *Proceedings of the Tcl/Tk 2005 Conference.*

Hertel, G., Niedner, S., & Hermann, S. (2003). Motivation of software developers in open source projects: An internet-based survey of contributors to the Linux kernel. *Research Policy, 32*(7), 1159–1177. doi:10.1016/S0048-7333(03)00047-7

Holck, J., & Jorgensen, N. (2004). Do not Check in on Red: Control Meets Anarchy in Two Open Source Projects. In S. Koch (Ed.), *Free/Open Source Software Development* (pp. 1–26). Hershey, PA: Idea Group Publishing.

Hossain, M. S., Bujang, J. S., Zakaria, M. H., & Hashim, M. (2015). The application of remote sensing to seagrass ecosystems: An overview and future research prospects. *International Journal of Remote Sensing, 36*(1), 61–114. doi:10.1080/0 1431161.2014.990649

Huang, J. S., Hsueh, K. A., & Reynolds, A. (2013). *A Framework for Collaborative Social, Economic and Environmental Development.* Paper presented at the 2013 7th IEEE International Conference on Digital Ecosystems and Technologies (DEST), Menlo Park, CA. http://web2.research.att.com/techdocs/TD_101166.pdf

Huger, J. W. (Interviewer) & Bergmann, F. (Interviewee). (2013). *Open source project management on the rise.* [Interview transcript]. Retrieved from the business section at the opensource.com website: http://opensource.com/business/13/5/open-project-interview

Hugos, M. (2012). *Enterprise Games: Using Game Mechanics to Build a Better Business.* O'Reilly Media Incorporated.

Hunicke, R., Leblanc, M., & Zubek, R. (2004). MDA: A Formal Approach to Game Design and Game Research. In *Proceedings of the 19th National Conference of Artificial Intelligence.* Retrieved from http://www.cs.northwestern.edu/~hunicke/MDA.pdf

Hunter, B. (2010). Moving Open Access to Open Source: Transitioning an Open-Access Journal into the Open Journal Systems Journal Management System. *Technical Services Quarterly*, 28(1), 31–40. doi:10.1080/07317131.2010.500972

Huotari, K., & Hamari, J. (2012). Defining gamification – a service marketing perspective. In *Proc 15th MindTrek conference*.

Iansiti, M., & Levien, R. (2004). Strategy as ecology. *Harvard Business Review*, 82(3), 68–78.

Iansiti, M., & Levien, R. (2004). Strategy as Ecology. *Harvard Business Review*, 82(3), 68–81. PMID:15029791

Iansiti, M., & Richards, G. L. (2006). Information technology ecosystem: Structure, health, and performance, The. *Antitrust Bull.*, 51(1), 77–110.

Illanas, A., & Llorens, F. (2011). Los retos Web 2.0 de cara al EEES. In C. Suarez-Guerrero & F. J. García-Peñalvo (Eds.), *Universidad y Desarrollo Social de la Web* (pp. 13–34). Editandum.

IMS AF. (2003). *IMS Abstract Framework Specification*. Retrieved February 13, 2015, from http://imsglobal.org/af/index.html

IMS LTI 2.0. (2015). *IMS Learning Tools Interoperability 2.0*. Retrieved February 13, 2015, from http://www.imsglobal.org/lti/#lti2.0

IMS LTI. (2010). *IMS Learning Tools Interoperability*. Retrieved February 13, 2015, from http://www.imsglobal.org/lti/index.html

IMS Tutorials. (2015). *The basic overview on how LTI works*. Retrieved February 13, 2015, from http://developers.imsglobal.org/tutorials.html

ISO/IEC. (2008). *ISO/IEC 38500:2008 Corporate governance of information technology*. Retrieved from http://www.iso.org/iso/catalogue_detail?csnumber=51639

ISO/IEC. (2015). *ISO/IEC 3850 Information technology — Governance of IT for the organization. Second Edition*. Retrieved from https://www.iso.org/obp/ui/#iso:std:62816:en

ITE-UA. (2016). *Servicio de Informática*. Grupos de Innovación Tecnológico-Educativa. Retrieved from http://si.ua.es/ite/gite

Jacomy, M., Venturini, T., Heymann, S., & Bastian, M. (2014). ForceAtlas2, a Continuous Graph Layout Algorithm for Handy Network Visualization Designed for the Gephi Software. *PLoS ONE*, *9*(6), 1–12. doi:10.1371/journal.pone.0098679 PMID:24914678

Jansen, S., Cusumano, M. A., & Brinkkemper, S. (2013). *Software Ecosystems: Analyzing and Managing Business Networks in the Software Industry*. Edward Elgar Publishing. doi:10.4337/9781781955635

Jansen, S., Finkelstein, A., & Brinkkemper, S. (2009). A sense of community: A research agenda for software ecosystems. In *Proceedings of 31st International Conference on Software Engineering* (pp. 187-190). IEEE.

Jasemi & Piri. (2012). Knowledge Management Practices in a Successful Research and Development Organization. *Open Journal of Knowledge Management*, (5).

Jasperson, J., Carter, P., & Zmud, R. (2005). A comprehensive conceptualization of post-adoptive behaviors associated with information technology enabled work systems. *Management Information Systems Quarterly*, *29*(3), 525–557.

Jorgensen, N. (2001). Putting it All in the Trunk: Incremental Software Engineering in the FreeBSD Open Source Project. *Information Systems Journal*, *11*(4), 321–336. doi:10.1046/j.1365-2575.2001.00113.x

Juiz, C., & Toomey, M. (2015). To govern IT, or not to govern IT? *Communications of the ACM*, *58*(2), 58–64. doi:10.1145/2656385

July, G. S. (2005). ABC of Knowledge Management. Published by Community of Knowledge.

Kampath, N., & Röglinger, M. (2010). Operational and work system-related success factors for customer relationship management in "product sales" and "solution sales"–a descriptive case study. In *Proceedings of ECIS 2010, the 18th European Conference on Information Systems*.

Kapp, K. M. (2012). *The Gamification of Learning and Instruction: Game-based Methods and Strategies for Training and Education*. San Francisco, CA: Wiley.

Kapp, M. K. (2012). *The gamification of learning and instruction: game-based methods and strategies for training and education*. Pfeiffer - John Wiley & Sons, Inc.

Karmacracy. (2013). *Karmacracy*. Retrieved 21 April 2016 from https://karmacracy.com

Kates, R. W. (2010). *Readings in Sustainability Science and Technology* (C. f. I. Development, Trans.). CID Working Paper. Cambridge, MA: Harvard University.

Kates, R. W. (2011). What kind of a science is sustainability science? *Proceedings of the National Academy of Sciences of the United States of America*, *108*(49), 19449–19450. doi:10.1073/pnas.1116097108 PMID:22114189

Kates, R. W., Clark, W. C., Corell, R., Hall, J. M., Jaeger, C. C., & Lowe, I. et al. (2001). Environment and development:sustainability science. *Science*, *292*(5517), 641–642. doi:10.1126/science.1059386 PMID:11330321

Keim, D. A. (2002). Information visualization and visual data mining. *IEEE Transactions on Visualization and Computer Graphics*, *8*(1), 1–8. doi:10.1109/2945.981847

Kemerer, C. F., & Slaughter, S. (1999). An Empirical Approach to Studying Software Evolution. *IEEE Transactions on Software Engineering*, *25*(4), 493–509. doi:10.1109/32.799945

Keskin, S. (2013). Communication and Management of Knowledge in Research and Development (R&D) Networks. *Journal of US-China Public Administration*.

Kidane, Y. H., & Gloor, P. A. (2007). Correlating temporal communication patterns of the Eclipse open source community with performance and creativity. *Computational & Mathematical Organization Theory*, *13*(1), 17–27. doi:10.1007/s10588-006-9006-3

Kidwell, J. J., Vander Linde, K. M., & Johnson, S. L. (2000). Applying Corporate Knowledge Management Practices in Higer Education. EDUCAUSE Quarterly, 4.

Kidwell, J. J., Vander Linde, K., & Johnson, S. L. (2000). Applying Corporate Knowledge Management Practices in Higher Education. EDUCAUSE Quarterly, 23(4), 28–33.

Kitchenham, B., Brereton, O. P., Budgen, D., Turner, M., Bailey, J., & Linkman, S. (2009). Systematic literature reviews in software engineering – A systematic literature review. *Information and Software Technology*, *51*(1), 7–15. doi:10.1016/j.infsof.2008.09.009

Kitchenham, B., & Charters, S. (2007). *Guidelines for performing Systematic Literature Reviews in Software Engineering. Version 2.3*. School of Computer Science and Mathematics, Keele University.

Klein, H. K., & Myers, M. D. (1999). A Set of Principles for Conducting and Evaluating Interpretive Field Studies in Information Systems. *Management Information Systems Quarterly, 23*(1), 67–93. doi:10.2307/249410

Knowledge Management and Business Model Innovation. (2000). doi:10.4018/978-1-878289-98-8

Koch, S. (2004). Profiling an open source project ecology and its programmers. *Electronic Markets, 14*(2), 77–88. doi:10.1080/10196780410001675031

Koch, S. (2008). Effort Modeling and Programmer Participation in Open Source Software Projects. *Information Economics and Policy, 20*(4), 345–355. doi:10.1016/j.infoecopol.2008.06.004

Koch, S., & Neumann, C. (2008). Exploring the Effects of Process Characteristics on Products Quality in Open Source Software Development. *Journal of Database Management, 19*(2), 31–57. doi:10.4018/jdm.2008040102

Koch, S., & Schneider, G. (2002). Effort, Cooperation and Coordination in an Open Source Software Project: Gnome. *Information Systems Journal, 12*(1), 27–42. doi:10.1046/j.1365-2575.2002.00110.x

Komiyama, H., & Takeuchi, K. (2006). Sustainability science: Building a new discipline. *Sustainability Science, 1*(1), 1–6. doi:10.1007/s11625-006-0007-4

Korpela, M. M., Eerola, A., Häkkinen, A., & Toivanen, H. (2004). IS research and development by activity analysis and development: Dead horse or the next wave? In Relevant Theory and Informed Practice: Looking Forward from a 20- Year Perspective on IS Research 15-17 July 2004, Manchester (pp. 453–471). Kluwer Academic Publishers.

Koster, R. (2005). *A theory of fun for game design*. Scottsdale, AZ: Paraglyph Press.

Koster, R. (2014). *Theory of Fun for Game Design* (2nd ed.). O'Reilly Media, Inc.

Kozaki, K., & Mizoguchi, R. (2015). A Keyword Exploration for Retrieval from Biomimetics Databases. In *Proc. of 4th Joint International Conference* (JIST 2014) (LNCS), (vol. 8943, pp. 361-377). doi:10.1007/978-3-319-15615-6_27

Kozaki, K., Hirota, T., & Mizoguchi, R. (2011). Understanding an Ontology through Divergent Exploration. *Proc. of 8th Extended Semantic Web Conference (ESWC2011)*:305-320.

Kozaki, K., Saito, O., & Mizoguchi, R. (2012). A Consensus-Building Support System based on Ontology Exploration. In *Proc. of International Workshop on Intelligent Exploration of Semantic Data (IESD 2012)*.

Krishnamurthy, S. (2002). Cave or community? An empirical investigation of 100 mature open source projects. *First Monday, 7*(6). doi:10.5210/fm.v7i6.960

Kumazawa, T., & Matsui, T. (2014). *Description of social-ecological systems framework based on ontology engineering theory*. The 5th Workshop on the Ostrom Workshop (WOW5).

Kumazawa, T., Kozaki, K., Matsui, T., Saito, O., Ohta, M., Hara, K., … Mizoguchi, R. (2014). Initial Design Process of the Sustainability Science Ontology for Knowledge-sharing to Support Co-deliberation. *Sustainability Science, 9*(2), 173-192. doi: 10.1007/s11625-013-0202-zK

Kumazawa, T., Kozaki, K., Matsui, T., Saito, O., Ohta, M., Hara, K., et al. (2009). Development of ontology on sustainability science focusing on building a resource-circulating society in Asia. In *Proceedings of the 6th international symposium on environmentally conscious design and inverse manufacturing* (EcoDesign 2009).

Kumazawa, T., Matsui, T., Hara, K., Uwasu, M., Yamaguchi, Y., & Yamamoto, Y. et al. (2008). Knowledge structuring process of sustainability science based on ontology engineering. In *Proceedings of the 8th international conference on eco balance*.

Kumazawa, T., Saito, O., Kozaki, K., Matsui, T., & Mizoguchi, R. (2009). Toward knowledge structuring of sustainability science based on ontology engineering. *Sustainability Science, 4*(2), 315. doi:10.1007/s11625-009-0076-2

Kurz, S., Podwyszynski, M., & Schwab, A. (2008). A Dynamically Extensible, Service-Based Infrastructure for Mobile Applications. In *Proceedings of Advances in Conceptual Modeling – Challenges and Opportunities*. Springer. Retrieved February 13, 2015, from http://luisa.atosorigin.es

Laakso, M., Welling, P., Bukvova, H., Nyman, L., Björk, B. C., & Hedlund, T. (2011). The development of open access journal publishing from 1993 to 2009. *PLoS ONE, 6*(6), e20961. doi:10.1371/journal.pone.0020961 PMID:21695139

Laanpere, M. (2012). *Digital learning ecosystems: Rethinking virtual learning environments in the age of social media*. Paper presented at the IFIP-OST'12: Open and Social Technologies for Networked Learning, Taillin.

Laanpere, M. (2012). *Digital Learning ecosystems: rethinking virtual learning environments in the age of social media*. Paper presented at the IFIP-OST'12: Open and Social Technologies for Networked Learning, Taillinn, Estonia.

LACE. (n.d.). *LACE – Learning Analytics Community Exchange*. Retrieved 21 April 2016 from http://www.laceproject.eu

Lakhani, K. R., & Wolf, R. G. (2005). Why Hackers Do What They Do: Understanding Motivation and Effort in Free/Open Source Software Projects. In J. Feller, B. Fitzgerald, S. A. Hissam, & K. R. Lakhani (Eds.), *Perspectives on Free and Open Source Software* (pp. 3–22). Cambridge, MA: MIT Press.

Larsen, P. O., & von Ins, M. (2010). The rate of growth in scientific publication and the decline in coverage provided by science citation index. *Scientometrics*, *84*(3), 575–603. doi:10.1007/s11192-010-0202-z PMID:20700371

Lazzaro, N. (2004). *Why We Play Games: Four Keys to More Emotion Without Story*. XEODesign,® Inc.

Lee, A. S., & Baskerville, R. L. (2003). Gerneralizing Generalizability in Information Systems Research. *Information Systems Research*, *14*(3), 221–243. doi:10.1287/isre.14.3.221.16560

Leonardi, P. M. (2011). When flexible routines meet flexible technologies: Affordance, constraint, and the imbrication of human and material agencies. *Management Information Systems Quarterly*, *35*(1), 147–167.

Leonardi, P. M., & Barley, S. R. (2010). What's Under Construction Here? Social Action, Materiality, and Power in Constructivist Studies of Technology and Organizing. *The Academy of Management Annals*, *4*(1), 1–51. doi:10.1080/19416521003654160

Lerís, D., & Sein-Echaluce, M. L. (2011). La personalización del aprendizaje: Un objetivo del paradigma educativo centrado en el aprendizaje. *Arbor*, *187*(3), 123-134.

Llorens, F. (2009). La tecnología como motor de la innovación educativa. Estrategia y política institucional de la Universidad de Alicante. *Arbor*, *185*, 21-32.

Llorens, F. (2011). La biblioteca universitaria como difusor de la innovación educativa. Estrategia y política institucional de la Universidad de Alicante. *Arbor*, *187*(3), 89-100.

Llorens, F., Molina, R., Compañ, P., & Satorre, R. (2014). Technological Ecosystem for Open Education. Smart Digital Futures, 262, 706–715.

Llorens, F., Molina, R., Compañ, P., & Satorre, R. (2014). Technological Ecosystem for Open Education. In R. Neves-Silva, G. A. Tsihrintzis, V. Uskov, R. J. Howlett, & L. C. Jain (Eds.), *Smart Digital Futures 2014* (Vol. 262, pp. 706–715). IOS Press.

Llorens, F., Molina, R., Compañ, P., & Satorre, R. (2014). Technological ecosystem for open education. In R. Neves-Silva, G. A. Tsihrintzis, V. Uskov, R. J. Howlett, & L. C. Jain (Eds.), *Smart digital futures 2014: Frontiers in artificial intelligence and applications* (pp. 706–715). IOS Press.

Llorens-Largo, F. (2007). *Strategic Plan of the University of Alicante (Horizon 2012)*. Retrieved from http://web.ua.es/en/peua/horizon-2012.html

Long, P. D., & Siemens, G. (2011). Penetrating the fog: Analytics in learning and education. *EDUCAUSE Review*, *46*(5), 30–32.

Long, P. D., & Siemens, G. (2011). Penetrating the Fog: Analytics in Learning and Education. *EDUCAUSE Review*, *46*(5), 30–32.

Long, Y., & Siau, K. (2007). Social network structures in open source software development teams. *Journal of Database Management*, *18*(2), 25–40. doi:10.4018/jdm.2007040102

Lopez-Fernandez, L., Robles, G., & Gonzalez-Barahona, J. M. (2004). Applying social network analysis to the information in CVS repositories. In *International Workshop on Mining Software Repositories* (pp. 101-105). doi:10.1049/ic:20040485

Lungu, M. F. (2009). *Reverse Engineering Software Ecosystems*. (Doctoral dissertation). University of Lugano.

Lungu, M., Lanza, M., Gîrba, T., & Robbes, R. (2010). The small project observatory: Visualizing software ecosystems. *Science of Computer Programming*, *75*(4), 264–275. doi:10.1016/j.scico.2009.09.004

MacCormack, A., Rusnak, J., & Baldwin, C. Y. (2006). Exploring the structure of complex software designs: An empirical study of open source and proprietary code. *Management Science*, *52*(7), 1015–1030. doi:10.1287/mnsc.1060.0552

Madey, G., Freeh, V., & Tynan, R. (2005). Modeling the Free/Open Source software community: A quantitative investigation. *Free/Open Source Software Development*, 203-221.

Magnier-Watanable, Berrton, & Daisenoo. (2011). *A study of Knowledge Management enablers across countries*. KMR&P.

Malone, T. W., & Lepper, M. R. (1987). Making Learning Fun: A Taxonomy of Intrinsic Motivations for Learning. *Aptitude, Learning and Instruction: III. Cognitive and affective process analyses.* Academic Press.

Malone, T. W. (1981). Towards a theory of intrinsically motivating instruction. *Cognitive Science, 4*(4), 333–369. doi:10.1207/s15516709cog0504_2

Manikas, K., & Hansen, K. M. (2013). Software ecosystems – A systematic literature review. *Journal of Systems and Software, 86*(5), 1294–1306. doi:10.1016/j.jss.2012.12.026

Mann, F., von Walter, B., Hess, T., & Wigand, R. T. (2009). Open access publishing in science. *Communications of the ACM, 52*(3), 135–139. doi:10.1145/1467247.1467279

Marczewski, A. (2012). *An Interview with Richard Bartle about Gamification.* Retrieved from http://www.gamified.uk/2012/12/31/an-interview-with-richard-bartle-about-gamification/

Mars, M. M., Bronstein, J. L., & Lusch, R. F. (2012). The Value of a Metaphor: Organizations and Ecosystems. *Organizational Dynamics, 41*(4), 271–280. doi:10.1016/j.orgdyn.2012.08.002

Maruta, R. (2014). The creation and management of organizational knowledge. *Knowledge-Based Systems, 67*, 26–34. doi:10.1016/j.knosys.2014.06.012

Max Planck Society. (2003). *Berlin Declaration on Open Access to Scientic Knowledge.* Retrieved from http://oa.mpg.de/lang/en-uk/berlin-prozess/berliner-erklarung

McGonigal, J. (2011). *Reality Is Broken: Why Games Make Us Better and How They Can Change the World.* Penguin Group US.

Merriman, J. (2003). *Redefining interoperability. The Open Knowledge Initiative (OKI).* Retrieved February 13, 2015, from http://www.okiproject.org/view/html/node/2916

Messerschmitt, D. G., & Szyperski, C. (2005). Software ecosystem: Understanding an indispensable technology and industry. *MIT Press Books, 1*.

Meyer, J. P., & Allen, N. J. (1991). A three-component conceptualization of organizational commitment. *Human Resource Management Review, 1*(1), 61–89. doi:10.1016/1053-4822(91)90011-Z

Michavila, F. (2013). Prólogo del informe Tendencias Universidad: En pos de la educación activa. In F. Llorens Largo (Ed.), *En pos de la educación activa* (pp. 5–7). Madrid: Cátedra UNESCO de Gestión y Política Universitaria de la Universidad Politécnica de Madrid.

Michlmayr, M. (2005). Software Process Maturity and the Success of Free Software Projects. In K. Zielinski & T. Szmuc (Eds.), *Software Engineering: Evolution and Emerging Technologies* (pp. 3–14). Amsterdam, The Netherlands: IOS Press.

Mintzberg, H. (1978). Patterns in Strategy Formation. *Management Science, 24*(9), 934–948. doi:10.1287/mnsc.24.9.934

Mizoguchi, R. (2010). *YAMATO: yet another more advanced top-level ontology.* Available online at: http://www.ei.sanken.osaka-u.ac.jp/hozo/onto_library/upper-Onto.htm

Mizoguchi, R. (2005). *Ontology Kougaku.* Ohmsha. (in Japanese)

Mizoguchi, R. (2012). *Ontology Kougaku no Riron to Jissen.* Ohmsha. (in Japanese)

Mockus, A., Fielding, R., & Herbsleb, J. (2002). Two case studies of open source software development: Apache and Mozilla. *ACM Transactions on Software Engineering and Methodology, 11*(3), 309–346. doi:10.1145/567793.567795

Moore, G. A. (2014). *Crossing the Chasm* (3rd ed.). HarperCollins.

Moore, J. F. (1993). Predators and prey: A new ecology of competition. *Harvard Business Review, 71*(3), 75–86.

Mozilla OpenBadges. (n.d.). *Open Badges.* Retrieved 21 April 2016 from http://openbadges.org

Nachira, F. (2002). *Towards a network of digital business ecosystems fostering the local development.* Retrieved from http://www.digital-ecosystems.org/doc/discussionpaper.pdf

Nan, N., & Kumar, S. (2013). Joint effect of team structure and software architecture in open source software development. *IEEE Transactions on Engineering Management, 60*(3), 592–603. doi:10.1109/TEM.2012.2232930

Neumann, G., Sobernig, S., & Aram, M. (2014). Evolutionary Business Information Systems. *Business & Information Systems Engineering, 6*(1), 33–38. doi:10.1007/s12599-013-0305-1

Neus, A., & Scherf, P. (2005). Opening minds: Cultural change with the introduction of open-source collaboration methods. IBM Systems Journal, 44(2), 215–225. doi:10.1147/sj.442.0215 doi:10.1147/sj.442.0215

Nolan, R. L. (1982). *Managing the Data Resource Function* (2nd ed.). St. Paul, MN: West Publishing Company.

Nonaka, I., & Takeuchi, H. (1995). *The knowledge-creating company: how Japanese companies create the dynamics of innovation*. New York: Oxford University Press.

Norden, P. V. (1960). On the anatomy of development projects. *IRE Transactions on Engineering Management*, 7(1), 34–42. doi:10.1109/IRET-EM.1960.5007529

Norman, D. (1999). Affordance, conventions, and design. *Interaction*, 6(3), 38–43. doi:10.1145/301153.301168

Nunamaker, J. F., Briggs, R. O., & Vreede, G. J. (2001). From Information Technology to Value Creation Technology. In G. W. Dickson & G. DeSanctis (Eds.), *Information Technology and the Future Enterprise*. Prentice Hall.

O'Mahony, S. (2003). Guarding the commons: How community managed software projects protect their work. *Research Policy*, 32(7), 1179–1198. doi:10.1016/S0048-7333(03)00048-9

O'Mahony, S., & Bechky, B. A. (2008). Boundary Organizations: Enabling Collaboration among Unexpected Allies. *Administrative Science Quarterly*, 53(3), 422–459. doi:10.2189/asqu.53.3.422

O'Mahony, S., & Ferraro, F. (2007). The Emergence of Governance in an Open Source Community. *Academy of Management Journal*, 50(5), 1079–1106. doi:10.5465/AMJ.2007.27169153

Oakley, A. (2003). Research evidence, knowledge management and educational practice: Early lessons from a systematic approach. London Review of Education, 1(1), 21–33. doi:10.1080/14748460306693 doi:10.1080/14748460306693

Oauth 2.0. (n.d.). *Oauth 2.0 Security Protocol*. Retrieved February 13, 2015, from http://www.oauth.net

Oezbek, C., Prechelt, L., & Thiel, F. (2010). The onion has cancer: Some social network analysis visualizations of open source project communication. In *Proceedings of the 3rd International Workshop on Emerging Trends in Free/Libre/Open Source Software Research and Development* (pp. 5-10). ACM.

Oh, W., & Jeon, S. (2007). Membership herding and network stability in the open source community: The Ising perspective. *Management Science, 53*(7), 1086–1101. doi:10.1287/mnsc.1060.0623

Ondari-Okemwa. (2006). Knowledge Management in a Research Organisation: International Livestock Research Institute. *Libri, 56*, 63–72.

Open H. U. B. (2015). *The OpenACS Open Source Project on Open Hub*. Retrieved May 8, 2015, from https://www.openhub.net/p/openacs

Orlikowski, W. J., & Iacono, C. S. (2001). Research Commentary : Desperately Seeking the " IT " in IT Research — A Call to Theorizing the IT Artifact. *Information Systems Research, 12*(2), 121–134. doi:10.1287/isre.12.2.121.9700

Ousterhout, J. K. (1989). *Tcl: An Embeddable Command Language (No. UCB/CSD-89-541)*. Berkeley, CA: EECS Department, University of California.

Papaioannou, T., Wield, D., & Chataway, J. (2009). Knowledge ecologies and ecosystems? An empirically grounded reflection on recent developments in innovation systems theory. *Environment and Planning. C, Government & Policy, 27*(2), 319–339. doi:10.1068/c0832

Pardo, A., & Delgado Kloos, C. (2011). Stepping out of the box: Towards analytics outside the learning management system. In *Proceedings of the 1st International Conference on Learning Analytics and Knowledge* (pp. 163-167). ACM.

Pardo, A., & Delgado Kloos, C. (2011). Stepping out of the box: Towards analytics outside the learning management system. In *Proceedings of the 1st International Conference on Learning Analytics and Knowledge* (pp. 163-167). New York, NY: ACM.

Pata, K. (2011). *Meta-design framework for open learning ecosystems*. Paper presented at the Mash-UP Personal Learning Environments (MUP/PLE 2011), London, UK.

Pätzold, S., Rathmayer, S., & Graf, S. (2008). Proposal for the Design and Implementation of a Modern System Architecture and integration infrastructure in context of e-learning and exchange of relevant data. In *ILearning Forum* (pp. 82–90). European Institute For E-Learning.

Paulk, M. C., Curtis, B., Chrissis, M. B., & Weber, C. V. (1993). *Capability Maturity Model for Software, Version 1.1* (No. CMU/SEI-93-TR-024, ESC-TR-93-177). Pittsburgh, PA: Software Engineering Institute, Carnegie Mellon University. Retrieved from http://www.sei.cmu.edu/reports/93tr024.pdf

Petersson, J. (2008). Work system principles. In *Proceedings of the 3rd International Conference on the Pragmatic Web Innovating the Interactive Society - ICPW '08* (pp. 69–76). doi:10.1145/1479190.1479200

Phillips, R., Maor, D., Preston, G., & Cumming-Potvin, W. (2012). *Exploring Learning Analytics as Indicators of Study Behaviour*. Paper presented at the World Conference on Educational Multimedia, Hypermedia and Telecommunications 2012, Denver, CO.

Pickett, S. T. A., & Cadenasso, M. L. (2002). The ecosystem as a multidimensional concept: Meaning, model, and metaphor. *Ecosystems (New York, N.Y.)*, *5*(1), 1–10. doi:10.1007/s10021-001-0051-y

Píriz Duran, S. (2015). *UNIVERSITIC 2015: Análisis de las TIC en las Universidades Españolas*. Madrid: Conferencia de Rectores de las Universidades Españolas.

Pitarch, A., Álvarez, A., & Monferrer, J. (2007). *e-PEL: paradigma de gestión de portfolios educativos*. Paper presented at the Congreso Español de Informática (CEDI 2007).

Polydoratou, P., & Moyle, M. (2008). Scientific journals, overlays and repositories: A case of costs and sustainability issues. Lecture Notes in Computer Science, 5362, 154–163.

Popp, K., & Meyer, R. (2010). *Profit from Software Ecosystems: Business Models*. Norderstedt, Germany: Ecosystems and Partnerships in the Software Industry.

Prensky, M. (2006). *"Don't bother me Mom, I'm learning!": how computer and video games are preparing your kids for twenty-first century success and how you can help!* St. Paul, MN: Paragon House.

Prensky, M. (2007). *Digital Game-Based Learning*. St. Paul, MN: Paragon House.

Putnam, L. H. (1978). A general empirical solution to the macro software sizing and estimating problem. *IEEE Transactions on Software Engineering*, *4*(4), 345–361. doi:10.1109/TSE.1978.231521

Radoff, J. (2011). *Game On: Energize Your Business with Social Media Games*. Indianapolis, IN: Wiley Publishing Inc.

Raymond, E. S. (1999). *The Cathedral and the Bazaar*. Cambridge, MA: O'Reilly & Associates.

Razak, N. A. (2009, August). E-Rakan Universiti: A Portal for bridging knowledge and digital divide among the varsity and the community. In *Computer Science and Information Technology, 2009. ICCSIT 2009. 2nd IEEE International Conference on* (pp. 429-432). IEEE. doi:10.1109/ICCSIT.2009.5234676 doi:10.1109/ICC-SIT.2009.5234676

Riehle, D. (2007). The Economic Motivation of Open Source Software: Stakeholder Perspectives. *IEEE Computer*, *40*(4), 25–32. doi:10.1109/MC.2007.147

Roberts, J. A., Hann, I.-H., & Slaughter, S. A. (2006). Understanding the Motivations, Participation, and Performance of Open Source Software Developers: A Longitudinal Study of the Apache Projects. *Management Science*, *52*(7), 984–999. doi:10.1287/mnsc.1060.0554

Robey, D., Schwaig, K. S., & Jin, L. (2003). Intertwining material and virtual work. *Information and Organization*, *13*(2), 111–129. doi:10.1016/S1471-7727(02)00025-8

Robles, G., Koch, S., & Gonzalez-Barahona, J. M. (2004). Remote analysis and measurement of libre software systems by means of the CVSanalY tool. In *ICSE 2004 - Proceedings of the Second International Workshop on Remote Analysis and Measurement of Software Systems* (RAMSS '04) (pp. 51–55). doi:10.1049/ic:20040351

Rodriquez, Anuro, & Stanishy. (2004). Knowledge Management Analysis of the Research and Development & Transference Process at HERO's. *Journal of Universal Computer Science*.

Rogers, E. M. (2003). *Diffusion of Innovations* (5th ed.). Free Press.

ROLE. (n.d.). *Project*. Retrieved 21 April 2016 from http://www.role-project.eu

Romero, C., & Ventura, S. (2007). Educational data mining: A survey from 1995 to 2005. *Expert Systems with Applications*, *33*(1), 135–146. doi:10.1016/j.eswa.2006.04.005

Romero, C., & Ventura, S. (2010). Educational Data Mining: A Review of the State of the Art. *Systems, Man, and Cybernetics, Part C: Applications and Reviews. IEEE Transactions on*, *40*(6), 601–618.

Romero, C., & Ventura, S. (2010). Educational data mining: A review of the state of the art. *IEEE Transactions on Systems, Man and Cybernetics. Part C, Applications and Reviews*, *40*(6), 601–618. doi:10.1109/TSMCC.2010.2053532

Rubio, E., Ocón, A., Galán, M., Marrero, S., & Nelson, J. C. (2004). *A personal and corporative process-oriented knowledge manager*. Retrieved from http://www.cicei.com/index.php/publicaciones/congresos/111-congresos/425-a-personal-and-corporative-process-oriented-knowledge-manager-suricata

Saito, O., Kozaki, K., Hirota, T., & Mizoguchi, R. (2011). The application of ontology engineering to biofuel problems. In *Sustainability Science: A Multidisciplinary Approach (Sustainability Science 1). United Nations University Press.*

Santos, O. C., Boticario, J. G., Raffenne, E., & Pastor, R. (2007). *Why using dotLRN? UNED use cases.* Paper presented at 1st International Conference on FLOSS: Free/Libre/Open Source Systems.

Saviotti, P. P. (1996). *Technology Evolution, Variety and the Economy.* Cheltenham, UK: Edward Elgar Publishing.

Scacchi, W. (2010, November). The future of research in free/open source software development. In *Proceedings of the FSE/SDP workshop on Future of software engineering research* (pp. 315-320). ACM. doi:10.1145/1882362.1882427 doi:10.1145/1882362.1882427

Scacchi, W., Feller, J., Fitzgerald, B., Hissam, S., & Lakhani, K. (2006). Understanding Free/Open Source Software Development Processes. *Software Process Improvement and Practice, 11*(2), 95–105. doi:10.1002/spip.255

Schaffert, R., & Hilzensauer, W. (2008). On the way towards Personal Learning Environments: Seven crucial aspects. *eLearning Papers, 2*(9), 1-11.

Schwaber, K. (2007). SCRUM Development Process. In J. Sutherland, C. Casanave, J. Miller, P. Patel, & G. Hollowell (Eds.), *Business Object Design and Implementation. OOPSLA '95 Workshop Proceedings* (pp. 117-134). London, UK: Springer London. doi:10.1007/978-1-4471-0947-1_11

Sein-Echaluce Lacleta, M. L., Fidalgo-Blanco, Á., García-Peñalvo, F. J., & Conde-González, M. Á. (2015). A knowledge management system to classify social educational resources within a subject using teamwork techniques.*Proceedings of the 17th International Conference, HCI International 2015.* Los Angeles, CA: Springer International Publishing. doi:10.1007/978-3-319-20609-7_48

Serrano, N., & Sarriei, J. M. (2006). Open source software ERPs: A new alternative for an old need. *IEEE Software, 23*(3), 94–97. doi:10.1109/MS.2006.78

Sharma, A., & Adkins, R. (2006). OSS in India. In C. DiBona, D. Cooper, & M. Stone (Eds.), Open Sources 2.0 (pp. 189–196). Sebastopol, CA: O'Reilly Media, Inc.

Shen, C., & Monge, P. (2011). Who connects with whom? A social network analysis of an online open source software community. *First Monday*, *16*(6). doi:10.5210/fm.v16i6.3551

Shimomura, M. (2012). Engineering Biomimetics: Integration of Biology and Nanotechnology. In Design for Innovative Value Towards a Sustainable Society, (pp. 905-907). Academic Press.

Shuen, A. (2008). *Web 2.0: A Strategy Guide*. Sebastopol, CA: O'Reilly Media Inc.

Siemens, G. (2012). Learning analytics: envisioning a research discipline and a domain of practice. In *Proceedings of the 2nd International Conference on Learning Analytics and Knowledge* (pp. 4-8). New York, NY: ACM.

Siggelkow, N. (2007). Persuasion With Case Studies. *Academy of Management Journal*, *50*(1), 20–24. doi:10.5465/AMJ.2007.24160882

SI-UA. (2016). *Servicio de Informática*. Retrieved from http://si.ua.es/vertice/

Smith, K. R. (2006). Building an innovation ecosystem: Process, culture and competencies. *Industry and Higher Education*, *20*(4), 219–224. doi:10.5367/000000006778175801

Smokotin, V. M., Petrova, G. I., & Gural, S. K. (2014). Theoretical Principles for Knowledge Management in the Research University. Procedia: Social and Behavioral Sciences, 154, 229–232. doi:10.1016/j.sbspro.2014.10.141 doi:10.1016/j.sbspro.2014.10.141

SNOLA. (2016). *SNOLA*. Retrieved 21 April 2016 from http://snola.net

SOLAR. (2016). *Society for Learning Analytics Research (SoLAR)*. Retrieved 21 April from https://solaresearch.org

Solomon, D. J. (2007). Handbook of research on open source software: Technological, economic, and social perspectives. IGI Global.

Stackoverflow. (n.d.). *Stack Overflow*. Retrieved 21 April 2016 from http://stackoverflow.com

Stewart, K. J., Ammeter, A. P., & Maruping, L. M. (2006). Impacts of license choice and organizational sponsorship on user interest and development activity in open source software projects. *Information Systems Research, 17*(2), 126–144. doi:10.1287/isre.1060.0082

Stiglitz, J. E., & Greenwald, B. C. (2014). *Creating a learning society: a new approach to growth, development, and social progress.* New York: Columbia University Press. doi:10.7312/columbia/9780231152143.001.0001

Still, K., Huhtamäki, J., Russell, M. G., & Rubens, N. (2014). Insights for orchestrating innovation ecosystems: The case of EIT ICT Labs and data-driven network visualisations. *International Journal of Technology Management, 66*(2-3), 243–265. doi:10.1504/IJTM.2014.064606

Taleb, N. N., & Mosquera, A. S. (2008). *El cisne negro: El impacto de lo altamente improbable.* Barcelona: Paidós Ibérica.

Tatnall, A., & Davey, B. (2004). Improving the chances of getting your IT curriculum innovation successfully adopted by the application of an ecological approach to innovation. *Informing Science: International Journal of an Emerging Transdiscipline, 7,* 87–103.

Tian, J., Nakamori, Y., & Wierzbicki, A. P. (2009). Knowledge management and knowledge creation in academia: A study based on surveys in a Japanese research university. Journal of Knowledge Management, 13(2), 76–92. doi:10.1108/13673270910942718 doi:10.1108/13673270910942718

Toomey, M. (2009). *Waltzing with the elephant: a comprehensive guide to directing and controlling information technology.* Belgrave South, Australia: Infonomics.

Toral, S. L., Bessis, N., Martinez-Torres, M. R., Franc, F., Barrero, F., & Xhafa, F. (2011, November). An exploratory social network analysis of academic research networks. In *Intelligent Networking and Collaborative Systems (INCoS), 2011 Third International Conference on* (pp. 21-26). IEEE. doi:10.1109/INCoS.2011.49 doi:10.1109/INCoS.2011.49

Toral, S. L., Martínez-Torres, M. R., & Barrero, F. (2010). Analysis of virtual communities supporting OSS projects using social network analysis. *Information and Software Technology, 52*(3), 296–303. doi:10.1016/j.infsof.2009.10.007

Tuomi, I. (2004). Evolution of the Linux credits file: Methodological challenges and reference data for open source research. *First Monday, 9*(6). doi:10.5210/fm.v9i6.1151

Turkle, S. (2011). *Alone Together: Why We Expect More from Technology and Less from Each Other*. Basic Books.

Uceda Antolín, J., & Barro Ameneiro, S. (2010). *UNIVERSITIC 2010: Evolución de Las TIC en el Sistema Universitario Español 2006-2010*. Madrid: Conferencia de Rectores de las Universidades Españolas.

Urban, R. A., Bakshi, B. R., Grubb, G. F., Baral, A., & Mitsch, W. J. (2010). Towards sustainability of engineered processes: Designing self-reliant networks of technological–ecological systems. *Computers & Chemical Engineering, 34*(9), 1413–1420. doi:10.1016/j.compchemeng.2010.02.026

Valverde, S., & Solé, R. V. (2007). Self-organization versus hierarchy in open-source social networks. *Physical Review E: Statistical, Nonlinear, and Soft Matter Physics, 76*(4), 046118. doi:10.1103/PhysRevE.76.046118 PMID:17995071

Vargo, S. L., & Lusch, R. F. (2011). It's all B2B…and beyond: Toward a systems perspective of the market. *Industrial Marketing Management, 40*(2), 181–187. doi:10.1016/j.indmarman.2010.06.026

Vickers, S. P., & Booth, S. (2014). Learning Tools Interoperability (LTI): a Best Practice Guide. CeLTIc developers Project.

Walsham, G. (1995). Interpretive Case Studies in IS Research : Nature and Method. *European Journal of Information Systems, 4*(2), 74–81. doi:10.1057/ejis.1995.9

Walsham, G. (2006). Doing Interpretive Research. *European Journal of Information Systems, 15*(3), 320–330. doi:10.1057/palgrave.ejis.3000589

Wareham, J., Fox, P. B., & Cano Giner, J. L. (2014). Technology Ecosystem Governance. *Organization Science, 25*(4), 1195–1215. doi:10.1287/orsc.2014.0895

Watanabe, C., & Fukuda, K. (2006). National innovation ecosystems: The similarity and disparity of Japan-US technology policy systems toward a service oriented economy. *Journal of Service Research, 6*(1), 159–186.

Wenger, E. (1998). Communities of Practice. Learning as a social system. *The Systems Thinker, 9*(5), 2–3.

Wenger, E. (2007). *Learning in communities of practice: a journey of the self*. Academic Press.

Compilation of References

Werbach, K., & Hunter, D. (2012). *For the Win: How Game Thinking Can Revolutionize Your Business*. Wharton Digital Press.

Wexler, S., Dublin, L., Grey, N., Jagannathan, S., Karrer, T., Martinez, M., & van Barneveld, A. (2007). *Learning management systems. The good, the bad, the ugly,... and the truth. Guild Research 360 Degree Report*. Santa Rosa, CA: The eLearning Guild.

Willinsky, J. (2005). Open Journal Systems. *Library Hi Tech, 23*(4), 504–519. doi:10.1108/07378830510636300

Wilson, S., Liber, O., Johnson, M., Beauvoir, P., Sharples, P., & Milligan, C. (2007). Personal Learning Environments: Challenging the dominant design of educational systems. *Journal of e-Learning and Knowledge Society, 3*(3), 27-38.

Witt, N., McDermott, A., Peters, M., & Stone, M. (2007). A knowledge management approach to developing communities of practice amongst university and college staff. In ICT: Providing choices for learners and learning. Proceedings ASCILITE. Academic Press.

Yeo, B., Liu, L., & Saxena, S. (2006). When China dances with OSS. In C. DiBona, D. Cooper, & M. Stone (Eds.), Open Sources 2.0 (pp. 197–210). Sebastopol, CA: O'Reilly Media, Inc.

Yin, R. K. (2009). *Case Study Research: Design and Methods* (4th ed.). Thousand Oaks, CA: Sage Publications.

Yu, E., & Deng, S. (2011). Understanding software ecosystems: A strategic modeling approach. In S. Jansen, J. Bosch, P. Campbell, & F. Ahmed (Eds.), *IWSECO-2011 Software Ecosystems 2011:Proceedings of the Third International Workshop on Software Ecosystems* (pp. 65-76). Aachen, Germany: CEUR.

Yukselturk, E., Ozekes, S., & Türel, Y. (2014). Predicting dropout student: An application of data mining methods in an online education program. *European Journal of Open, Distance and E-Learning, 17*(1).

Yukselturk, E., Ozekes, S., & Türel, Y. (2014). Predicting Dropout Student: An Application of Data Mining Methods in an Online Education Program. *European Journal of Open, Distance and E-Learning, 17*(1).

Zacharakis, A. L., Shepherd, D. A., & Coombs, J. E. (2003). The development of venture-capital-backed Internet companies. An ecosystem perspective. *Journal of Business Venturing, 18*(2), 217–231. doi:10.1016/S0883-9026(02)00084-8

Zara, O. (2008). Le management de l'intelligence collective: vers une nouvelle gouvernance (2nd ed.). Paris: M21 Editions.

Zicherman, G., & Linder, J. (2010). *Game-based Marketing – Inspire Customer Loyalty Through Rewards, Challenges, and Contest*. Hoboken, NJ: John Wiley & Sons Inc.

Zichermann, G., & Cunningham, C. (2011). *Gamification by Design Implementing Game Mechanics in Web and Mobile Apps*. Sebastopol, CA: O'Reilly Media.

Zichermann, G., & Linder, J. (2013). *The Gamification Revolution - How Leaders Leverage Game Mechanics to Crush the Competition*. McGraw-Hill Education.

About the Contributors

Francisco José García-Peñalvo completed his undergraduate studies in Computing at the University of Salamanca and University of Valladolid and his Ph.D. at the University of Salamanca. Dr. García-Peñalvo is the head of the research group GRIAL (Research Group Interaction and eLearning). His main research interests focus on eLearning, Computers & Education, Adaptive Systems, Web Engineering, Semantic Web and Software Reuse. He has led and participated in over 50 research and innovation projects. He was Vice Chancellor for Innovation at the University of Salamanca between March 2007 and December 2009. He has published more than 300 articles in international journals and conferences. He has been guest editor of several special issues of international journals (Online Information Review, Computers in Human Behaviour, Interactive Learning Environments...). He is also a member of the program committee of several international conferences and reviewer for several international journals. At present, he is the Editor-in-Chief of the International Journal of Information Technology Research and the Education in the Knowledge Society Journal. Besides, he is the coordinator of the multidisciplinary PhD Programme on Education in the Knowledge Society.

* * *

Marc Alier (1971) received an Engineering degree in Computer Science and a PhD in Sciences in the Universitat Politècnica de Catalunya – BarcelonaTech (UPC). He is an associate professor at UPC and director at ICE (the UPC Institute of Education Sciences) http://www.ice.upc.edu . The last 17 years has worked in research and development related to the usage of ICT in education innovation. He has participated in the development of several LMS and authoring tools, and has been an online teacher. Since 2001, he has taught project management, computer science history and computing ethics. He is and has been director of a master's program in software for organization management and several post degree courses at UPC School. Since early 2004, he has been a developer of the http://moodle.org community contributing with third part modules and core functionalities such as the Wiki module and the Webservices layer. He is the co-founder of the http://moodbile.org open source project. He is the lead researcher of the http://sushitos.essi.upc.edu research group. He is author of a radio program about technology http://mossegalapoma.cat.

Patricia Compañ-Rosique has a PhD in Computer Science (University of Alicante, 2004). She has held positions of leadership and management since she joined the University of Alicante: Deputy Head of Computer Engineering of the Polytechnic School (2009-2012) and deputy director of the Polytechnic School (2012-2013). In these periods she was directly involved in the development of new curricula in the Computer Engineering Degree and Master's. She has taught various subjects throughout her teaching career, especially computer programming and artificial intelligence. Her research lines are within the application of AI techniques: evolutionary algorithms for solving mathematical problems and neural networks applied to coastal engineering problems. Furthermore she works in game development and the application of digital technologies to education. She has had several papers published related to the use of stereoscopic vision for segmentation and recognition as well as the reconstruction of space from grammatical models. All these lines have a common denominator, which is the use of AI techniques to deal with a wide range of different problems. She participates in many educational innovation projects related to the EEES. She is a member of AENUI (Association of University teachers of Informatics). She is part of the research team involved in the ByteRealms trademark, whose objective is the design and construction of serious and innovative games in different fields, especially in education.

Miguel Ángel Conde holds a PhD in Computer Science (2012, University of Salamanca). From 2002 to 2004 he was working in educational environment teaching in several courses related to computers. In 2004 he decided to begin working on software development environments and he worked for GPM, a web development and multimedia company. In 2005 he began working for Clay Formación Internacional R&D department where he was involved in different eLearning projects. From 2010 to 2012 he was researching at the University of Salamanca and also working there as a teacher. During 2013 he worked in the Informatics and Communications Service of the University of León and as assistant lecturer in that university. Now he works as an assistant professor at the University of León. He is a member of the Robotics research group of the University of León and GRIAL research group of the University of Salamanca. His PhD thesis is focused on the merging of informal, non-formal and formal environments. He has published more than 100 papers about different topics such as eLearning, Service Oriented Architectures, Learning Analytics, Mobile Learning, Human-Computer Interaction, Educational Robotics, etc.

Dhananjay S. Deshpande has been recently awarded by Doctorate in Computer Application and Management (Dr. B.A.M. U., Aurandabad), his research area is knowledge management, data science and information science.He was focused on challenges of Academic Research Community and need of the knowledge management in research.He has proposed a Knowledge Management Model and System for research community under university.He has completed M. Phil. in Information Technology (YCMOU, Nashik). He has postgraduate degrees Master in Computer Applications(Punjab Technical University, Jalandhar), Master in Computer Management (SPPU, Pune) and also completed his dual Graduation in subjects Science (B.Sc from Dr. B.A.M.U., Aurangabad.) and Education (B.Ed. from Shivaji University, Pune). He is having total 18 years of experience in Academics and IT - Industry. He is a founder member of K-MARG (Knowledge Management and Academic Research Group).

Angel Fidalgo-Blanco is Director of the Laboratory for Innovation in Information Technology at the Polytechnic University of Madrid and has participated actively as principal investigator in R&D projects. He has organised seminars and conferences over many years and is currently President of the organising committee for the International Conference of Learning, Innovation and Competitiveness (CINAIC, Spanish abbreviation). His work as an active researcher in educational innovation, knowledge management, educational technologies and educational communities based on social networks has generated numerous publications and information products.

André Pimenta Freire is a professor of Human-Computer Interaction at the Universidade Federal de Lavras. BSc and MSc in Computer Science by the University of São Paulo and PhD in Computer Science by the University of York.

Francisco J. Gallego-Durán started programming, developing computer games and artificial intelligence in 1988. Got its Computer Science Degree by the University of Alicante (UA) in 2003. Researcher of the Artificial Intelligence and Industrial Informatics (i3a) group since 2004. Teaches Computer Science, Game Developing and Artificial Intelligence at the UA since 2005 Has designed and developed many computer games, including Mad University, Screaming Racers, P84Attack, PLMan, MindRider and La Plantación. Has also designed and developed complete Game Engines like WiseToad Framework or CPCtelera. Is also Technical Director at ByteRealms (UA trademark for Game Development) since 2008. Has developed many experiences related to educational innovation using automated systems, Gamification and Serious Games. These experiences have been combined with Project Based Learning methodologies, and they are actually being used for fourth year's at

Computer Science and Multimedia degrees at the UA. His present research is focused in Neuroevolution, Machine Learning, Computer Games and their educative uses.

Ángel Hernández-García is M.Sc. in Telecommunication Engineering, Master SAP in Integrated Information Systems, and Ph.D. in Information Systems by the Universidad Politécnica de Madrid. Ángel is Assistant Professor at the UPM's School of Telecommunication Engineering. Currently, Ángel's research lines cover information systems' acceptance and educational technologies, with special focus on learning analytics and educational data mining methods and applications. Ángel has been guest editor of, and published research papers in international journals. He has also participated as chair in several international conferences and is member of the editorial board and reviewer for leading journals in the fields of technology enhanced learning, information systems and business.

Jenny S. Huang has more than 25 years of ICT industry experiences, working at international alliances and standards policy setting level. She specializes in enterprise architecture and infrastructure design to facilitate organization's business agility, service innovation and value creation in a digital world. Ms. Huang also serves as a director of research for iFOSSF (International Free and Open Source Solutions Foundation), a non-profit organization focused on the science and advocacy of digital infrastructure required for collaborative sustainable development.

Santiago Iglesias-Pradas is M.Sc. and Ph.D. in Telecommunication Engineering and MBA by the Universidad Politécnica de Madrid (UPM). He is Associate Professor in Economics and Information Systems at the Business Administration Department of the UPM. Santiago is member of the "Innovation, Industrial Property and Technology Policy" research group at the UPM. He is author of several papers and articles about interactions between Information Technologies and Organizations in international journals and conferences.

Özgün Imre is recently a PhD student in Linköpings University, Sweden. His research interests are investment decisions for integrated information systems and has been working on open source ERP implementation decisions. Also he has worked on academic publication strategies of PhD students.

Stefan Koch is Professor and Chair at Bogazici University, Department of Management. He received his Ph.D. from WU – Vienna University of Economics and Business. His current research interests include user and open innovation, the open source development model, the management and governance of information systems, ERP systems, and software business. He has published over 30 papers in peer-reviewed journals, including Information Systems Journal, Information Economics and Policy, Decision Support Systems, Empirical Software Engineering, Information and Software Technology, Electronic Markets, Information Systems Management, Journal of Database Management, Journal of Software Maintenance and Evolution, Enterprise Information Systems, Journal of Services Marketing, Journal of Global Information Technology Management and Wirtschaftsinformatik, and over 30 in international conference proceedings and book collections. He also serves as Editor-in-Chief of the International Journal on Open Source Software & Processes.

Kouji Kozaki is Associate Professor at the Department of Knowledge Science, the Institute of Scientific and Industrial Research, Osaka University. He received his Bachelor, Master and Doctoral degrees of Engineering in 1997, 1999 and 2002 from Osaka University, respectively. His research interest includes ontology building, fundamental theory of ontological engineering (especially for role and identity), ontology development system, ontology-based application. A major theme of his research is a development Hozo (http://www.hozo.jp), which is an environment for building/using ontologies, and ontology building in several domains such as clinical medicine, bioinformatics, environmental engineering.

Pradeep R. Kulkarni is working as Professor & HOD - Department of Commerce in senior college. He has received his Ph.D. degree from Dr. B.A.M. University, Aurangabad in commerce under the faculty of Commerce. He has 30+ years of experience in the field of teaching and industry. He is a research guide of Dr. B.A.M. University, Aurnagabad.

Terukazu Kumazawa is an assistant professor in the Center for Research Promotion, Research Institute for Humanity and Nature (RIHN), Japan.

Faraón Llorens-Largo obtained his B.Sc. and M.Sc. in Computer Science in 1993, and a PhD in Computer Science by the University of Alicante in 2001. He also has a B.Sc. in Education since 1982. He has been head of the Higher Polytechnic School of Alicante (2000-2005) and Pro-Vice-chancellor of Technology and Educative Innovation at the University of Alicante (2005-2012). He is now head of the Santander-UA Digital Transformation Chair. He has received many awards related to education, like the Professional Sapiens 2008 award, from the Official Association of Computer Scientists of Valencia, or the AENUI award to educative quality and innovation 2013. He is currently professor at the University of Alicante and his research interests are focused on the uses of Artificial Intelligence, games and Gamification to improve education.

Enric Mayol is an associate professor at Universitat Politècnica de Catalunya·BarcelonaTech (UPC) where he has been teaching software engineering, information systems management and project management. He received his PhD and engineering degree in computer science at UPC. His current research work is related to the application of information technologies in genealogy research and the application of mobile technologies in education. He is a member of the SUSHITOS research group (http://sushitos.essi.upc.edu) and deputy director of innovation at the Education Sciences Institute of the UPC (ICE).

Pravin S. Metkewar has received his Ph.D. degree from SRT University, Nanded in computer science under the faculty of science in Aug 2005. He has 17 years of experience in the field of teaching, R & D (Research) centre and industry. His specialization in Information Systems, Neural networks, Fuzzy Logic, OOAD and UML. He has presented and published 25 research papers and 02 books in his account. He is a research guide of Symbiosis International University, Pune. He is a CSI life member.

Miroslav Minović is an Associate professor at University of Belgrade and Senior researcher in the Multimedia Lab. He obtained his PhD in Informational Technology in the area of Educational Games. He also participated in TRAILER EU funded project as a team leader for development of educational game module. He published lot of journal and conference papers on the topic of games application in education. His main research interests are HCI, Multimedia and Gamification.

Rafael Molina-Carmona received his B.Sc. and M.Sc. in Computer Science from the Polytechnic University of Valencia, Spain in 1994, and his Ph.D. in Computer Science from the University of Alicante, Spain in 2002. He is a professor at the University of Alicante, and he belongs to the department of Computer Science and Artificial Intelligence. He is also a researcher at the Industrial Computing and Artificial Intelligence research group and his interests are mainly in the application of Artificial Intelligence to different fields: computer-aided design and manufacture, computer graphics, learning, gamification and information representation, among other. His first works were focused on Artificial Intelligence applied to computer-aided design and manufacture, space reconstruction and grammatical models for virtual worlds generation. He has published more than 20 papers and he has also directed three Thesis in this fields. Moreover, he is now participating in a other research lines about technology-enhanced learning and creativity, including videogames, gamification, learning analytics and information representation. He has co-authored more than 10 papers and he has co-directed two Thesis in this field.

Gustaf Neumann is Chair of Information Systems and New Media at the University of Economics and Business Administration (WU) in Vienna, Austria. Before joining WU he was Chair of the department of Information Systems and Software Techniques at the University of Essen. Gustaf Neumann is native of Vienna, Austria. He joined the faculty of WU in 1983 as Assistant Professor at the MIS department and served as head of the research group for Logic Programming and Intelligent Information Systems. Before becoming a full professor at the University of Essen, Gustaf Neumann was working for 5 years as a scientist at IBM's T.J. Watson Research Center in Yorktown Heights, NY, in the field of deductive databases and object orientation. Gustaf Neumann has received several research awards and published books and papers in the areas of program transformation, data modeling, and information systems technology. He has developed several widely used open source products and is author of the Extended Object Tcl programming language the Next Scripting Framework. Gustaf Neumann was awarded with the Tcl community service award and mentored several Google Summer of Code Projects. He was heading as scientific lead nine research projects funded by the European Community. He is as heading the Learn@WU project, which is one of the most intensively used e-learning platforms worldwide.

Fabrício Horácio Sales Pereira is an undergraduate student at Federal University of Lavras, UFLA. Researches on Human-Computer Interaction and Accessibility.

André Lima Salgado is an undergraduate student at Federal University of Lavras, UFLA. Researches on Human-Computer Interaction, Smart Toys and Information Architecture.

Rosana Satorre-Cuerda holds a degree in Computer Science (Polytechnic University of Valencia, 1993) and she is Doctor in Computer Engineering (University of Alicante, 2002). Her specialty includes programming, stereoscopic vision, educational games, engineering education, and teacher training in ICT. She works as a lecturer in the Department of Computer Science and Artificial Intelligence at the University of Alicante (Alicante, Spain) since 1994, where she is Full Professor since 2008. She hold the position of Deputy Director of Department between 2000 and 2004, acting Director of Department between 2004 and 2005, Deputy Director of Computer Studies at the Polytechnic School between 2005 and 2009, and Secretary of the Polytechnic School. Her thesis was related to issues of stereoscopic vision, although since her inception she has devoted many efforts to education and teacher training in ICT. In her period as Deputy Director of Computer Studies, she coordinated the development of new curricula of Degree in Computer Engineering, implanted at this time at the University of Alicante, to adapt it to the European Higher Education Area. She is member of the Spanish Association of University Teachers of Computers (AENUI).

María Luisa Sein-Echaluce is Director of Virtual Campus and Professor of Applied Mathematics in the School of Engineering and Architecture at University of Zaragoza. She is the main researcher of the Research and Innovation Group in Training supported by Information and Communication Technology (GIDTIC, Spanish abbreviation). She is the president of the scientific committee of the International Conference of Learning, Innovation and Competitiveness (CINAIC, Spanish abbreviation) and takes part in evaluation committees of the local calls of innovation projects and of the international conferences. Her research is currently focused on technologies applied to cooperative methodologies and the usage of Open Source LMS and other tools for online adaptive learning.

Velimir Štavljanin is an Associate professor in the area of Marketing and Multimedia at the Faculty of organizational sciences University of Belgrade. His main research is in the area of digital marketing, brand management, product management, multimedia and gamification. His current research explores application of gamification in different areas of business. Štavljanin holds an BS in mechanical engineering, an MSc, and an PhD in marketing, all from University of Belgrade.

Raj Vayyavur has more than 15 years of successful senior technical leadership and implementation experience delivering innovative and high quality solutions in areas of information technology including Project/Program/Portfolio (PPM) Management, Solution/Software Engineering, Architecture, Implementation, Product Development, ERP, EAI, Quality Assurance, Lean Six Sigma, Change Management etc. Raj has a Bachelor of Science degree in Computer Science, Master degree in Applied Computing, Master degree in Business Administration and is currently pursuing his Doctorate degree in Information Systems and Enterprise Resource Management. He is certified PMI Project Management Professional (PMP), CA Clarity PPM technology professional, Six Sigma Black Belt and Microsoft Certified Professional.

Carlos J. Villagrá-Arnedo achieved a degree in Computer Science from the Faculty of Computer Science at the Polytechnic University of Valencia in 1994. He is currently a professor of Computer Science and Artificial Intelligence department at the University of Alicante since 2002. He has just obtained the PhD in Computer Science at this university in January 2016. He was head of studies of the Multimedia Engineering degree from 2010 to 2013. He teaches in Computer Science Engineering and Multimedia Engineering degrees, and his research focuses on the fields of artificial intelligence, video games and its educational potential.

Index